CAMBRIDGE LIBRARY COLLECTION

Books of enduring scholarly value

History

The books reissued in this series include accounts of historical events and movements by eye-witnesses and contemporaries, as well as landmark studies that assembled significant source materials or developed new historiographical methods. The series includes work in social, political and military history on a wide range of periods and regions, giving modern scholars ready access to influential publications of the past.

Aureretanga: Groans of the Maoris

When George William Rusden (1819–1903) was fourteen, his family emigrated from England to Australia, where he later became a prominent educationalist and civil servant, responsible for establishing national schools. In 1883, after retiring to England, he published histories of Australia and New Zealand, both of them sympathetic to the indigenous populations. The latter proved controversial and resulted in a libel case against Rusden, which he lost. *Aureretanga*, first published in 1888, was written with the purpose of exposing British abuses of the Treaty of Waitangi, which had ceded New Zealand to the Crown in 1840. Drawing on government documents, official correspondence, court records, petitions and press reports, Rusden lists the hardships and injustices inflicted on the Maori, asserting that the actions of the British-led government 'dishonoured the name of England'. His book provides intriguing contemporary insights into the harsh realities of even supposedly enlightened colonialism.

T0352086

Cambridge University Press has long been a pioneer in the reissuing of out-of-print titles from its own backlist, producing digital reprints of books that are still sought after by scholars and students but could not be reprinted economically using traditional technology. The Cambridge Library Collection extends this activity to a wider range of books which are still of importance to researchers and professionals, either for the source material they contain, or as landmarks in the history of their academic discipline.

Drawing from the world-renowned collections in the Cambridge University Library, and guided by the advice of experts in each subject area, Cambridge University Press is using state-of-the-art scanning machines in its own Printing House to capture the content of each book selected for inclusion. The files are processed to give a consistently clear, crisp image, and the books finished to the high quality standard for which the Press is recognised around the world. The latest print-on-demand technology ensures that the books will remain available indefinitely, and that orders for single or multiple copies can quickly be supplied.

The Cambridge Library Collection will bring back to life books of enduring scholarly value (including out-of-copyright works originally issued by other publishers) across a wide range of disciplines in the humanities and social sciences and in science and technology.

Aureretanga:
Groans of the Maoris

EDITED BY G.W. RUSDEN

CAMBRIDGE
UNIVERSITY PRESS

CAMBRIDGE UNIVERSITY PRESS

Cambridge, New York, Melbourne, Madrid, Cape Town,
Singapore, São Paolo, Delhi, Tokyo, Mexico City

Published in the United States of America by Cambridge University Press, New York

www.cambridge.org
Information on this title: www.cambridge.org/9781108040006

© in this compilation Cambridge University Press 2012

This edition first published 1888
This digitally printed version 2012

ISBN 978-1-108-04000-6 Paperback

AURERETANGA;

GROANS OF THE MAORIS;

EDITED BY

G. W. RUSDEN,

FELLOW OF THE ROYAL ASIATIC SOCIETY.

―――――

" Τοὐλεύθερον δ'ἐκεῖνο, Τις θέλει πόλει
Χρηστον τι βούλευμ' εἰς μέσον φέρειν, ἔχων;
Καὶ ταυθ' ὅ χρήζων, λαμπρὸς ἔσθ· ὁ μὴ θέλων
Σιγα· τί τούτων ἐστ' ἰσαίτερον πολει ;"

Euripides.

―――――

" If thou seest the oppression of the poor, and violent perverting of judgment and justice in a province, marvel not at the matter ; for he that is higher than the highest regardeth ; and there be higher than they."—*Ecclesiastes.*

―――――

"And he looked for judgment, but behold oppression ; for righteousness, but behold a cry."—*Isaiah.*

―――――

LONDON:

WILLIAM RIDGWAY, 169, PICCADILLY.

AND SOLD BY ALL BOOKSELLERS.

―――

MDCCCLXXXVIII.

More than three hundred years ago a humane Spaniard was reviled for denouncing cruelties committed, not by all, but by some of his countrymen, against the Americans.

Bryan Edwards, the historian of the West Indies, depicted those cruelties in terms which can never be forgotten. *
"All the murders and desolations of the most pitiless tyrants that ever diverted themselves with the pangs and convulsions of their fellow-creatures fall infinitely short of the bloody enormities committed by the Spanish nation in the conquest of the New World:— a conquest, on a low estimate, effected by the murder of ten millions of the species. But, although the accounts which are transmitted down to us of this dreadful carnage are authenticated beyond the possibility of dispute, the mind shrinking from the contemplation, wishes to resist conviction, and to relieve itself by incredulity.†

Such at least is the apology which I would frame for (Robertson) the author of the American History, when I find him attempting in contradiction to the voice and feelings of all mankind, to palliate such horrible wickedness."

At page 110, Edwards, declaring that his hand trembled as he wrote, and his heart devoutly wished that the statement could be proved false, quoted, from Las Casas, the fearful record—
' I once beheld four or five principal Indians roasted alive at a slow fire . . .".

My own hand refuses to transcibe the atrocious particulars which follow the above words.

---

* Vol I. p, 105·

† Thus benevolence is called in aid of cruelty, and apathy among many becomes in time an accomplice in the crimes of a few.

Las Casas failed to arrest, though perhaps he modified the injustice of his own time ; but Robertson (arraigned by Edwards for palliating the wrongs done) was compelled to acknowledge "the malevolent opposition of Las Casas' adversaries," and to accord "great praise to his humane activity, which gave rise to various regulations that were of some benefit to the unhappy people " whose cause he espoused.

Robertson himself testifies that the Spaniards robbed the Americans of their lands—parted the despoiled owners as slaves in time of peace—and in "war paid no regard to those laws which by a tacit convention between contending nations, regulate hostility, and set some bounds to its rage." He tells us also that Las Casas, in pleading for the Americans, "censured the conduct of his countrymen settled there with such honest severity as rendered him universally odious to them."

It may be hoped that hatred of "honest severity" was not so universal as the historian supposed, and that some just men concurred with Las Casas; for few Spanish civilians can have resembled Roldan, nor can all Spanish Commanders have been so base and brutal as Ovando.

A later historian paid a higher tribute to the philanthropist. Not denying that Las Casas, like other men, was liable to error, Prescott says : "He was inspired by one great and glorious idea. . . . It was this which urged him to lift the voice of rebuke in the presence of Princes, to brave the menaces of an infuriated populace, to cross seas, to traverse mountains and deserts, to incur the alienation of friends, the hostility of enemies, to endure obloquy, insult, and persecution. . . Who shall say how much of the successful efforts and arguments since made in behalf of persecuted humanity may be traced to the example and writings of this illustrious philanthropist?"

Thus did Prescott write of one whom he nevertheless blamed for "exaggeration and over-colouring."

"Great and glorious ideas" are seldom entertained without enthusiasm, and, unless an author feels deeply, he will not stir the sympathy of his readers.

Strong colours are required in depicting startling events ; and the world is generally too much absorbed in its pleasures and profits, its *panem et Circenses*, to allow its attention to be readily diverted to remote occurrences.

What less sorrows can command attention when my lost friend, the hero of our time, has been allowed to pass away beguiled by an appeal for his help in the sacred name of patriotism, thwarted, betrayed, maligned, abandoned to starvation or death, and yet standing alone on the ramparts of Khartoum contending for the honour of his country, whose rulers were earning "indelible disgrace" by his fate ?

History will in due time fasten that disgrace upon those to whom it is due; but who can aver that the people of England, in the day of disgrace, did their duty to punish its authors ?

Las Casas, in a worldly sense, failed in his crusade on behalf of humanity. But the day has come when his "actions blossom in the dust," and his detractors are only known as an ignoble herd because they were his detractors.

For myself, although I have laboured in the cause of humanity, I have as yet failed to bring before my countrymen, as I desired, the manner in which infractions of a solemn Treaty have inflicted hardships on the Maori race, and, in my humble judgment, dishonoured the name of England.

The pages of general history are so crowded with events, that it is perhaps impossible to enforce sufficiently in them the consideration of special grievances. A shorter work may effect my purpose better ; and, therefore, I have compiled from the most authentic sources, and in the most unimpassioned manner, the following brief record of a few of those dealings which have caused the groans of the Maoris, to which the following pages are devoted in the hope that past wrongs may yet in some degree be atoned for.

Some portions of their father-land still remain in the hands of the Maoris; and the "system of fraud, under the authority of law," denounced by Dr. Pollen in the New Zealand Parliament, may yet be applied at Waikato, Kawhia, and elsewhere, unless a healthy public opinion can be aroused.

AURERETANGA:

GROANS OF THE MAORIS.

LONG before the flag of England was hoisted in token that the sway of Queen Victoria was extended to New Zealand, in 1840, British subjects had trafficked with Maoris, and many of them had taken up their abode in the North Island.

When the Rev. Samuel Marsden yearned to make known the Gospel to the Maoris, he wrote in 1814:—"They are as noble a race of men as are to be met with in any part of the world. I trust I shall be able, in some measure, to put a stop to those dreadful murders which have been committed upon the island for some years, both by the Europeans and the natives. They are a much-injured people, notwithstanding all that has been said against them."

Marsden's labours can be learned from general history.

The "dreadful murders" became the subject of legislation in England in 1817. An Act (57 Geo. III., cap. 53) provided a mode of trial for the "grievous murders and manslaughters" committed "by the masters and crews of British ships, and other persons, who have, for the most part, deserted from and left their ships." . . .

But the plague was not stayed. In 1830, a frightful atrocity, in which a British subject was an actor—stirred the Governor of New South Wales (General Darling) to action. He considered that the character of the nation was implicated in the "atrocious conduct of Captain Stewart and his crew, and that every possible exertion should be used to bring the offenders to justice." Like many others who strive to remedy the wrongs of their fellow-creatures, Governor Darling failed in this instance. His legal advisers "entertained doubts whether there were sufficient grounds for putting the parties on their trial." Witnesses were spirited away. Able counsel took the cause of the criminal in hand; complained against his being held to "bail for an indefinite period;" and though, perhaps, none doubted his guilt, he was finally "discharged on his own recognizance in the sum of £1,000." But a Committee of the House of Commons declared in 1836 that "those who might have been witnesses were suffered to leave the country. Thus, then, we see that an atrocious crime, involving the murder of many individuals, has been perpetrated through the instrumentality of a British subject, and that yet, neither he nor any of his accomplices have suffered any punishment."

Nevertheless, Governor Darling made his power felt in the repression of what he denounced as the "barbarous traffic" in human heads in which some British subjects were engaged at New Zealand. A Secretary of State (Lord Goderich) did not wait for the opinion of the House of Commons on the failure of justice in the case of Stewart. He wrote to Darling's successor:—"It is impossible to read without shame and indignation these details."

The English Government took various measures to vindicate the character of the nation.

They appointed a British Resident (Mr. James Busby) in 1832. In 1834, they recognized a New Zealand flag, which was formally saluted by the commander of a British ship of war.

In 1835, the British Resident, at the Bay of Islands, aided thirty-five chiefs in a declaration of their independence, at a time when they suspected that "the tribe of Marion" (the French) were about to take away their land.

They were designated as "the United Tribes of New Zealand." The conduct of the Resident was approved in England.

But, however kindly might be the disposition of the Government, there were terrible evils to which the Maoris were exposed by the irruption of a dissolute European population on the island.

Samuel Marsden, whose missionary work had prospered to an unexpected degree, lamented bitterly in his later years the evils to which his Maori disciples were subjected by contact with uncontrolled Europeans. "These are," he said, "generally men of the most infamous character—runaway convicts and sailors, and publicans, who have opened grog-shops in the pahs, where riot, drunkenness, and prostitution are carried on daily. . . . Some civilized Government must take New Zealand under its protection, or the most dreadful evils will be committed by runaway convicts, sailors, and publicans."

The good tidings conveyed by Marsden and some others had done much. The Bishop of Australia (Broughton), after a visit to the Bay of Islands, in 1838, reported to the Church Missionary Society that "the chief and the slave stood side by side with the same holy volume in their hands."

Captious men have disputed whether the extinction of slavery in Europe was the work of Christianity. None can deny that such was the case in New Zealand. When England abolished slavery in the Colonies, she gave pecuniary compensation to the slave-owners. At a great price she bought human creatures from her own subjects in order to make them free.

In New Zealand, touched by the wand of Christianity, the slave-owners themselves, the hereditary lords of their fellow-men—wielding the power of life and death, commanding without resistance, and almost worshipped by their dependents—of their free will enfranchised all their slaves. Cruel in war, and savage in many customs, the Maori has been depicted elsewhere by me without concealment of his faults. But the giving of freedom to their slaves may stand as an almost unrivalled act of self-sacrifice and charity on the part of the Maori chiefs, and though it has found few admirers.in this world, it may not be forgotten in the next. When the noble Bishop Selwyn went to New Zealand in 1842 (twenty-eight years after Marsden's first visit), he thus described its people:—" We see here a whole nation of pagans converted to the faith. A few faithful men, by the Spirit of God, have been the instruments of adding another Christian people to the family of God. Young men and maidens, old men and children, all with one heart and with one voice praising God; all offering up daily their morning and evening prayers; all searching the Scriptures to find the way of eternal life; all valuing the Word of God above every other gift; all, in a greater or less degree, bringing forth and visibly displaying in their outward lives some fruits of the influences of the Spirit. Where will you find, throughout the Christian world, more signal manifestations of that Spirit, or more living evidences of the kingdom of Christ ? "

Such was the aspect of one side of the shield. On the other were the gloomy portents described and dreaded by Marsden, and not unrecognized by the Committee of the House of Commons in 1836, when it denounced the " atrocious" and unpunished crime of Stewart.

A Committee of the House of Lords took evidence also in 1838.

Efforts were made in 1837, 1838 and 1839 to found a British Colony in New Zealand.

A Bill for founding a Colony was rejected at the second reading by the House of Commons.

How the able and energetic Gibbon Wakefield dispensed with Parliamentary sanction, and in what manner Her Majesty's Government were induced to found the Colony of New Zealand in 1840, may be read in history.

These pages must be mainly confined to certain grievances inflicted on the Maoris in defiance of the terms of the solemn Treaty made with them in the name of the Queen on the foundation of the Colony.

In instructing Captain Hobson, who, under guidance of the able Governor of New South Wales (Sir George Gipps), was to arrange that Treaty, the Secretary of State (the Marquis of Normandy) announced (14 August, 1839), that Her Majesty's Government concurred with the Committee of the House of Commons in 1836 " in thinking that the increase of national wealth and power, promised by the acquisition of New Zealand, would be a most inadequate compensation for the injury which must be inflicted on this kingdom itself, by embarking on a measure essentially unjust, and but too certainly fraught with calamity to a numerous and inoffensive people whose title to the soil and to the sovereignty of New Zealand is indisputable, and has been solemnly recognized by the British Government."*

It was established, Lord Normandy said, " that about the commencement of the year 1838, a body of not less than two thousand British

---

* Parliamentary Papers, 1841.

subjects, had become permanent inhabitants of New Zealand; that amongst them were many persons of bad or doubtful character—convicts who had fled from our penal settlements, or seamen who had deserted their ships; and that these people, unrestrained by any law, and amenable to no tribunals, were alternately the authors and the victims of every species of crime and outrage."

Lest such persons should "repeat, unchecked in that quarter of the globe the same process of war and spoliation," and "to mitigate and if possible to avert these disasters, and to rescue the emigrants themselves from the evils of a lawless state of society," it had been determined to found a Colony, and this could only be honourably done by a Treaty with the Maoris.

The manner in which the Treaty was made has often been narrated. Its text is given as follows in a Parliamentary Return, 27 July, 1840.*

'Her Majesty Victoria, Queen of the United Kingdom of Great Britain and Ireland, regarding with Her Royal favour the native chiefs and tribes of New Zealand, and anxious to protect their just rights and property, and to secure to them the enjoyment of peace and good order, has deemed it necessary (in consequence of the great number of Her Majesty's subjects who have already settled in New Zealand, and the rapid extension of emigration, both from Europe and Australia which is still in progress) to constitute and appoint a functionary, properly authorised to treat with the aborigines of New Zealand for the recognition of Her Majesty's sovereign authority over the whole or any part of the islands. Her Majesty therefore being desirous to establish a settled form of civil government with a view to avert the evil consequences which must result from the absence of the necessary laws and institutions, alike to the native population and to Her subjects, has been graciously pleased to empower and to authorize me, William Hobson, a captain in Her Majesty's Royal Navy, Consul and Lieutenant Governor over such parts of New Zealand as may be, or hereafter shall be, ceded to Her Majesty, to invite the confederated and independent chiefs of New Zealand to concur in the following articles and conditions:—

Article the First.—The chiefs of the confederation of the United Tribes of New Zealand and the separate and independent chiefs who have not become members of the confederation, cede to Her Majesty, the Queen of England absolutely, and without reservation all the rights and powers of sovereignty which the said confederation or independent chiefs respectively exercise or possess over their respective territories, as the sole sovereigns thereof.

Article the Second.—Her Majesty the Queen of England confirms and guarantees to the chiefs and tribes of New Zealand, and to the respective families and individuals thereof, the full, exclusive and

---

* Parliamentary Papers, 1840 [560]. By order of the New Zealand Government a fac-simile of the original document and signatures was published in New Zealand in 1877, together with the declaration of independence of 1835.

undisturbed possession of their lands and estates, forests, fisheries and other properties which they may collectively or individually possess, so long as it is their wish and desire to retain the same in their possession. But the chiefs of the United Tribes, and the individual chiefs, yield to Her Majesty the exclusive right of pre-emption over such lands as the proprietors thereof may be disposed to alienate, at such prices as may be agreed upon between the respective proprietors and persons appointed by Her Majesty to treat with them in that behalf.

Article the Third.—In consideration thereof, Her Majesty, the Queen of England, extends to the natives of New Zealand her Royal protection, and imparts to them all the rights and privileges of British subjects.—W. Hobson.

Now therefore we, the chiefs of the confederation of the United Tribes of New Zealand, being assembled in congress at Waitangi, and we, the separate and independent chiefs of New Zealand, claiming authority over the tribes and territories which are specified after our respective names, having been made fully to understand the provisions of the foregoing Treaty, accept and enter into the same in the full spirit and meaning thereof.

In witness whereof we have attached our signatures or marks at the places and dates respectively specified.

Done at Waitangi this 6th day of February in the year of our Lord, 1840." (Many Maori names were subscribed).

Hobson wrote to Sir George Gipps that "The Treaty was signed by forty-six head chiefs in presence of at least five hundred of inferior degree." He also deputed British officers to carry the Treaty throughout the islands of New Zealand. Major Bunbury, 80th Regiment, was specially enjoined while engaged in obtaining the signatures of chiefs to "offer a solemn pledge that the most perfect good faith would be kept by Her Majesty's Government, that their property, their rights and privileges should be most fully preserved."

Sir George Gipps transmitted the Treaty of Waitangi to Lord John Russell, the Secretary of State who succeeded Lord Normanby, and Lord John Russell replied that "Her Majesty's Government entirely approve of the measures which you adopted, and of the manner in which they were carried into effect by Captain Hobson."*

The Treaty was as formally ratified by the Queen as by the Maoris. The Blue Books and Hansard abound with tributes to its binding nature upon the British people and upon the Colonists.

On one occasion a representative of the New Zealand Company wrote to Lord Stanley (who in Sir Robert Peel's ministry had become Secretary of State),—"We did not believe that even the Royal power of making treaties could establish in the eye of our Courts such a fiction as a native law of real property in New Zealand. We have always had very serious doubts whether the Treaty of Waitangi, made with naked savages by a Consul invested with no plenipoten-

---

* Parliamentary Papers, 1840, [560].

tiary powers could be treated by lawyers as anything but a praise-worthy device for amusing and pacifying savages for the moment." The company objected to being "required to prove that in every instance, every native with whom our agent contracted *understood the full force and meaning of the contract which he made.*"

Lord Stanley answered (Feb. 1843), that he was "not prepared as Her Majesty's Secretary of State to join with the Company in setting aside the Treaty of Waitangi after obtaining the advantages guaranteed by it. even though it might be made with 'naked savages,' or though it might be treated by lawyers as a praiseworthy device for amusing and pacifying savages for the moment.

Lord Stanley entertains a different view of the respect due to obligations contracted by the Crown of England, and his final answer to the demands of the Company must be that, as long as he has the honour of serving the Crown, he will not admit that any person or any government, acting in the name of Her Majesty, can contract a legal, moral, or honorary obligation to despoil others of their lawful and equitable rights."*

At a later date, 13 June, 1845, he wrote to a Governor in New Zeaand,† "In the name of the Queen I utterly deny that any Treaty entered into and ratified by Her Majesty's command, was or could have been made in a spirit thus disingenuous, or for a purpose thus unworthy. You will honourably and scrupulously fulfil the conditions of the Treaty of Waitangi."

Sir Robert Peel, speaking in Parliament (19 June, 1845), asked if the House could resist the appeal made by the Ngapuhi chief Waka Nene to the equity and honour of the English nation. "I will say (he added) that if ever there was a case where the stronger party was obliged, by its position, to respect the demands of the weaker, if ever a powerful country was bound by its engagements with the weaker, it was the engagement contracted under such circumstances with these Native chiefs."

The Treaty has never been cancelled. No Governor of New Zealand has done otherwise than declare to the Maoris that it is sacred.

The Constitution Act of 1852 (15 & 16 Vict. cap. 72) contained no word of disparagement of the Treaty: but it did contain clauses which enabled Her Majesty to preserve rights guaranteed to the Maoris.‡

Clause 71 enabled her to set apart particular districts in which the "Laws, Customs and Usages" of the Natives should be maintained "any Law, Statute, or Usage in force in New Zealand, or in any part thereof, in anywise notwithstanding."

---

* House of Commons Blue Book, 1844, Vol. XIII. App. No. 2, p. 36.

† House of Commons Blue Book, 1844, Vol. XXX. (337).

‡ This Act was carried by Sir John Pakington in the ministry of Lord Derby. It is often asserted that acts of liberality to the Colonies have sprung from so-called Liberal ministries. The truth is that the control over their revenues, the administration of the Crown lands, the discontinuance of transportation to Tasmania—all of which had been denied by Whig Governments—were conceded by Sir John Pakington (the first two in reply to Wentworth's famous "Remonstrances" to which Earls Russell and Grey turned uncompliant ears and gave offensive answers.)

Clause 73 retained for Her Majesty the sole right to acquire or accept from the Natives land "belonging to, or used or occupied by them in common as tribes or communities."

The 58th clause enabled Her Majesty to dis-allow Bills passed in New Zealand, and the 59th deprived of any force any reserved Bill to which the assent of Her Majesty might not be given.

The Treaty spoke so plainly for itself that it needed some effrontery to question its meaning. But greed for land and the exigencies of an embarrassed company prompted the use of arguments of which the arguers might well have been ashamed; and which, while Sir Robert Peel was Prime Minister, and Lord Derby was at the head of the Colonial Department, had no power to warp the English nation to wrong the Maoris, or to permit others to do so,

The pages of Hansard show how Captain Rous, Sir H. Douglas, Mr. Cardwell, Sir James Graham, and Sir Robert Peel defended the cause of justice in the House of Commons in 1845, when Lord Stanley had taken his seat in the House of Lords.

The constant endeavour of those who desired to defraud the Maoris was to depreciate the Treaty. In the House of Commons one member complained that Sir Robert Peel had repeated " all the flummery about the Treaty; " but the House declined to listen to such unworthy counsels.

When the Treaty has been violated in later years, it can hardly be said that either Englishmen or Colonists generally have been aware of what was being done by the prime movers in the wrong.

It requires a robust morality, however, to intervene to undo a wrong by means of which a worldly advantage is supposed to be procurable. I have always been careful to recognize the fact that the Colonists were not active accomplices in many of the wrongs inflicted on the Maoris. Those who wished to extirpate the Maori race, cared little whether that end was accomplished in the field, or by decay. The cumbering Maoris were to be destroyed. The bulk of the Colonists had no such desires, but their humanity did not assume the form of controlling the inhumanity of others.

As a motive for exposing iniquities it has seemed to me possible that a wider revelation of the wrongs done in the name, but not by command of the Queen, may tend to lighten the oppression which has so long been inflicted upon a race which reposed its trust in her.

With such a motive one may hope that all, whose good opinion is valuable, will sympathize.

The instance already given of the manner in which the New Zealand Company besought Lord Stanley to break faith with the Maoris must suffice for these pages. Many others might be adduced.

The Company had friends in England, and sought to damage the Treaty through a Committee of the House of Commons in 1844.

A Committee of fifteen, amongst whom was a member of the Company, did, in effect, carry resolutions which alluded to the " so-called Treaty of

Waitangi," and suggested that maugre the clear terms of the Treaty it would not have been unjust to claim " all unoccupied land" for the Crown.

Mr. Cardwell's counter-proposition that the Treaty was " binding in conscience and policy on the British Government" was only lost in the Committee by one vote: and the House never adopted the Report of the Committee. But it had been printed, and when Clarke, the Protector of the Aborigines in New Zealand, saw it, he warned the Governor, Captain Fitzroy, that " Your Excellency (to secure you from the effect of such publications) has need of both steamers and an army to ensure the peace of the country," which could not but be disturbed by the circulation of the Report. Fitzroy himself wrote " I cannot believe that those most dangerous resolutions of the House of Commons in 1844, respecting unoccupied land can be adopted by Her Majesty's Government." Fortunately they were Resolutions not of the House, but of a Committee.

In spite of Fitzroy's precautions the Report was sufficiently known to enable designing persons to stir suspicion amongst the most impressible of the Maoris. It was believed by many that the attack upon Kororarika would not have been made by Honi Heke in 1845 if the suggestions of the Report had not been represented to him as disloyal to the Treaty.

That it was not mere rumour among the thoughtless which attributed mischief to the Report, was proved by the fact that the sagacious Sir George Gipps, the Governor of New South Wales, expressed his "fear that the want of troops to keep in check the natives, and to preserve peace between the two races would be more extensively felt in proportion as the late Report of the Select Committee of the House of Commons should become generally known in the Colony."

The eagerness with which the New Zealand Company strove to work their will in England is shown by the fact that Sir Robert Peel (18th March 1845) adverted to their activity in the House of Commons thus—" There were eight gentleman, therefore, on the opposite benches, and seven out of the eight were members of the New Zealand Company." While Sir Robert Peel was in power the House of Commons, though vehemently urged, refused to sanction any violation of the Treaty of Waitangi.

But that great minister fell before a mean coalition in 1846.

Earl Grey succeeded Lord Stanley at the Colonial office. He having as Lord Howick, in the House of Commons, joined in assailing the the integrity of the Treaty of Waitangi, now (like Lord Stanley) was in the House of Lords; and promptly availed himself of his position as Minister by causing " the Groans of the Maoris " to be heard in England with an accompaniment of sympathy from some of the noblest Englishmen who stood on the soil of New Zealand.

His position as an incoming Minister enabled him to pass a Bill without delay. With the new Statute he sent (December 1846) to the Governor (Grey) a new Charter and new Instructions. The latter were to elicit groans and indignant remonstrance from men of such high mark that the Earl was fain to abandon his schemes.

It is more with the remonstrances than with the Instructions that these brief pages must deal. It may be stated broadly that the latter expressly denied to the Maoris the rights expressly guaranteed by the Treaty of Waitangi; and that the Earl wrote that he "entirely dissented" from the doctrine that "aboriginal inhabitants of any country are the proprietors of every part of its soil of which they have been accustomed to make any use, or to which they have been accustomed to assert any title."

The Governor not only abstained from publishing but cogently remonstrated against the Instructions before their purport was publicly known in the Colony.

When they became known there in June 1847, Bishop Selwyn made a "formal and deliberate" protest against them.

"It is my duty also to inform Your Excellency that I am resolved, God being my helper, to use all legal and constitutional measures befitting my station to inform the natives of New Zealand of their rights and privileges, and to assist them in asserting them and maintaining them, whether by petition to the Imperial Parliament, or other loyal and peaceable methods."

Another noble-minded man, William Martin, Chief Justice of New Zealand, aided the Bishop. In a pamphlet printed (1847) but not published—"England and the New Zealanders"—he laid bare the injustice which Earl Grey's instructions contemplated.

A petition from the Bishop, the Chief Justice, and others, prayed that the Instructions might be revoked as derogatory to the honour of the Queen.

Governor Grey, while abstaining from promulgating the Instructions strove to allay the excitement which rumours about them had produced.

Captain Sotheby of H.M.S. Racehorse, with the Ngapuhi chief Waka Nene, visited many chiefs and assured them on the "authority of the Governor that there was no truth in the report that the Government claimed all land "not under tillage." This was true inasmuch as the Governor was included in the word Government. But if Earl Grey's Instructions had been carried out the possession of Maori "lands and estates, forests, fisheries, and other property," solemnly guaranteed in the Treaty of Waitangi, would have been taken away.

The tact displayed by the Governor in dealing with the position must be read in general History.

The Groans of the Maoris are the subject of these pages.

The great chief Te Whero Whero, and his friends, winged their words to the Queen. "O Madam the Queen . . . hearken to our words, the words of all the chiefs of Waikato . . . May God grant that you may hold fast our word, and we your word, for ever. Madam, listen; news is going about here that your Ministers are talking of taking away the land of the natives without cause, which makes our hearts dark.

But we do not believe this news, because we heard from the first Governor that the disposal of the land is with ourselves. And from the second Governor we heard the same word, and from this Governor.

They have all said the same. Therefore we write to you that you may be kind to us, to your friends that love you. Write your thoughts to us that peace may prevail among the natives of these islands."

A Wesleyan Mission Committee in London, armed with complaints from missionaries in New Zealand, swelled the volume of protests against the violation of the Treaty.

The result was that Te Whero Whero and his brother chiefs were informed that there was " no foundation for the rumours to which they allude, and that it never was intended that the Treaty of Waitangi should be violated by dispossessing the tribes which are parties to it. . . On the contrary, Her Majesty has always directed that the Treaty should be scrupulously and religiously observed.'

Thus, the " Groans of the Maoris " when they were powerful, aided by the noble Selwyn and Martin,* averted evil in 1847.

A new measure was intro uced in the English Parliament. In debate the conduct of Bishop Selwyn was defended by Mr. Roundell Palmer (now Lord Selborne) and others ; Mr. Gladstone declared (Hansard, Vol. XCVI. p. 342.) that " as far as England was concerned there was not a more strictly and rigorously binding treaty in existence than that of Waitangi ; " Mr. Labouchere pledged the government to respect the Treaty ; and great power was left in the hands of Governor Grey, who had shown marked ability in the difficult position into which Earl Grey's instructions had forced him.

Another notable occasion on which Maoris made their complaints known in England, was one on which they again received aid from Bishop Selwyn and Sir William Martin.

It would be tedious to insert here, a detailed statement of the Waitara case.

One remarkable testimony to the accuracy of my view of the matter has recently been furnished by the high authority of Mr. Fenton who was for many years Chief Judge of the Native Land Court in New Zealand.

---

* Chief Justice Martin, whose "Remarks " on Earl Grey's Despatch had been printed and forwarded to statesmen in England, and Selwyn, were upbraided for their " perilous appeal to the feelings of the natives," and some persons thought the Chief Justice's office was in danger. He calmly left it to Her Majesty's Government to decide whether his conduct in striving to secure peace was justifiable, and whether it would be for the public advantage that he should still retain the office entrusted to him.

Selwyn also officially replied that " we all with one voice, as the friends and advisers of this native people, have persuaded them to put their trust in the good faith of England ; and with one voice we will protest against any infringement, either in word or act, of the rights of British subjects which they acquired by cession of their independent sovereignty." To a friend the Bishop wrote that he would rather that Earl Grey " cut me in pieces than induced me by any personal compliments to resign the New Zealanders to the tender mercies of men who avow the right to take the land, and who would not scruple to use force for that purpose."

A few lines will state the broad facts of the case. Those who care to follow all its windings will find them in other volumes.

Te Rangitake, better known among the colonists as Wiremu Kingi, or William King, was a notable chieftain of the Ngatiawa tribe.

That tribe held possessions in various parts of the North Island.

The powerful section of it which dwelt at Waitara on the West Coast had, by co-operation with Rauparaha the Ngatitoa chief, acquired lands at Waikanae and in Cook's Straits; and Te Rangitake, with his father and others, had (about the year 1827) gone to Waikanae to possess the land.

They left many members of their tribe at the Waitara, but in accordance with custom, common in other places as well as in New Zealand, they retained their titles to their original lands, while they went to occupy their new acquisitions.

It was notorious that Te Rangitake himself constantly declared his intention to return to his native place.

One of the pretended purchases made by the New Zealand Company comprehended Te Rangitake's land at the Waitara.

They were elastic enough to comprehend places of which the pretending buyer had never even heard.

Mr. Spain, a Commissioner deputed by the English Government to examine all of them, formally reported thus:—" It appears to me as the evidence has gone;—that all the Company's purchases were made in a very loose and careless manner; that the object of the Company's agents, after going through a certain form of purchase, seems to have been to procure the insertion in their deeds of an immense extent of territory, the descriptions of which were framed from maps, and by obtaining the names of ranges of mountains, headlands and rivers, and were not taken from the native vendors; and that such descriptions were generally written in the deeds before the bargain for the purchases was concluded :

That these parcels contained millions of acres, and in some instances, degrees of latitude and longitude :

That the agents of the Company were satisfied with putting such descriptions in their deeds, without taking the trouble to enquire, either at the time of, or subsequently to the purchase, whether the thousands of Aboriginal inhabitants occupying the surface of these vast tracts of country had been consenting parties to the sale.

I am further of opinion that the natives did not consent to alienate their pahs, cultivations, and burying-grounds : That the interpretation between the Aborigines and the agents of the Company in the alleged purchases was exceedingly imperfect, and tended to convey in but a very slight degree, any idea to the former of the extent of territory which the latter by these purchases pretended to have acquired, and that the explanation by the interpreters of the system of reserves was perfectly unintelligible to the Natives."*

* This passage was reprinted in a work, The New Zealand Question, published London in 1848, by T. C. Newby. It was contained in a Report to the government in New Zealand.

When there seemed some risk that the New Zealand Government was about to recognize claims of the New Zealand Company at the Waitara, Te Rangitake wrote to Governor Fitzroy (June 8th, 1844.) "Waitara shall not be given up . . . The Ngatiawas are constantly returning to their land, the land of their birth. . . Friend, Governor, do you not love your land—England, the land of your fathers—as we also love our land at Waitara?"

The Governor (Fitzroy) and Bishop Selwyn, whose influence was already great, hastened to the spot. Mr. Donald McLean, the Rev. Mr. Whiteley (a Wesleyan Missionary), Mr. Forsaith, and others, were there to assist: and the Governor decided the matter in a way against which those who wished to do injustice to the Maoris never ceased to rail.

Mr. Spain, the Commissioner, not recognizing the full claims of absentee owners, had recommended an award, which Governor Fitzroy, having full power so to do, declined to adopt; and, aided in his inquiries by those best acquainted with the Maoris and versed in their customs, he obtained the consent of the Maoris to an arrangement by which a block of land was secured for the New Zealand Company by payment of a small sum of money.

One writer sneered at the Governor for giving weight to the "customs of barbarism," for being "blinded by maudlin sentimentality," and "spurred on by the missionary clique to dispossess the Company of the finest territory they had ever acquired."

It was indeed the richness of territory which whetted the appetite of the Governor's detractors; and which, from 1844 to 1881, spurred on the unscrupulous to practise every wile, and shrink from no injustice, in order to wrest the land from its rightful owners.

A few lines may be quoted here from a statement made by myself as to the rights of those owners. I cite them, instead of using others, because they have been approved of by the high authority of Mr. Maning, the author of "Old New Zealand, by a Pakeha Maori."

Mr. Maning was an inhabitant of New Zealand before the English Colony was founded; but his sagacity and power were recognized by the Colonial Government, when he was long afterwards appointed a Judge of the Native Land Court. On seeing my statement he wrote to me (30th April, 1883) :—" I cannot help writing to say that I admire your short and correct description of the tenure of land by the Maoris amongst themselves. The Ariki was trustee for the whole tribe, and had the right of veto on any alienation, which was exercised at Waitara unsuccessfully by Wi Kingi te Rangitake."

The passages commended by Mr. Maning were as follows :—

"The land was the domain of the people, and though by separate cultivation a man had a right to the product, he acquired no fee simple of the land. Over the whole domain the tribe hunted, and as the kiore or native rat was snared in distant places, the boundaries of each territory were well known, and, if necessary, defined by marks.

"Alienation to a foreigner could not be the act of the separate occupier. Only common consent could alienate the common property.

"In the same manner, if a hapu, or sub-tribe, of a neighbouring clan, was invited to settle on the lands of a tribe, the new-comers, under the general tribal sanction, acquired such rights as any occupier of the inviting tribe could have possessed. Inheritance was from father to son. . .

"Where land was proverbially a cause of war, titles orally preserved became hopelessly involved. The paramount authority of the chief, his 'mana,' was the only safeguard. Chiefs descended from the leaders of the emigration from Hawaiki were deemed to have special 'mana' over the tribal land. The chief could not sell the village of his friends, nor the patrimony of any of them; but the tribe required his sanction to make good their own transactions.*

"Strange rights accrued and multiplied. A fishing right possessed by a man's father entitled him to compensation, and the owner of the spot could not sell without satisfaction to the claimant. Marriage relations conferred partial rights. One man claimed compensation because his grandfather had been murdered on land, another because his own grandfather committed the murder. If wise counsels could not allay strife, fresh fighting conferred fresh rights. Conquest—absolute conquest with occupation—gave indefeasible title. But if a remnant of a defeated tribe escaped death or captivity, it preserved its rights, except as to those portions of its birthright which the conquerors chose to occupy, to till or to hunt or fish over."

There are other characteristics of Maori land-law and usages, but it is unnecessary to dwell upon them.

The incidents of tenure among the Maoris are not peculiar to them among the families of the world.

Many of them are almost identical with those described by Tacitus as prevailing among the Teutonic ancestors of the bulk of the English nation. Sir Henry Maine tells us that the "village community of India exhibits resemblances to the Teutonic township which are much too strong and numerous to be accidental."

The absence of cattle-ownership in New Zealand, entailed a difference with regard to the waste or common land (on which, in Germany the Teutonic cattle were fed), but the fishing and forestry rights were co-extensive with the tribal domain.

As in Germany, so in Maoria, the community, to use the language of Sir Henry Maine, "inhabited the village, held the common mark

---

* This fact was strongly impressed upon Mr. Commissioner Spain, the lawyer entrusted by Lord John Russell with the duty of inquiring into land-claims in New Zealand. Spain had agreed to meet some chiefs at Ohau, to discuss a proposed purchase. The paramount chief, Rauparaha, heard of the conference and arrested it. "Breaking at once into the midst of the meeting, he made a long and violent speech, in which, in a loud tone, and with angry gestures, he bade us go on our way to Manawatu, forbade the natives to proceed with the sale, and denounced the whole affair in no measured terms." Thus, as early as in 1844, the function of a chief in forbidding a sale was recognized by a British Land Commissioner.

in mixed ownership, and cultivated the arable mark in lots appropriated to the several families."

The "power of absorption" of visitors in a tribe, which Sir Henry Maine says that the village communities may "be inferred to have possessed in the earlier stages of development," was a recognized practice among the Maoris, and the Native Land Court in New Zealand has decided that the visitors thus received, acquired by Maori custom well known and recognized rights in the soil, constituting them owners along with the inviting tribe.

With much similarity to the choice of leaders in war, which Tacitus describes as extant in Germany, there was also in New Zealand a peculiarly important character ascribed to the Ariki, the hereditary head of the tribe, who was "*tapu*," or sacred, in the highest degree and without whose consent, according to the Maori usages which the Treaty of Waitangi guaranteed to the Maori chiefs and people, no tribal land could be alienated.

As the Maori possessed no flocks or herds, he became an assiduous cultivator.

His skill was noticed by Cook and Sir Joseph Banks in 1769. They saw plantations where "the ground was as well broken down and tilled as even in the gardens of the most curious people among us."

Though the cultivator was not the absolute owner of the land thus carefully tilled, he was protected by the whole tribal force in the use of it.

A marked feature in the Maori character was veneration for ancestors. To desecrate the place where their bones were deposited was a heinous offence, and it was incumbent upon all to avenge it, in ancient times. After the acceptance of the Sovereignty of the Queen, it was natural that in serious cases the authority of the Crown should be appealed to, to guard those interests, whether of the chief or of the tribe, whether collective or individual, which the Queen had solemnly undertaken to protect.

It is a lamentable fact that the most signal instance of the vain groans of the Maoris, and of the futile protests of their noble champion, Bishop Selwyn, was furnished in the case of a chief whose joint interest in the land seized by the Local Government was indisputable, and who also had the paramount right of chieftainship to forbid a sale, if even he had had by descent no special interests in the particular plot. Moreover he had laid the colonists under deep obligation by dissuading his countrymen from an attack upon Wellington.*

His reward was the denial of a legal enquiry as to his rights, the rough seizure of his land, the advance of troops into his territory, and consequent wars in which with the aid of ten thousand British troops

---

* Sir W. Fox, and Sir Dillon Bell wrote in an elaborate Report made in 1880—
"It is worthy of remark that the settlement of Wellington was probably saved from destruction by the act of Wiremu Kingi Te Rangitake. . . We believe that if his loyalty had been requited as it ought to have been, we might never have known him otherwise than as a friend." Blue Book 1882. (C. 3382) p. 49.

many Maori tribes were beaten down and left at the mercy of those whosought to plunder them.

Great interest seems to have been brought to bear in England in order to reverse the judgment of Governor Fitzroy as to the Taranaki land-claim put forward by the New Zealand Company.

Fitzroy had over-ruled, as he had the power to over-rule, the opinion of Spain, the Commissioner who had erroneously ignored the rights of absentee Ngatiawas to their Taranaki lands. Such rights were clearly unimpeachable in Maori law; and, supported by Bishop Selwyn, by Clarke, the Protector, by the Rev. Mr. Whiteley, a Wesleyan Missionary, Mr. Forsaith, the interpreter, and some others, Fitzroy after careful enquiry recognized those rights.

It is impossible to say in what manner the Company's agents brought influence to bear in England. But in July, 1846, Mr. Gladstone, then Secretary of State, wrote to the new Governor, Grey— " I indulge the hope that you may have found yourself in a condition to give effect to the award of Mr. Spain; . . . unless, indeed, which I can hardly think probable, you may have seen reason to believe that the reversal of the Commissioner's judgment was a wise and just measure."

Thus tempted by his casuistical superior, the Governor endeavoured, but vainly, to dissuade Te Rangitake from his long meditated return to the land of his birth. The present Agent-General in England for New Zealand, Sir F. Dillon Bell, stated in 1860 in the New Zealand Parliament that " At one of the meetings, Te Rangitake declared the intention of himself and his people to return to the Waitara. Sir George Grey refused to grant them permission to do so, and Te Rangitake said he should return without it, and defied the Governor to prevent him."

The language of rhetoric perhaps coloured this description of the conduct of Te Rangitake, who had ever been the friend of the English. He returned in 1848, with about five hundred and eighty-seven souls, to his birth-place, and re-occupied it with all necessary ceremonies.

A section of the Colonists viewed his return with animosity, because they coveted those rich lands which the New Zealand Company had pretended to purchase by obtaining signatures almost at random and inventing boundaries in the same manner.

A Wesleyan Missionary, Rev. J. Buller, thus described the proceedings of their Agent Colonel Wakefield—"He had bought—or was presumed to have bought—territories by degrees of latitude while in ignorance of the rightful owners." In the case of the alleged purchase at Taranaki, Wakefield had deputed an ignorant interpreter to act for him. Finding it "impossible to collect the chiefs whose consent was requisite for the transfer of the land from Manawatu to Mokau under at least a week" Wakefield reported that he left his ignorant agent "to secure this fine territory," and to "assemble the numerous chiefs resident on a coast line of 150 miles in a month's time when I am to return . . . and receive the written assent of the chiefs." Within the space thus roughly spoken of, were domains of about ten different tribes.

I will not multiply these pages by inserting in them the full particulars which may be read by the curious, elsewhere. It is sufficient to say here that great efforts were made to induce some Maoris to sell land in defiance of the refusal of the majority of their tribe;—that after the intervention of a Land Commissioner in these forbidden transactions there were quarrels, and lives were lost, among the dissentient Maoris; that the Acting-Governor, General Wynyard, visited Taranaki and appealed to Te Rangitake to prevent the English from being molested in the armed turbulence caused by their own solicitations for unlawful transactions, and that Te Rangitake answered "Yes, our father, we will guard against all evil to the Pakeha . . I will go into the midst of them, and the evil shall fall on me."

In 1855, Bishop Selwyn was on the spot; and Major Nugent, 58th Regt. reported that the Bishop's presence had "considerable influence in re-assuring the natives," whose suspicions were aroused by the proceedings of the Superintendent and Council of Taranaki, (then one of the six Provinces into which the Colony was divided).

The Council complained to the Governor that Rawiri, when about to cut the boundary of land he was offering "to the Government with the sanction of the resident Land Commissioner, was shot by Katatore, who claimed an interest in the land and opposed the sale."

It was true that Rawiri was thus shot, but not without repeated warning to desist, and the language of the Provincial Council showed that Rawiri found abettors among the settlers in violating the intended safeguards of the Treaty of Waitangi as to the tribal proprietary rights.

Bishop Selwyn endeavoured to stand between the wrong doers. He rebuked Katatore for shooting Rawiri. He declined to aid the settlers in their schemes. A Taranaki newspaper reviled him for sympathy with Katatore. In a pastoral letter to his flock at Taranaki the Bishop mentioned that he had condemned the murder of Rawiri "in the strongest language, even in the presence of the murderer." He added that it was strange that their advisers in the "newspapers who dwell so much upon the sixth commandment, should forget altogether that the same law has said, Thou shall not covet. . . I offer to my countrymen my best assistance and influence with the native people in all their just and lawful desires, but I have no fellowship with covetousness, which Ahab found to be the first step to blood-guiltiness."

On some minds the Bishop's manly justice made no impression. A newspaper had accused him of "lending his blighting influence to New Zealand" and " using his undoubted influence to shield notorious criminals from justice."

The Bishop informed his flock that he would urge the Maoris to sell land amicably; but would "resist by all lawful means, every attempt to carry out any other interpretation of the Treaty of

Waitangi than that in which it was explained to the natives by Governor Hobson, and understood and accepted by them."

The land sold at Taranaki already was, he said, 30,000 acres and it had cost only ten-pence an acre! [After the death of Rawiri, a friend named Ihaia took up his cause, and when his pah was besieged some of the settlers aided him.]

A new Governor, Colonel Gore Browne, visited Taranaki in 1855 and informed the Secretary of State that he had "given the strongest assurances of protection in all their rights to the Maoris, and declared his determination neither to interfere in native questions, *nor to permit the purchase of lands until the owners are united in desiring to sell them, and have agreed upon the terms.*" He "disapproved of the conduct of Cooper, the sub-commissioner, in commencing a survey of land before he was assured that all who had even a disputed title desired it should be sold."

Thus, without approving the killing of Rawiri, Governor Browne coincided with Bishop Selwyn in condemning the acts which led to his death.

Other advisers besides the Bishop, advised the Governor well. Mr. Riemenschreider, a Wesleyan missionary, assured him that not only the Ngatiawa but other tribes recognized Te Rangitake as "the real and true chief of Waitara."

The Governor appointed a Board to investigate the land question generally, in 1856, and their Report reiterated what was known already to all intelligent persons who had studied the subject.

They found that "each native has a right in common with the whole tribe over the disposal of the land of the tribe," and that "the chiefs exercise an influence in the disposal of the land, but have only an individual claim like the rest of the people to particular portions."*

Mr. Donald McLean and the Rev. Mr. Whiteley a Wesleyan minister, concurred. A Maori witness, Riwai-te-ahu, said "I consider there is no individual claim. They are all entangled or matted together—the children of our common ancestor claiming the land bequeathed to them"

There was no doubt as to the Maori land-law, nor was there any doubt as to the guarantee in the Treaty of Waitangi that the law should be maintained.

But a section of the community hated the law and the Treaty, and at the coveted land at Taranaki they eventually induced the Governor to do what they required.

The Governor's general anxieties were somewhat increased in 1857 by the election of a so-called King in Waikato.

It was by gross mismanagement on the part of some of Governor Browne's advisers that Te Waharoa, the King-maker, was driven to the resort of creating a King because the local Government failed to appreciate their duty and would not aid the Governor in doing his.

The King-movement, as the election of Te Whero Whero as King

---

* Blue Book 1861. (1341.) Presented by command, p. 200.   c

Potatau was called, was linked in many minds with the land feuds at Taranaki : but the connection was not obvious, and did not perhaps exist.

It was also said that there was an organized anti-land-selling league to refuse to sell any land to the Government, but this was denied by many.

The determination to set aside the Treaty of Waitangi in obtaining land, could not but induce resistance to that determination, and that resistance would necessarily take form in some kind of organization.

Te Waharoa said the causes of setting up the Maori King "were many." Amongst them was the injury done to his countrymen by the introduction of spirituous liquors contrary to the law and in spite of his constant efforts to arrest it.

At Taranaki the old blood-feud was suddenly revived in 1858, by an act of Ihaia, already mentioned as befriended by that section of the settlers which reviled Bishop Selwyn.

Ihaia laid a plot for the murder of Katatore, who was accordingly murdered in January, 1858, on the first occasion of being seen unarmed ; and the murder was committed, and the body was mangled, in sight of Europeans.

Te Rangitake, "the head of the tribe," took steps to punish the murderer, who took shelter in a pah. Strange sympathy was shown towards Ihaia by some Europeans. In May, 1858, the Speaker of the Provincial Council at Taranaki pleaded for him as having, "by his friendly, honest character, gained a foremost place in the esteem of the settlers. . . If at any time he has evinced hostility to the Government, he has always been actuated by a sincere desire to serve what he thought the cause of the settlers." The petition fitly entreated the Governor to compel the natives to give up their lands. Governor Browne replied that, "in reference to a proposal to coerce a minority of native proprietors, who might be disinclined to sell," he had already expressed an opinion that such a course would be unjust and impolitic, and Her Majesty's Government had conveyed to him "their unqualified approval of his views."*

Governor Browne was ashamed of the support afforded to Ihaia. He wrote (Jan. 1858), "I have expressed strong disapprobation of the conduct of the gentleman who communicated with Ihaia after the murder ; " (in April, 1858), "as the settlers' sympathies are generally with the besieged (Ihaia and friends), there is constant danger of collision between them and Te Rangitake."

A lurid light is thrown on the whole transaction by a passage written in May, 1858, by Governor Browne. Te Rangitake, who had "threatened to fire on the troops, or any one else who attempted to interfere on behalf of Ihaia" . . submitted at once to my decision in reference to the removal of Ihaia, but the latter, "*having received reinforcement and promise of further aid,* declined to accept the interference which he so earnestly solicited in his letter. . . I

---

* Blue Book, 1860. Vol. XLVII.

should also add that the settlers *openly avow their desire to possess the land*, which was the original cause, and is now the chief subject of dispute. . ."

By one outspoken settler, it was urged upon the Governor "that the Treaty of Waitangi, being no longer valuable to us, should be broken," but the Governor declined to trouble the Secretary of State with any remarks "on such a document."

Of the class to which the writer belonged, the Governor wrote (20th Sept., 1859), "The Europeans covet these lands, and are determined to enter in and possess them, *recte si possint, si non, quocunque modo*. This determination becomes daily more apparent."*

There can be no doubt that Governor Browne wrote these words sincerely. But Governors are surrounded by others who warp events, and sometimes induce results differing widely from those which upright Governors would approve of.

Such was the case in New Zealand in 1860, and from that time till the present "the Groans of the Maoris" have arisen on account of a trampled Treaty, and Englishmen have been shamed by the rejection of the prayers of Bishop Selwyn and Sir William Martin, and by the dishonour done to their country.

Efforts were made to poison the mind of the Governor against Te Rangitake, the old friend of the English, who was believed to have saved Wellington from being sacked.†

The Governor wrote in 1858 "Te Rangitake has no sort of influence with me or the Colonial Government. We believe him to be an infamous character, but I will not permit the purchase of land over which he has any right, without his consent."

The history of the war of 1860, which was the cause and precursor of the greater war of 1863, would occupy too much space in these pages. It must be perused elsewhere.

It is enough to say here that the Governor was induced to accept personally an offer by a prompted Maori, named Teira, to sell land which Teira had no power to sell, and in which Te Rangitake had a direct and tribal interest, as well as that rangatiratanga, or full right of chieftainship, which the Treaty of Waitangi had guaranteed to him and his countrymen.

Te Rangitake protested in vain. His appeals to the Governor and to his friends were scorned. His words were distorted into the opposite sense to that in which they were used.‡

---

* Blue Book. Accounts and Papers. Return; House of Commons, 1860, Vol. XLVII., p. 78.

† *Vide* note, p. 14, supra.

‡ Mr. Swanson complained of this in the New Zealand Parliament in 1881. " Why, the very Gazettes were falsified, The Maori was on one side and the English on the other, and there were falsehoods on the face of it. The English said, ' The land is Teira's, but I will not allow it to be sold.' What was on the Maori side ? ' The land was Teira's, but it is no more his property than the property of the rest of us, and I will not allow it to be sold,' which made all the difference. . . . It was nothing but an attempt to rob Te Rangitake of his land; one of the most unjust things ever done." N.Z. Hansard, 1881 vol. 40. p. 359.

Though, as the principal chief, he could forbid the sale, his attempt to do so was represented to the Governor as disloyalty to the Queen, to whom he all the while was appealing.

After his pah was attacked, it was charged against him that the Maoris had commenced the warfare, Fortunately, a military eye-witness, Lieutenant-Colonel Carey, has recorded the truth.[*] He tells us that it was after the destruction of Te Rangitake's pah that some Europeans were "attacked and killed on the Omata block." He tells us also that in spite of this fact, the coveters of Maori lands accused the Maoris of commencing the war. "The fact (p. 25) that the deaths above alluded to, took place eight or ten days after our attack on this pah was carefully kept in the background by the local papers, which tried to make it appear, and for a long time succeeded in doing so, that the Maori had commenced the war by the murder of unarmed, unwarned, and inoffensive settlers. Whereas, war having been begun by us, the natives, naturally enough, considered this retaliation a legitimate mode of fighting."

Colonel Carey testifies (p. 189) also that "the Colonists treated even the friendly tribes with the greatest brutality. The prisoners we took had to be most carefully guarded, not so much to prevent escape, as to save them from the un-English and unmanly attacks of the Europeans, who, when they could do so with safety, treated them with the greatest indignities. Widely different was the behaviour of the soldiers. . ."

It is true that the Maoris not only groaned, but fought, when they were attacked at Waitara. They knew that it was by pre-arrangement with some Europeans in Taranaki that Teira was put forward to offer the land to the Governor. They ought, perhaps, to have known that they would fail in warfare against British troops. But whither were they to go if their land was stolen? Te Rangitake wrote thus to Governor Browne, a few days before Teira was put forward to sell what was not his:—"These lands will not be given by us into your hands, lest we become like the birds of the sea, which are resting on a rock. When the tide flows, the rock is covered by the sea. The birds fly away because there is no resting place for them. . . I will not give you the land."

Dr. Featherston groaned in the New Zealand Parliament over the wrong done. Confiding in the good faith of England (he said) that "when Her Majesty's Government know that the greatest portion of the land is owned by natives who have either protested against the sale, or have never been consulted in the matter—that no investigation worthy of the name has ever been instituted into their claims;—when, Sir, the Home Government learn these facts I venture to predict that their answer to his Excellency's application for troops will be that those who have been guilty, while acting in Her Majesty's name, of so great a wrong, who have plunged the country into such a war, are no

---

[*] Narrative of the late War in New Zealand. By Lieutenant-Colonel Carey. Richard Bewley, London, 1863.

longer worthy of Her Majesty's confidence; and that, instead of reinforcements, Her Majesty's Government will send out peremptory instructions to bring the war to a close, and to prevent any further shedding of blood in so unjust a cause."

Mr. Forsaith also produced in the House, a letter from Te Rangitake, which said "My belief is the Governor is seeking to quarrel, as he is putting death before me. . . If the Governor without cause attacks me, and I am killed, there will be no help for it, because it is an old saying:—The man first, the land afterwards— that is, first kill, and then take possession."

Waharoa the Maori King-maker groaned thus about the murder of Katatore:—"He was waylaid and died by Ihaia. That was a foul murder. You looked on and made friends with Ihaia. That which we regard as a murder you set at nought; and you call that a murder which we deny to be one. . . Rangitake's pah was burned with fire: the place of worship was burnt; and a box containing Testaments; all was consumed—goods, clothes, all were consumed. The cattle were eaten by the soldiers; and the horses, 100 in number, were sold by auction by the soldiers.

It was this that disquieted the heart of Te Rangitake—his church being burnt with fire. Had the Governor given word not to burn his church, and to leave his goods and animals alone, he would have thought also to spare the property of the Pakeha."

A groan from one hundred and seventy chiefs on the East Coast (far from the scene of rapine at Waitara) was addressed to the Queen —"Mother, do not listen to the false reports which, perhaps, are sent to you. They are false. Know then that the quarrel relates to the land only. We think it desirable that you should appoint a judge for this quarrel that it may be put an end to." The Governor's advisers disparaged the petition; and, though sent to England, it was unheeded. One of the petitioners became in after-years an elected Maori member of the New Zealand Parliament.

It was not only by Maoris that Her Majesty's Government were implored to arrest the rape of the Waitara and the unjust war by which it was effected.

Bishop Selwyn and Sir William Martin spoke the words of wisdom and equity while the Governor's official supporters were darkening counsel and urging him to violence. While the Maoris sought the intervention of the Queen to maintain the Treaty, it was dinned into the Governor's ears, that Te Rangitake's desire to retain his land was an act of rebellion. A long despatch on Seignorial right was really a wordy repetition of this preposterous absurdity.

It was perfectly true that the head of the tribe had, by Maori law, the right to forbid a sale; but this right, far from being rebellious against the Queen, was one of those rights pertaining to Maori tenure which the Queen had guaranteed to the Maori chiefs, of whom Te Rangitake was one. He had indeed signed the Treaty with his own hand in 1840.

Te Rangitake had, of course, the other tribal rights which, as a

Ngatiawa, he would have enjoyed if he had not been the acknowledged head of the tribe at Waitara. The real state of the case was that those who urged the Governor to infringe Te Rangitake's rights were themselves, unwittingly, disloyal to their Queen.

Governor Browne had desired a permanent council on Native affairs : and he had urged that if Bishop Selwyn and Sir William Martin could be induced to take seats in such a council "calumny would fall harmless and unheeded. while the presence of men so well-known and so thoroughly trusted by the Maoris, would secure to it an influence which no other European body could possibly acquire." He wrote (2 June, 1859) that Martin held the "enviable distinction of being universally respected by all parties and both races."

Both Selwyn and Martin groaned bitterly at the seizure of Te Rangitake's land. After the attack on Rangitake's pah the Bishop sent a deliberate protest to the Government. He claimed (28 April, 1860) for the Maoris an investigation of all land titles before a regular tribunal, with the usual safeguards of evidence, counsel, and right of appeal, and demanded that military force should not be employed till all civil measures might fail.

The Bishop appealed in vain. The local Government kept back his appeal while they spent weeks in concocting an answer to it. Their arguments (if they deserve such a name) are recorded elsewhere and need not be repeated here. It may be well to state that they averred that if the Bishop "*desired to arouse and stimulate the hatred of race, he could not do so more effectually than by such assertions.*" As to a judicial trial of Te Rangitake's title, it "would under the circumstances, have been *something more ludicrous* than has yet been seen in our public dealing with the Maoris, which is saying a great deal." It is remarkable that the ministry which thus vilipended a legal trial contained several lawyers. The complaints of the late chief justice, Sir William Martin, took the form of a careful pamphlet on "the Taranaki question." So cogent was it that "Notes by the Governor on Sir William Martin's pamphlet" were prepared and officially promulgated.

A revised edition, not decorated with the Governor's name, was afterwards published. As the Notes contended that the words "tino rangatiratanga," or full rights of chieftainship, in the Treaty of Waitangi, meant "ownership" and not full "chiefship" as Sir W. Martin contended, one may presume that the Governor was glad to have his name withdrawn.

Ordinary tribesmen had a tribal ownership, but the attributes pertaining to a Rangatira or chief were necessarily something more, especially when he was the recognized head among the chiefs.

The groans of Sir W. Martin, besides exposing (in "Remarks" on the Revised Notes) what he deemed defiance of the Treaty, arraigned the acts of the local Government on general grounds. "It is not lawful for the Executive Government to use force in a purely civil question without the authority of a competent judicial tribunal. In this case no such authority has been obtained, no such tribunal has been resorted to. If there was no existing tribunal, the duty of the Government was to establish one. . . To acquire the Waitara land was not a necessity. To do justice to the Queen's subjects was a necessity."

Such a voice from the learned, the wise, and good, was unanswerable in the realms of reason. How would the reader think it was responded to? A member of the Government declared that Sir W. Martin's reasoning was "a public danger," and the Governor promulgated a notice that the right of discussion was "dangerous" sometimes, and that "such an occasion exists now in this colony." Thus piteously appeale to, Sir W. Martin, though his Remarks were privately printed, "abstained for the present from giving publicity within the colony" to them.*

"I have argued (he wrote) that the people of Waitara, being subjects of the Crown, have not been dealt with as subjects of the Crown." The Treaty of Waitangi guaranteed to them "all the rights and privileges of British subjects," and those rights "must mean at any rate the opposite of despotism." What was it that the Governor's advisers "called by the name of the Crown" in the Waitara case? "The Governor judging in this case is simply and in fact Mr. Parris. . . The Majesty of the Royal word, and the largeness of the national undertaking issue in the decision of an assistant Land Purchase Commissioner."

The war which followed the rape of the Waitara was not prosecuted without appeals or groans from the Bishop. But he was rudely told by a Minister that the latter denied the right of the clergy or Bishop to "interfere between Her Majesty's Government and her native subjects."

The noble Bishop replied that when others support a "policy which we believe to be unjust, we should be guilty of betraying the Native race, who resigned their independence upon our advice, if we did not claim for them all the rights and privileges of British subjects, as guaranteed to them by the Treaty of Waitangi."

No judicial enquiry as to Te Rangitake's rights was ever granted. The war of 1860 ended in 1861, and the greater war which the colonial government entered upon in 1863 by invading Waikato was also concluded, as regarded Waikato in 1864, though some of its embers in other districts were not quenched until 1865-6.

It has become a common practice with those who write without knowledge to assert, that so long as English troops were employed in

---

* The reader will observe that as my object is to set forth the condition of the Maoris and not to animadvert upon those who brought it about, I often abstain from using names of wrong-doers, except when they are needed to make the narrative intelligible. Of course in history, events must be told with greater fulness and precision. Mr. Maning, author of Old New Zealand, assured me that at this period he was implored not to publish his opinion that one of the acknowledged rights of a chief in Te Rangitake's position was to prevent the alienation of land, even if a majority should wish to alienate it. Mr. Maning declared to me that my opinions on the question were strictly correct. In 1860, he yielded to the entreaties made to him, which emanated from the highest quarters.

New Zealand, wars were badly managed, but that as soon as the Colonists were left to manage their own affairs, they speedily ended their troubles, and put down the Maoris.

Nothing can be farther from the truth. Ten thousand British troops smote down the Maoris in the war of 1863-4, after which period there was no organized resistance amongst the tribes.

It is believed that even in that war the Maoris had on no occasion so many as 600 men in their camp, or rather within their defences, in any one place, and it was not wonderful that from fortress to fortress, from Mere mere to Orakau, the English army swept the Waikato tribes from their path. Of Orakau the English General wrote: "It is impossible not to admire the heroic courage and devotion of the natives in defending themselves so long against overwhelming numbers. Surrounded closely on all sides, cut off from their supply of water, and deprived of all hope of succour, they resolutely held their ground for more than two days, and did not abandon their position until the sap had reached the ditch of their last entrenchment." When they did abandon their position they marched, in a phalanx, melting under fire, through a portion of the lines which surrounded them. Again, when near Tauranga, the British troops annihilated an inferior force of the Maoris at Te Ranga, Colonel Greer reported that the latter "fought with desperation, and when at length compelled by the bayonet to quit the trenches, in which they left more than a tenth of their number dead, it was strange to see them slowly climb up, and disdaining to run, walk away under a fire that mowed them down, some halting and firing as they retired, others with heads bent down stoically and proudly receiving their inevitable fate."

The British army thus crushed the Maori forces in 1864, and never afterwards was there any general resistance on the part of the natives. It may be added that in 1864, there were nearly ten thousand men in local forces acting with the British troops.

He who studies the annals of the time will find that while doing their duty, many British soldiers regretted the necessity which compelled them to destroy men who had been forced to fight for their land of which the Treaty of Waitangi had guaranteed their peaceful possession, but which some greedy persons coveted Colonel Carey's testimony as to the demeanour of the soldiery, as compared with that of some other persons, has been cited.

After the Maoris were crushed in 1864, there were terrible scenes in New Zealand. The Hau Hau superstition rose like an evil spirit from the ashes of past injustice and strife and stained the land. Bishop Selwyn, addressing a Synod of his church in 1865 said: "The war which seemed to have come to an end was renewed by the perversity of a few misguided men. Mixed with the *new element of the confiscation of land* it acquired a bitterness unknown before."

To soften the horrors of war, to attend to the wounded, he had himself accompanied the English troops in 1864, and he wrote to a friend that his doing so had exposed him "to the imputation of having led the troops. This has thrown me back in native estimation, more, I fear than my remaining years will enable me to recover." Confiscation of land would, to the Maori, look like premeditated spoliation. " Certainly nothing could look more like a determination to provoke a quarrel than the Waitara business. . . O, earth! earth! earth! such as been our cry. The Queen, law, religion, have been thrust aside in the one thought of the acquisition of land."*

What the Bishop deplored as "the new element of the confiscation of land," would not have been cast into the cauldron if the wise advice of the Secretary of State, Mr. (afterwards Lord) Cardwell had been taken.

When the British soldiery had taken the field in force, and the discomfiture of the Waikato tribes was a matter of certainty, the New Zealand Ministry (known as the Whitaker-Fox Ministry) introduced Bills called the "Suppression of Rebellion Bill," and the "New Zealand Settlements Bill," 1863. They became Acts.

Under the first, "suspected" persons might be tried by Court Martial. Nothing done under it could be investigated in the Supreme Court; the Habeas Corpus Act was dispensed with; and indemnity was given for all unlawful things already done.

The second enabled the Governor in Council to proclaim districts wherever "any native tribe, or section of a tribe (after 1st January, 1863), or any considerable number thereof, had been engaged in rebellion;"—and within such districts the Governor in Council might seize upon lands for settlement. Compensation to robbed Maoris might be awarded—excepting those who had warred or had " counselled, advised, induced, enticed, persuaded, or conspired with any person," to levy war.

As suspected owners might be hanged under the Suppression of Rebellion Act, the compensation provided by the Settlements Act might be kept down to a low rate; but the astute Whitaker devised a mode of defeating the operation of the compensation clause. It was provided that no claim should be "entertained unless preferred in writing to the Colonial Secretary within six months" (if the claimant were residing in the Colony) after proclamation of his land. (27 Vic. No 8. Sec. 7.)

Outlawed Maoris who had taken refuge from British bayonets, from rifles, from shot, and shell, by fleeing to distant fastnesses, were invited to enter into correspondence about their land; although, when they had done so before, in appealing to the Treaty of Waitangi, their letters had been thrust aside, and troops had been sent to drive them from their homes.

It so happened that in many tribes among the Maoris there were fast friends to the English, who had adhered to them through good and evil report. Notably at Taranaki, though it was only a minority which sided with Ihaia and Teira in pretending that they had power to sell the Waitara block, that minority had, nevertheless, tribal

---

* Letter to Rev. E. Coleridge, 26 Dec., 1865. "Life of Selwyn.' London, 1879.

rights deserving of respect within the scope of Maori land-laws, as guaranteed by the Treaty of Waitangi.

A natural consequence was, that no land could be confiscated without a breach of faith to those tribesmen who were still deemed loyal subjects.

Admitting that it was decent to break the Treaty, to rob a Maori, and to confiscate his share in land, for his resistance, there remained the difficulty that his share was only a joint right, and that on his death or removal, it accrued to the remainder of the tribe. He had no separate right which could be seized. All that he had was merged in the tribal stock.

Such a condition would have made most men adopt Mr. Cardwell's common-sense view, that if acquisition of land were deemed essential it should be brought about by a process known to Maori law; *i.e.*, cession by tribal arrangement; and not by rough contempt of Maori law—not by confiscation and seizure—which defied the rights guaranteed by the Treaty of Waitangi.

Mr. Cardwell's Despatches are models of perspicuity and honourable to English statesmanship.

For the latter reason they were not pleasing to the section of the Colonists of whom Governor Browne had written that they were "determined to enter in and possess the lands *recte si possint, si non, quocunque modo.*"

The official defence of the Settlements Act, by Messrs. Whitaker and Fox, was well calculated to cause groans among the Maoris.

The Attorney General (Whitaker) remarked that as Maoris owned little personal property, "the permanent loss of their landed possessions" was that which they would feel the most. "It will be observed," he added, "that the provisions of the Act may be made to include lands belonging to persons who have *not justly forfeited* their rights by rebellion. In order to carry out the scheme this is *absolutely necessary.* . . . The New Zealand native tenure of land is for the most part, in fact, with *little or no exception*, tribal; and if the principle were admitted that the *loyalty* or neutrality of a few individuals would preserve the lands of a tribe, the Act would for the most part be a dead letter, and that in districts where it is most required, and in which its operation would be perfectly just." In other words, when a man covets his neighbour's goods, and cannot obtain them by doing that which is lawful and right, it is *absolutely necessary* for him to do wrong.

Mr. Fox, Whitaker's colleague, grotesquely defended the Act, as exhibiting a kind of benevolence towards the Maoris. To allow "natives, rebels or others, to *retain possession of immense tracts of land*, that they neither use nor allow others to use, and which *maintains them* in a state of isolation from the European civilization," was "most "*prejudicial to the natives*," and contributed "*to the rapid extinction of the native race.*" Let it not be imagined that this was irony on the part of Mr. Fox. Dean Swift might have used such words in sarcasm: Mr. Fox seriously wrote them in reply to "Observations" (by Sir William Martin) "on the proposal to take native lands under an Act of the Assembly."

Sir W. Martin declared that he emitted this groan with a "feeling of sorrow, if not of shame;" but Sir W. Martin admitted (as I have always urged) that the majority of Colonists in New Zealand, ignor-ant of Maori history and rights, were comparatively innocent of those acts of which Bishop Selwyn said, "The Queen, law, religion, have been thrust aside in the one thought of acquisition of land."

Sir William Martin's and the Bishop's groans were alike ineffectual. The hearts of Whitaker and Fox were not softened at the time ; and many years afterwards, when the raid upon Parihaka had been con-summated, and Whitaker had become Prime Minister, the latter framed a solemn memorandum for the Governor to send to the Secre-tary of State, at the end of which, Whitaker—a prime proposer and champion of the Suppression of Rebellion and the New Zealand Set lements Acts—coolly wrote these words :—"It may indeed with confidence be asserted generally, that there is not, and has not been, anything on the Statute Book of the Colony, or in the conduct of the Colonial legislature, as regards the Maoris, to which reasonable ex-ception can be taken."[*]

Words which should indeed be graven in brass! and which, with the dire facts confuting them, I hope to preserve in these pages from the ravages of time.

The groans of the Maoris under these so-called laws, in 1864, I may well leave to the imaginations of my readers. But terrible tales might be unfolded. The homesteads of the Maoris were laid waste. Their very burial grounds were desecrated and rifled. I have stood with a Ngatimaniapoto chief by the spot where, in 1863, were his ancestral treasures, and where, in 1879, we found the site with diffi-culty on an allotment, seized under the name of confiscation, and occupied by a purchaser.

Was it wonderful that desperate thoughts filled some Maori minds ? Colonel Greer described how some of their warriors proudly met their inevitable fate on the field. A portion of the race plunged into fanatical orgies attended with unspeakable horrors.

Singularly enough, Sir W. Martin had in 1846 warned the Governor of such an effect as probable. He then wrote with regard to Earl Grey's instructions, which, if carried out, would have involved breach of Treaty and confiscation of land. "Hitherto (he said) confidence had on the whole prevailed, because no act of aggression has been committed by the Queen's Government. . . In particular those who have received Christianity are disposed to look up to us for guid-ance and Government. But let the *plan of confiscation or seizure* be once acted on, and all this will be at an end. The worst surmises of the natives will have become realities. To them we shall appear to be a nation of liars. All our means of exercising a moral influence over this people will have ceased, together with all the hopes (which

---

* Blue Book, 1883, c. 3689, p. 39.

we have nationally professed to hold most dear) of success in the work of civilizing and Christianizing them. The Christian faith itself has, from the necessity of the case, been received mainly upon our credit ; that is, in the belief that the Pakeha who proclaimed it, was a true man, honestly seeking to benefit in every way, those whom he instructed. If our dishonesty shall be seen, the Christian religion will be abandoned by the mass of those who now receive it. That such will in that case be the result, may be shown (as far as any result yet contingent can be shown at all) from the language and conduct of the natives, since the contents of Earl Grey's despatch became known. This consideration can scarcely be deemed a slight matter in the judgment of any Englishman ; certainly it cannot appear so in the judgment of any Christian man".

It was a dreary prophecy, and it was woefully accomplished in the Paimarire or Hau Hau superstition, into which a portion of the Maoris plunged, after their countrymen's groans for justice had been spurned, their land seized, and their blood shed in vain efforts to defend it.

One unqualified source of thankfulness remained. No Maori Gobel brought shame upon his profession of faith. One horror of France in 1793 was not repeated in Maori land. Bishop Selwyn, lamenting the falling away of some, declared—"Our native clergymen need not return, because they have not swerved; it may be said of each of them, like Milton's seraph Abdiel, among the faithless faithful only he. Though they be few in number, they have ever been faithful to that faith which they have espoused, and still the Native Church is full of vitality and hope."

It is hard to practise all the virtues when one's native soil is seized, the graves of one's ancestry are desecrated and rifled, and one's countrymen have fallen, as Colonel Greer described, before superior numbers and more destructive appliances of war.

Let those who will cast stones at the fallen Maori. My task is now to record his groans. I have not shrunk from recording his faults.

When Mr. Cardwell, in consideration of the entreaties of the New Zealand Ministry, determined not to recommend the immediate disallowance of the New Zealand Settlements Act, he laid down principles (26th April, 1864) by which he hoped to prevent it from being abused.

It was to be of brief duration, and he trusted in the will and capacity of the Governor, Sir George Grey, so to administer it as to foil evil desires of those who might strive to wrest the Act to manifest wrong-doing. " Considering that the defence of the Colony is at present effected by an Imperial force, I should perhaps have been justified in recommending the disallowance of an Act couched in such sweeping terms, capable therefore of great abuse, unless its practical operation were restrained by a strong and resolute hand ; and calculated if abused to frustrate its own objects, and to prolong instead of terminating the war. But not having received from you any expression of your disapproval, and being most unwilling to weaken your hands in the moment of your military success, Her Majesty's

Government have decided that the Act shall remain for the present in operation.

They are led to this conclusion not merely by a desire to sustain the authority of the Colonial Government, but also in no small degree by observing that no confiscation can take effect without your personal concurrence, and by the reliance which they so justly place on your sagacity, firmness, and experience, and your long-recognized regard as well for the interests of the colonists as for the fair rights and expectations of the native race." But cession, not confiscation, was desirable. Cession of lands should be obtained on condition of Her Majesty's clemency being extended. Only if cession should be found impossible, the Settlements Act might be brought into operation subject to reservations. It must be limited as to duration. A Commission, not removable with the Ministry, should enquire as to lands to be obtained. and the Governor's concurrence was to be no perfunctory assent, but to be withheld from any proposals unless he should be satisfied that they were just and moderate.

"I trust (wrote the wise Cardwell) that in accepting any cession, or authorizing confirmation of any forfeiture of land, *you will retain in your own hands ample power* of doing substantial justice to every class of claimant for restitution or compensation."

These instructions of the Secretary of State must be borne in mind in reading the terms of the Proclamation promulgated by Sir George Grey. Terms, which might be passed by without sufficient attention, become cogent axioms when studied with due regard to the principles by which their framer was bound.

Mr. Cardwell might reasonably hope that in the period of two years (laid down by him) Sir George Grey might define and arrange principles and details. He could hardly have anticipated that Sir G Grey would issue a proclamation qualified according to his instructions, and that seventeen years afterwards men would advocate in New Zealand a daring denial in practice of all those principles of justice which Mr. Cardwell had so earnestly commended to the Governor.*

For my present purpose it has been necessary to show under what limitations the Governor issued his Proclamations, and thus to make clear the meaning of the qualifying expressions they will be found to contain.

The Whitaker-Fox ministry did not live to see the Governor's Proclamation issued. They resented Mr. Cardwell's just words; but they were in difficulties, financial and otherwise, and reams of paper were consumed in discussions between them and the Governor.

In May 1864 they had submitted sweeping schemes to him, but he shrunk from them; declining to confound the innocent with the guilty, and to leave innocent families homeless.

---

* But even at the time there were mutterings. Mr. (now Sir W.) Fox denounced Mr. Cardwell's instructions as "directing things to be done which were physically impossible, and others to be attempted which were palpably absurd, and which if attempted to be carried out, could operate in no other way than to upset the plans of the Colonial Government." Fox's "History of the War in New Zealand."

The arrival of Mr. Cardwell's Despatch of 26th April 1864 strengthened the Governor's position; and on the 7th September Sir G. Grey prepared a proclamation drawn in compliance with Mr. Cardwell's instructions. He offered free pardon to all who might "come in on or before the 22nd October, take the oath of allegiance, and make cession of such territory as may in each instance be fixed by the Governor and Lieutenant General."

After discussion and wranglings in which Sir G. Grey declared that he would not seize any man's land more largely than justice would warrant merely because it might be wished to plant settlements, Mr. Whitaker declined (13th September) to acquiesce in the proposed proclamation.

Nevertheless, as the Treasurer of the Colony, Mr. Reader Wood, had in England assured Mr. Cardwell that he and his ministerial colleagues would "certainly co-operate with Sir George Grey in carrying out that just and temperate policy towards the native race embodied in the New Zealand Settlements Act, as limited in its operations by his instructions of April 26th" – it was difficult for the ministry to overbear the Governor and openly defy Mr. Cardwell. No proclamation of confiscation was issued while Whitaker and Fox were in office, but on the 2ᵗh October, 1864, Sir George Grey issued a Proclamation, offering pardon to all who would submit to his conditions as to cession, etc., before the 10th December, 1864. There was a list of persons excepted, on the ground that they were believed to have committed murders. There was much altercation between the Ministry and the Governor as to the terms of this Proclamation. He regarded the injunctions of Mr. Cardwell. They burned to abolish or evade them. This was inevitable, for Mr. Cardwell had seriously made known the desire of Her Majesty's Government that "the proposed appropriation of land should take the form of a cession imposed by yourself and General Cameron upon the conquered tribes;" and had written (26th May, 1864), "It is my duty to say to you plainly that if, unfortunately (your Ministers') opinions should be different from your own as to the terms of peace, Her Majesty's Government expect you to act on your own judgment, and to state to your Ministers explicitly that an army of 10,000 English troops has been placed at your disposal for objects of great Imperial, and not for the attainment of any mere local object; that your responsibility to the Crown is paramount, and that you will not continue the expenditure of blood and treasure longer than is absolutely necessary for the establishment of a just and enduring peace."

On the 26th July (reminding the Governor of the above injunctions) Mr. Cardwell added, "What I do feel it my duty to say to you plainly is, that the aid of the mother country, in men and money, is given to the Colony, on the understanding that the military measures which have, unhappily, become necessary. shall be directed by you in concert with the distinguished General in command."

Generally, such important despatches were promptly published for information in the Colony, but Whitaker and Fox resisted the usual course. They vacated office in November, 1864, without giving effect to their own sweeping demands for confiscation—indeed, without superintending the issue of any proclamation on the subject.

Mr. Weld became Prime Minister. In his uprightness all men could confide, but he was somewhat infected with the Rhadamanthine idea that it was reasonable to put down the Maoris by force, and find out afterwards whether they had been right or wrong in their contention about their lands.

The Proclamation issued after Mr. Weld's assumption of office, was dated the 17th December, 1864.*

The site of Orakau, far in the Waikato district, the Gulf of the Thames, the Waikato Heads, named in the Proclamation, attest the wideness of its terms. But there was a profession of respect for the rights of the loyal. Mr. Cardwell was not forgotten.

" The *land of those natives* who have adhered to the Queen, *sh allbe secured to them;* and to those who have rebelled, but who shall at once submit to the Queen's authority, portions of the land will be given back for themselves and their families.

The Governor will make no further attack on those who remain quiet. . . . To all those who have remained and shall continue in friendship, the Governor assures the full benefit and enjoyment of their lands.''

One paragraph intimated that the Governor would confiscate " between Wanganui and New Plymouth, and in the Province of Taranaki, such land belonging to the rebels as he may think fit."

It was not until the 2nd September, 1865, that the threatened Proclamation defining the land to be seized at Taranaki was issued. Then, under the " New Zealand Settlements Act, 1863 (or rather under an Amending Act), Sir George Grey, in Council, declared that he was " satisfied that certain Native tribes, or sections of tribes, having landed properties," had been " engaged in rebellion ; " and schedules to the Proclamation specified the area to be seized, at Waitara, Mount Egmont, Whanganui River, &c.

The Proclamation declared, nevertheless, " that *no land of any loyal inhabitant* within the said districts, whether held by native custom or under Crown grant, will be taken, *except so much* as may be absolutely necessary for the security of the country, *compensation being given for all land so taken ;* and further that all rebel inhabitants of the said districts who come in within a reasonable time and make submission to the Queen, will receive a sufficient quantity of land within the said district under grant from the Crown." Thus Sir G. Grey complied with Mr. Cardwell's injunction to retain in his own hands "ample

---

* It is contained in a New Zealand Parliamentary paper, 1879, A. — 8. A subsequent Proclamation, of 2nd September, 1865, described the area at Taranaki. That Proclamation, with a Proclamation of Peace of the same date, is in a New Zealand Parliamentary paper, 1879, A.—8. A.

power of doing substantial justice to every class of claimant for restitution or compensation."*

Simultaneously with this Proclamation of (qualified) confiscation, appeared a Proclamation of Peace.

The war was declared to be at an end. Excepting persons concerned in certain imputed murders, "all others are forgiven."

"Out of the lands which have been confiscated in the Waikato, and at Taranaki, and Ngaiiruanui the Governor will *at once*† restore considerable quantities to those of the Natives who wish to settle down upon their lands, to hold them under Crown grants, and to live under the protection of the law. For this purpose Commissioners will be sent *forthwith* into the Waikato, and the country about Taranaki, and between that place and Whanganui, who will put the natives who may desire it *upon lands at once*, and will mark out the boundaries of the blocks which they are to occupy. . . Her Majesty the Queen desires that equal laws and equal rights and liberties may be enjoyed by all her subjects in this Island, and to that end the Governor in the name of the Queen publishes this Proclamation."

I have said that no judicial investigation of Te Rangitake's rights at the Waitara was ever granted. ‡ To have called in ten thousand British soldiers to defend an act of rapine, and then to hold an enquiry, the result of which must inevitably have condemned that act—would have been galling. Therefore all Bishop Selwyn's and Sir W. Martin's entreaties for a judicial investigation of Te Rangitake's case were rejected.

The land was seized: the chief brooded in seclusion over his broken fortunes, and reflected how ill his exertions to save the settlement at Wellington in former years, had been rewarded.

But the spoil had to be divided. The false Teira and those who suborned him—his friends, and theirs—demanded payment. Raro antecedentem scelestum Deseruit pede pœna claudo.

---

* It cannot be said that intelligent persons misunderstood the Proclamation. Sir F. Dillon Bell, speaking of it in the New Zealand Parliament in 1879, said, "It was untrue to say that the whole of the land between the Waitotara and the White Cliffs had been confiscated. It never had been confiscated. The only instrument by which the claim of confiscation was ever set up, was the proclamation bearing the signatures of Sir George Grey as Governor, and of Mr. Fitzgerald as Native Minister in Mr. Weld's government. What did that say? It confiscated the land of those in rebellion; but it not only did not confiscate the land of those who remained loyal, it conserved their rights, and made the express promise to them that their land should not be taken. That was an undeniable fact." New Zealand Hansard, 1879, Vol. 34, p. 864.

† Doubtless the Governor was sincere in these promises in the name of the Queen. But it will be seen that they were never performed, and that finally in 1881 a large armed force, acting without law, destroyed a peaceful village, robbed its inhabitants, dragged them away by force, and obtained an Act of Indemnity for its misdeeds.

‡ Sir George Grey was not the Governor of the Colony when the Waitara land was seized in 1860. He became Governor for a second time in 1861, and finding, after inquiry through Captain Nugent (58th Regt.) that the seizure had been improper, he resolved to restore the block. But he could not abolish the war and its consequences. His opinion was assailed, and had no effect on the general state of affairs.

The Proclamation of September, 1865, had in a qualified manner confiscated a large district which comprised the Waitara block, but it promised that the Governor would at once restore land to natives desirous to " settle down upon their lands." . . The promised Commissioners were not sent *forthwith*, but Governors cannot always be blamed for a breach of faith which sometimes their ministers cause.

For many long years the promise was set at nought. But, though a legal trial of Te Rangitake's case was refused, its facts incidentally received the attention of a Court.

There was a Native Lands Court, and there was a Compensation Court. Mr. Fenton presided in both of them.

When an amended Native Lands Act was passed (in the administration of Mr. Weld) in 1865, not only Mr. Fenton, but Mr. Mantell, and Sir William Martin, made suggestions, and the latter drew up a paper which is still to be seen in the Blue Books, but was not sufficiently respected.

Some influence was exercised by Mr. Cardwell in tempering oppressive legislation.

He warned the Governor (October, 1865) that in cases touching the honour or interests of the Crown, the adherence to treaties entered into by Her Majesty, and other matters of an analogous kind, the Royal power of disallowing Acts was not abandoned, and would be exercised unless the ministry would moderate their demands, and limit the duration of the Settlements Act to a definite period.

Through his means the Act of 1863 was amended in 1864, and as it was still unsatisfactory, Mr. Cardwell held the power of disallowance over it while he communicated with the Governor as to its administration. In 1865 it was again amended, and the 3rd December, 1867, was fixed as the time when the Governor's power to proclaim districts and seize upon lands was to cease.

The Compensation Court, under Mr. Fenton as Senior Judge, and Judges Rogan and Monro, sat at Taranaki (New Plymouth) in 1866 to decide upon "the claims of persons to compensation on account of the taking under the authority of the New Zealand Settlements Act of the blocks of land in the province of Taranaki hereunder described."

Te Rangitake's ravished land at the Waitara was within the area described in the official announcement of the sitting of the Court. There was also a block called the Oakura block.

The Judges found a difficulty which they had no means of solving. The Confiscation Proclamation of 1865 had declared that "no land (of any loyal native) would be taken except so much as may be absolutely necessary for the security of the country, compensation being given for all land so taken."

It had proclaimed also that the Governor would "*at once restore*" lands to those natives who wished "to settle down upon their lands."

This promise had not been complied with. On the contrary,

the Agents for the Government had allotted to military settlers,"* so much land in the block that it was impossible to comply. with it.

A chief groaned over this injustice and breach of faith. "I demand that our compensation be within the block; the blood of my relations is on the land. Remember my services during the war. My cattle, my sheep, my pigs, and all my property went in the war; my wheat and my cultivations; and I never received any compensation for them, though the Pakehas (the Europeans) have all been compensated. What I did was not rewarded. Let the Government now fulfil its promises."

A Mr. Atkinson, Crown Agent, opposed the chief and his brethren. The Court examined their claims and found that seventy-six claimants were entitled to 7400 acres in the block, but that the Government Agents had so squandered the land that justice could not be done by the Court to the native rightful claimants.

Their own words (New Zealand P. Paper 1866. A. No. 13) were— "Having thus arrived at the, to us, unavoidable conclusion that the claimants before us were entitled to 7400 acres of *good land* in this block, and having accepted Mr. Atkinson's assertions that the *whole of the available land*, except 2,500 acres *had been appropriated* to military settlers, the question then arose, What are we to do? We thought that possibly the Government were not aware of the large majority of owners of this land who had remained loyal, and reflecting on the great public calamity which would be caused, and the serious embarrassment which would occur to the Government if we issued orders of the Court extending, as they would have done, over the lands of considerable numbers of these military settlers, we determined to despatch one of our number to Wellington to place the state of affairs before the Government and give them an opportunity of availing themselves of the power given to the Colonial Secretary by the 9th Clause of the Act of 1865."

The upshot was that the Minister for Native Affairs returned with the Judge and "effected an arrangement with the claimants." "What the terms were, the Court did not think it their duty to enquire. In consequence of this agreement having been come to no adjudication was made by the Court, as our jurisdiction was gone."

The groans of the chief, the blood of whose "relatives was on the land," availed not to restore him to his birthright.

Those who despised his groans poured upon Bishop Selwyn on one occasion at Taranaki the insults with which mobs salute those whom they dislike.

But they who thus assailed the Bishop were not of the class of which ordinary mobs are composed. They belonged to that section of

---

* The "military settlers ' did not settle. It was admitted that the majority of them secured their allotments merely to sell them. The children of the soil were cursed at by some persons for groaning when they saw their birthplace thus rent and gambled with.

whom Governor Browne wrote in 1859, that they "coveted the Maori lands, and were determined to enter in and possess them, *recte si possint, si non quocunque modo;* " and they have possessed them—and they dislike exposure.

The Compensation Court was called upon to hear evidence at Taranaki in 1866, respecting that block of land at Waitara which Teira had been put forward to sell to the Governor in 1859, and the seizure of which by the troops produced the wars of 1860 and 1863-4.

The claims of the paramount chief Te Rangitake were not before the Court. Resistance against robbery had made him a rebel. The loyal among his tribe shared his diminution. No Court was empowered to deal with their claims. The disloyal to him were called loyal to the Queen. Their "faith unfaithful made them falsely true," and they were permitted to put their claims for Compensation before the Court.

In examining those claims the Court was constrained to regard the abstract rights of Te Rangitake—not with a view to recognize them in themselves, but in order to prevent Teira and others from making exorbitant demands.

The examination proved how righteous had been the protests of Bishop Selwyn and Sir W. Martin. The Court discovered that even without reference to Te Rangitake's paramount position which enabled him to forbid any sale, he had superior claims of personal inheritance to those of Teira. The case itself I have described in a special chapter of another work and need not repeat here. But since that work was published notable evidence has been supplied by Mr. Fenton who presided at the Compensation Court in 1866; and I take the opportunity of quoting it.

On the 3rd September, 1885, Mr. Fenton while giving evidence before the Committee on Native Affairs in Wellington, referred to the fact of his having examined the Waitara case in 1866.

A New Zealand Parliamentary Paper (I 2B. 1885) reports thus:

"770. *Sir G. Grey.* You said that you heard the Waitara case? A. Yes.

771. Did you finish it? A. We finished it, but we did not give any judgment. There were three of us. Judge Monro, Judge Rogan, and myself.

772. Did you ascertain whether William King (*i.e.* Te Rangitake) had any right to the land? A. Yes, he was the principal owner; his was a very curious title. There was a man whose name I forget: he represented or his successors represented, two or three tribes, and in the curious way of transferring, it came out that the father belonged to the one tribe, and a son and a daughter might belong to another tribe.

A European cannot understand it. However, this man, seven or eight generations back had two daughters whose names I do not remember* . . They were what we would call in England coheiresses. There was descent, and descent from each of these until we come to William King (Te Rangitake) . . So that according to Maori custom in those days the *mana* of the land came to William King.

773. I assume that you mean that power over the tribe and over the land vested in him? A. He had the principal 'say' to use a somewhat vulgar term.

774. It had been overlooked in previous investigations? A. If there ever was one. The thing is perfectly clear; there is no doubt whatever about it.

775. This has never been put upon record, and I am anxious to have it put on record. I will therefore put it in this way, so that there may be no misapprehension: Was William King (*i.e.* Te Rangitake) the real owner of the land? A. He represented the owners: he was the principal man. There were other owners, of course, but he was the principal man." On the following day Mr. Fenton produced the "pedigree book" and added—

789. "When the Crown Officer appeared in Court and objected to Te Teira's title to the six-hundred acre block, I thought it a very singular proceeding, although I did not say anything. It occurred to me that possibly the Crown Officer was acting without instructions. I wrote a letter to Mr. Domett who was not in the Government, and asked him to be good enough to see the Government, and make them acquainted with what was being done. This, I should say, was a Compensation Court, not a Native Land Court. I adjourned the case (not the Court) for some days. It had progressed some length before I found out what was the real contest. After the expiration of some days a Minister came down to Waitara—a Minister I think it was, and the case came on on the day to which it had been adjourned. When called in Court there was no appearance. Of course I presumed from that that it was arranged out of Court. At any rate we had no further functions."

Such was the result of that kind of enquiry which Bishop Selwyn implored the Government in New Zealand to grant instead of plunging into war. But it came too late to do more than furnish information as to the trnth.

With Mr. Fenton's plain statement before us now, it is hard for any one not acquainted with New Zealand affairs to believe that when the Governor had been urged to seize the Waitara by force, one of his advisers, a lawyer, in an official memorandum (20th March, 1860,) demanding troops, wrote—"An occasion has now arisen on which it has become necessary to support the Governors authority by a military

---

* The reader who cares to do so, will find the names on a genealogical table (quoted by me elsewhere) in a New Zealand Parliamentary Paper. 1866. A. 23. He may find also an extract from an Auckland Newspaper showing that in 1879 a reporter saw Teira, and Teira "acknowledged that he had done wrong in insisting on the sale of Waitara in spite of Te Rangitake."

force. *The issue has been carefully chosen—the particular question being as favourable a one of its class as could have been selected.*"*

Bishop Selwyn, (April 1860, vide Blue Book 1861, p. 48) in a letter to the Government, claimed " on behalf of the New Zealanders,

1. An investigation of all questions relating to their title to land, before a regular tribunal, with the usual safeguards against partiality or error; viz. evidence on oath, arguments of counsel, and a right of appeal.

2. That military force shall not be employed till the civil power shall have been tried and shall have been found insufficient to carry out the judgment of the Court."

Sir W. Martin's protests were equally noble and equally disregarded. Those who care to study the matter after seeing that a Judge who heard the case, pronounced Te Rangitake's rights irrefragable, will find in the Blue Book above quoted a Despatch (4th December, 1860) occupying with enclosures eighty-six pages, in which Governor Browne was made to contend that Te Rangitake had no rights at all. It may be supposed that, if the scribes who framed that Despatch could have foreseen that in order to diminish Teira's claims a Court of Justice would be at last set in motion to try the matter and Te Rangitake's title would be made clear, the Despatch would never have been written.

On the 17th and 18th March, 1860, artillery, rockets, and other appliances were brought to bear to drive Te Rangitake from his land,† and "after much labour," his pah "was taken to pieces and burnt," by the officer commanding the forces in New Zealand.

On the 27th March the Maoris retaliated by killing "three settlers and two boys."‡

On the 11th April, the Rev. T. Buddle, a Wesleyan minister, heard some of the groans of the Maoris at Waikato, and reported them. Tapihana said : "I mourn for the blood of Te Rangitake; my blood is the blood of Te Rangitake."

Karamoa said: "Alas! for me; my affliction is great. I have talked about land till I am weary, now I sit in my grief; my very vitals move. I shake like the leaves of the weeping fern-tree for my children. Come you, and tell us of death; you have come from the scenes of death. Bring your grief to us; pour out your sorrow. I am here sympathizing and weeping for my children. . . Am I not a man ? The very fountain of blood in the heart will burst with the depth of my feeling."¶

Such were the groans heard at the beginning of the strife caused

---

* Blue Book 1861. (1341) Recent Disturbances in New Zealand, p. 274. "Copy of Memorandum from Mr. C. W. Richmond to Colonel Gore Browne." The Governor of New South Wales, Sir W. Denison, when asked for troops, sent them ; but in a careful letter (ib. 277,278 of Blue Book) animadverted on the "immoral and impolitic" nature of the proposed treatment of the Maoris, as explained in Mr. Richmond's Memorandum.

† Blue Book, 1861 (1341), p. 16.

‡ ib., p. 24.   ¶ ib. p. 39.

by the rape of the Waitara, and such they remained during the larger
strife, when the Waikato was invaded in 1863, and a gallant British
soldiery struck down the Maoris.

Despair made the worser spirits amongst them savage, and the
abominable superstition of Hauhauism reared its head, proving the
truth of Sir W. Martin's prediction of the consequence of linking the
Government with oppression and falsehood.

But always there were some who appealed to the Queen to interpose
mercifully, and allow law to prevail.

One hundred and seventy chiefs at Napier sent their petition to
her : "Mother, do not listen to the false reports which, perhaps, are
sent to you. They are false. Know, then, that the quarrel relates
to the land only. We think it desirable that you should appoint a
Judge for this quarrel, that it may be put an end to." Their petition
was vilipended in the Colony, and probably never seen by the Queen.

On one point, in 1862, the Secretary of State, the Duke of New-
castle, respected the rights of the Maoris.

The New Zealand Ministry desired to seize Maori lands for roads,
in defiance of the Treaty of Waitangi. Mr. F. D. Fenton doubted
the legality of the attempt. The Attorney General, Whitaker, wrote
(21st February, 1863) : "It may be objected that this would be contrary to the Treaty of Waitangi. To this I answer that a positive
enactment of the legislature would prevail over the terms of the
Treaty if there were any conflict." How many contracts between Europeans would be broken if one of the contracting parties could, by
his sole resolution, free himself from obligations !

The Duke wrote that he would "hesitate to admit as a strict matter
of law that Her Majesty had the power, without any legislative sanction, of appropriating for any purpose the acknowledged property of
her subjects. But even if it were true that the peculiar legal condition of New Zealand authorized the application of this arbitrary
principle, I am of opinion that the question cannot be dealt with as
one of strict law." Policy and justice required that the Treaty of
Waitangi should be respected by the Government, and in a war undertaken to seize land for roads, however convenient for the settlers
at Taranaki, "Her Majesty's troops ought not to be employed."

The reader will find that in later years a Secretary of State, Lord
Kimberley, received, without apparent demur, accounts of making
roads through Maori cultivated fields, and of the seizure and sale of
the fields themselves.

Departments, like men, may become familiar with that which once
presented to them a hateful mien.

But ever and anon, some strong man signalizes his presence. Such
was Mr. Cardwell, who wrote to Governor Grey, in 1864 : "It is my
duty to say to you plainly that if, unfortunately, your Ministers'
opinion should be different from your own as to the terms of peace,
Her Majesty's Government expect you to act upon your own judg-

ment, and to state to your Ministers explicitly that an army of 10,000 English troops has been placed at your disposal for objects of great Imperial, and not for the attainment of any mere local object; that your responsibility to the Crown is paramount, and that you will not continue the expenditure of blood and treasure longer than is absolutely necessary for the establishment of a just and enduring peace."

The groans which reached Mr. Cardwell's ears received consideration. Many failed to reach them.

When war was resumed in 1863, it was reported that some volunteers desecrated a native burial-ground at Papakura. The upright William Swainson, formerly Attorney General of the Colony, wrote: "The act is a disgrace to our cause . . . if it be not publicly censured by the authorities, the Government of New Zealand will be irretrievably disgraced. If the natives had thus desecrated one of our burial-grounds! The bodies were not even the bodies of enemies."

Can it be wondered at that the Maoris groaned over these things, or that some of them resorted to savage and unjustifiable revenge?

There is something touching in the words of Tamati Ngapora (uncle of the Maori King), and of Te Waharoa, the King-maker, with regard to desecration of burial-grounds.

The English troops had always Maori allies, and after the capture of Rangiriri with more than 180 of its Maori garrison, in 1863, one of these allies—the well-known, high-bred chief, Te Wheoro—went with a message from General Cameron to his defeated countrymen.

Mindful, perhaps, of the deeds condemned by Swainson, they handed to Te Wheoro the flagstaff of the King, saying: "We give over this flagstaff to you, with those buried here and at Ngaruawahia, for you to give over to the General and to the Governor. Especially let not the remains of the dead be ill-treated by the soldiers."*

History tells how the submission was slighted, and how, groaning over the result, a friendly chief wrote to one of the Ministers that some Maoris distrusted the Government, fearing ill-treatment after surrender. "This is the cause of their sadness, and in persisting in their evil course until death."

The Minister was not affected by the appeal, and considered the friendly suppliant "not disinterested," because some of his relatives were prisoners of war.

---

* All the fighters were, perhaps, included in the term. Colonel Carey's statement as to the different conduct of the soldiers and settlers at Taranaki has been quoted. At Rangiriri, in Waikato, when the remnant of the Maori garrison surrendered—" the soldiers sprang in amongst them, and commenced shaking hands with the Maoris " —and General Cameron wrote to the Governor: " I hope the prisoners will be treated generously, for everyone must admire the gallant manner in which they defended their position to the last." History shows that the prisoners were not treated generously, and that Sir George Grey had much contention with his Ministers on the subject. Mr. Cardwell eventually promised to uphold the Governor in his views, which were in favour of clemency.

Fighting or groaning, the Maori gained nothing.

Let it not be supposed, however, that no noble spirits yearned for nobler treatment of the Maoris. Even in 1862 Mr. Fitzgerald moved resolutions in the New Zealand Parliament, recognizing the rights of the Maoris to "full and equal enjoyment of civil and political privileges," and asserting that such recognition "necessitated the personal aid of one or more native chiefs in the administration of the Government of the Colony—the presence of members of the Maori nobility in the Legislative Council, and a fair representation in this House of a race which constitutes one-third of the population of the Colony."

Mr. Fitzgerald was unsuccessful. Instead of yielding the equal rights guaranteed by the Treaty of Waitangi, the Governor's advisers asked for more British troops. The total male Maori population in the North Island, including children, was less than 30,000, and the groans of the New Zealand Ministers, backed by the recommendations of Governor Browne, induced Her Majesty's Government to send 10,000 soldiers to beat down the resistance of those who clung to their birth-places which a solemn Treaty had guaranteed that they should retain. And when the two or three thousand who composed the fighting force scattered throughout the Island had been beaten down, as they were sure to be, they who had petitioned for an army to quell the Maori resistance, boasted that they were able to manage their affairs without help! And they supply the bulk of the literature on the subject. And when any man tears away the veil which conceals the truth, they revile him.

If Mr. Cardwell could have anticipated the use to which the Acts for Confiscation of Land would have been put, it may safely be said that they would not have been sanctioned in England. He advocated cession rather than confiscation, and told the Governor: "I trust that in accepting any cession, or authorizing confirmation of any forfeiture of land, you will retain in your own hands ample power of doing substantial justice to every class of claimant for restitution or compensation."

Mr. Cardwell's instructions appear reasonable to ordinary understandings. But those inured to the groans of their fellow-creatures despised them. One of the New Zealand Ministers of 1864, Mr. (now Sir William) Fox, published a book, in which he denounced Mr. Cardwell for "directing things to be done which were physically impossible, and others to be attempted which were palpably absurd, and which, if attempted to be carried out, could operate in no other way than to upset the plans of the Colonial Government."

Mr. Cardwell had declared that the "Imperial and Colonial Governments were bound to adjust their proceedings to the laws of natural equity, and to the expectations which the Maoris had been encouraged or allowed to form." Natural equity was repulsive to those who coveted Maori lands.

Some attempt to respect it was embodied in the terms of Sir George Grey's Proclamation of Peace in 1865 (already quoted), but as those terms were not loyally adhered to by some New Zealand Ministries, Mr. Cardwell's wholesome injunctions failed to produce the desired effect.

The War in New Zealand was practically ended in 1864, but there were desultory operations afterwards. In 1865 troops were employed on the West Coast, and General Cameron thought that the operations were made to subserve a desire for land. " I have made enquiries about the purchase of the Waitotara block (he wrote 28th January) and have reason to believe that it was a more iniquitous job than that of the Waitara block. I am not surprised that the natives have opposed our road-making. The government at home ought to be made acquainted with the true history of the business."

The groans of the Maoris reached the General's ears; but could not of course, arrest him in the execution of duty.

There can be no doubt that some horrors occurred which the commanding officers strove to prevent. When General Cameron was in the Waikato in 1864, and Bishop Selwyn nobly accompanied the army, hoping to soften the rigours of the strife, an event occurred which was doubtless unseen not only by the Bishop, but by the General. The General's report of it was that " the few natives who were found in the place (Rangiaohia) were quickly dispersed, and the greater part escaped, but a few of them taking shelter in a whare made a desperate resistance until the Forest Rangers and a company of the 65th Regiment surrounded the whare which was set on fire, and the defenders either killed or taken prisoners." No doubt the report to the General was to this effect. A soldier of the 65th, to whom I spoke in after years, was by no means proud of the occurrence, and did not claim it as the act of his corps, but rather of the local force—the Forest Rangers.

A chief, Whitiora te Kumete, who had won admiration from the English soldiery at Rangiriri in 1863, thus described the occurrence to Mr. Firth, in June, 1869. " General Cameron told us to send our women and children to Rangiaohia, where they should remain unmolested; but he went away from Paterangi with his soldiers after them, and the women and children were killed and some of them burnt in the houses. You did not go to fight the men; you left them, and went away to fight with the women and little children. These things you conceal, because they are faults on your side, but anything on our side you set down against us, and open your mouths wide to proclaim it. That deed of yours was a foul murder, and yet there is nobody to proclaim it."

When a petition from Te Waharoa, noble in every sense of the word, was presented to the House in New Zealand by Mr. Fitzgerald in 1865, the same dolorous complaint was found.

Te Waharoa had been dwelling at his place " great darkness and sorrow of heart," groaning over his country's woes; he had always sought peace, and condemned savage practices; but they had been wreaked upon his own people, and he moaned "because of my women and children having been burnt alive in the fire, which was suffered, rather than the edge of the sword, to consume their flesh. I would not have regarded it, had it been only the men."*

In 1865 the atrocities committed by the Hau-haus induced other military operations, and many friendly Maoris co-operated in putting down their fanatical countrymen.

In September, 1865, the Governor's Proclamation of Peace declared that absolute war was at an end.

In 1866 the Governor, Sir George Grey, had peaceful interviews with Maoris recently at war on the East Coast and at Waikato. The king-maker, Te Waharoa, whom he saw at the latter place, promised to visit Wellington to give information as to Maori affairs. He kept his promise.

After his promise (made in May, 1866) there were encounters at the East and at the West.

Near Napier, Mr. Donald McLean, Superintendant of Hawke's Bay, in October, mustered men to disperse Hau-haus at Omaranui and reported that with the help of his native allies—"Nearly all the turbulent spirits are now killed or taken." On the West, in August, an undefended village named Pokaikai was attacked at night by a colonial force and many of its inmates were slain. One woman complained that her father and mother were shot. The attack was made, she said, "at night; at midnight when the people were asleep. The sleep was the sleep of fools; for the words of the Governor, sent through Te Ua, had lulled us. My children were lying around me in fancied security."

Also at Pungarehu on the West Coast a village was surprised and burnt. Twenty-one dead bodies were counted, but it was reported that "others could not be counted as they were buried in the burning ruins of the houses." (Blue Book, 1869, (307,) p.29.)

Lord Carnarvon (28 Dec. 1866,) called for some explanation about the attacks on Omaranui and Pungarehu, which the newspapers spoke of. Mr. (now Sir) Edward Stafford said that such a mode of "warfare may not accord with War Regulations, but it is one necessary for and suited to local circumstances." (ib. p. 25.)

The groans of the women and children were piteous, but they were not heard in England; whether any of them were stifled at Pungarehu, is not reported.

Even desultory warfare was at an end in 1866, and the Governor, Sir George Grey, visited the districts where it had raged in 1864, at Tauranga and Waikato.

A proclamation of peace was issued, and a Bill of Indemnity for all severities practised against the Maoris was passed. It was so

---

* Whitiora's speech is in the English Blue Book of 1870, C. 83 p. 30. Te Waharoa's petition is in the New Zealand Parliamentary Papers.

wide in its scope that the Secretary of State declined to recommend
it for Her Majesty's approval, because its terms protected any wanton
destroyer, who, without any order from civil or military authority,
might have destroyed the property of the innocent. In deference to
his opinion an altered Bill became law in 1867. But those who
had suffered in such a manner that the large terms of the Bill of
1866 were demanded to condone unlawful acts, still groaned ineffect-
ually. To some it seemed vain labour to seek restitution from those
who had laid waste their houses and cultivations. Some who had
ever been friendly to the local Government sent their petitions to the
Throne, but intervening Departments impeded their progress.

They deplored the seizure of their lands; they knew not whether
the confiscations had been sanctioned by the Queen. Could not
some at least, of the land be restored? They complained that no
Maori voice could be raised in the legislature against wrong, and
thus evils were perpetuated. The Land Court was odious;—"An
unjust Court is summoned and much money is wasted; the Court sits
and all is in confusion—the spirit is wearied. , . . O Queen!
let your love for us be expressed. (They had fought for her.) If
you behold this letter let your reply float over the ocean to us—to
your loving children."

Loyal as Mete Kingi, Hori Kingi, Rangihiwinui and their brother
petitioners had been, their prayer was not suffered to reach the Queen.
They were told to apply through the Governor.

One part of their prayer was accomplished soon afterwards.

That which Mr. Fitzgerald had aimed at in 1862 was brought about.
Maori members took their seats in the Parliament of New Zealand
on the 9th of July, 1868, and they could officially record their groans,
even though they might fail to remedy wrong. Sir G. Grey proposed
in 1865 to "obtain a parliamentary representation of the native
race." and within three years his object was attained.

He was Governor when the enabling Act was passed (10th October,
1867), and the man who carried it through its different stages in
the House was Mr. Donald McLean. Sir George Grey in his speech
closing the Parliament said, the Act would "commend itself to the
Maori race, and tend to confirm the peaceful and friendly disposition
which is everywhere spreading throughout the tribes recently in
rebellion." Doubtless, such was its tendency, but Sir G. Grey
had not quitted New Zealand long, before, in addition to the
enduring wrongs of confiscation, and to the sporadic, though
not general, ill-treatment of the Maoris, two special acts of folly
brought about, not a state of war, but partisan risings which produced results of a terrible character.

During operations on the East Coast against the Hau-haus in
1865, Te Kooti Rikirangi, friendly to the Colonists, was blunderingly
arrested, and without trial or even enquiry, deported, and imprisoned
at the Chatham Islands.

A member of the New Zealand Parliament procured a Return which proved this, and he said in the House (N.Z., Hansard 1882, Vol. xliii. p. 913.) "It is perfectly notorious that the whole of these natives were taken down to the Chatham Islands without any warrant whatever, and entirely against the law; that they were imprisoned and detained there against the law, and that when they effected their escape by seizing a vessel, they behaved with extreme moderation under the circumstances."

Bishop Selwyn said of them in the House of Lords, "They were told if they conducted themselves well, at the end of two years they would be set at liberty.

They behaved in the most exemplary manner; but at the expiration of the two years they were informed that they were not to be set at liberty, whereupon a look of despair at once came over them, as if every hope they had of life had been cut off."

Mr. Ritchie. a resident at the Chatham Islands, urged, in April 1868, that enquiry should be made about their cases, but the Premier, Mr. (now Sir Edward) Stafford, made light of Mr. Ritchie's requests.

In July 1868, Te Kooti seized a vessel, landed near Poverty Bay, and though immediately attacked, beat off his assailants, and marked his path with blood for years, until he took shelter in the Waikato country with the Maori king, as Tawhiao was called.

The atrocities of Te Kooti were in no manner supported by the Maori race. They were suppressed mainly by Maoris, Rangihiwinui, Ropata, Topia Turoa, and their followers.

Daring and active as he was in guerilla warfare, Te Kooti had no power to cause what could be called a New Zealand war, though he made his lawless treatment by the government a costly blunder to the colonists. His career I have told elsewhere without drawing any veil over his ferocity. Here it is only necessary to show that the New Zealand government did not even pretend that ordinary law or usages restrained their own conduct towards him.

With the help of Ropata, the Ngatiporou chief, the Colonial forces attacked Te Kooti at Ngatapa in January 1869.

The official return of the result is contained in one grim line—

"3rd and 5th January 1869.

Ngatapa; killed 136; captured none; total 136."*

As the women accompanied Te Kooti's band, it might be inferred from this return that many women were slaughtered; but, the commanding officer, Colonel Whitmore, reported "I think very few women, and those only by accident have been killed." (Blue Book, (307,) 1869, New Zealand, p. 341.) As no prisoners were spared the women must fortunately have been fleet of foot.

In a work, "Reminiscences of the War in New Zealand," by T. W. Gudgeon, the killing of the prisoners taken is told thus (p. 252.) "The system was simple; they were led to the edge of the cliff, stripped of the clothing taken by them from the murdered settlers, then shot, and their bodies thrown over the cliff where their bones

* N. Z. Parl Papers, 1869. A. No. 3. G. The Return is also in the English Blue Book C. 83 of 1870, p. 78.

lie in a heap to this day. Some of the pursuers were two days absent, and even these brought in prisoners. In all, about 120 Hauhaus were killed including one chief of high rank Nikora Te Whakaunua of Taupo. Weakened by his wound, he was unable to escape."

The official report of the commander of the Colonial forces thanked Mr. J. C. Richmond, one of the Ministry, "who was present during the whole of the operations." A reward of £1,000 was offered for Te Kooti at this time, alive or dead.

In July 1868 a newspaper in Wellington (Wellington Independent 21 July) had recommended that "no prisoner should be taken. Let a price be put on the head of every rebel, and let them be slain without scruple, wherever the opportunity is afforded. We must smite and spare not."

Another paper said, "Give a reward for every rebel's head that is brought to head quarters. " *The Hawke's Bay Times* said, in December 1868, 'The fatal clause which requires the rebels to be brought in alive will completely nullify the effect intended.' Soon afterwards it seems that the misnamed clause was modified. Statements about it found their way to England, and Lord Granville wrote (26 Feb. 1869)—"I find it said that the escape of a large proportion of the prisoners from the Chatham Islands is to be ascribed to the fact that they had been taken there with the expectation or promise that they should be brought back to New Zealand after a given time; that it was only when this expectation or promise was left unfulfilled that they made their escape, and that on their return to their country they did not offer any violence to the settlers till attempts were made to hunt them down." (This refers to Te Kooti.)

I find it also said that the disturbances on the West Coast arose from an arbitrary seizure of two natives as pledges or hostages for the return of two horses which were retaken by the natives after having been captured by General Chute. (This was the case of Titokowaru.)*

"I see it stated in the newspapers that you (Governor Sir G. F. Bowen) have offered a reward of £1000 for the person of the Maori chief Titokowaru, I infer alive or dead, and £5 for the person of every Maori rebel brought in alive. I do not pronounce any opinion at present as to the propriety of these steps. But I must observe that they are so much at variance with the usual laws of war, and appear at first sight so much calculated to exasperate and extend hostilities, that they ought to have been reported to me by you officially, with the requisite explanation which I shouldnow be glad to receive."†

The inept reply of the Governor is to be found in the English Blue

---

* Most of these facts are in the English Blue Books, 1869. (307) and 1870, C. 83. The Native Minister reported (as to the Maoris wrongfully arrested as horse-stealers)—"Two of the prisoners were quickly released as nothing could be proved against them ; the third was detained, but subsequently made his escape." (Blue Book, 1869 (307.)p. 159.)

† Blue Book, 1870 (C. 83.) p. 184.

Book of 1870. He sent a memorandum from his Premier, Mr. Stafford who wrote—"Earl Granville asks for information respecting an alleged offer of a reward of one thousand pounds for the capture of the chief Titokowaru. The report which has reached the Colonial office is exactly true, as also the inference drawn by his Lordship, that it was implied in the offer that the reward would be given for the body of Titokowaru, alive or dead.

Ministers regret if this offer has not been reported in the copious Minutes of events furnished to His Excellency for transmission by every mail. It is now right to add that a similar reward on the same terms has been offered for the body of Te Kooti." Mr. Stafford did not say that law justified such offers—he could not even allege that martial law had been proclaimed—but he thought that, after study of the subject, Earl Granville would conclude that the atrocities of Titokowaru and Te Kooti were "happily as exceptional as the course adopted with a view to their punishment."

Earl Granville accepted the explanations furnished as " full and satisfactory." Whether if Titokowaru aud Te Kooti had defended themselves in like manner, their explanations would have been deemed equally "full and satisfactory,' cannot be inferred. Under the circumstances they could not communicate with the Earl. Titokowaru once sent a letter to an officer of the Colonial forces under a flag of truce, but his two messengers were seized and imprisoned—a fact duly recorded in the New Zealand Parliamentary Papers of 1869 (A. No. 10) but which I have failed to discover amongst the voluminous papers sent to England. It may nevertheless be amongst the thousands of pages sent. Mr. Gudgeon mentions the incident in his ' Reminiscences.'

The Despatches of the time contain many requests from the Governor that the 18th Regiment might remain in the Colony.

So serious was the result of provoking Titokowaru by the seizure of Maoris against whom it was admitted that "nothing could be proved"—that the magistrates at Wanganui on the 29th September, 1868, prayed for Imperial troops, the House of Representatives at Wellington on the 2nd October addressed the Governor in the same strain, and he repeatedly urged similar requests upon Lord Granville.

On the 20th of April, 1869, The Earl wrote* to the Governor, Sir G. Bowen, that he had seen " with very great concern " the following words in a New Zealand newpaper:— " The Hon. Mr. Richmond has offered a reward of £50 for the head of Nikora, £500 for that of Te Kooti, and I hear £1 per head for any of the others......the good effect has been seen in the arrival of a great many prisoners who are shot as soon as they arrive."

"I trust (the earl added) you will be able to inform me that it is "untrue, and I am led to hope this, both by the doubtful words of "the writer, and by the circumstance that you have not reported to

---

* Blue Book, 1869.   Papers relating to New Zealand, p 430.

" me a measure, the gravity of which you can scarcely have under-
" rated......But the general offer to savages of £1 for every head
" brought in would be evidently calculated to produce undiscriminat-
" ing murders, to intensify among our own allies the worst character-
" istics of the Maori nature, and to leave behind among those who
" escaped this unmeasured punishment, or who were connected with
" them by blood, alliance, or a sentiment of nationality, a permanent
" intention of revenge."

There was indeed nothing left for the Maori to do but to fight with
desperation, or to groan, or to die without groaning (as an eye-wit
ness informed me that he saw an old chief die on the steep of
Ngatapa when put to death in cold blood on the occasion animadverted upon by Earl Granville.)

Sir G. Bowen consulted Mr. Richmond, who hoped that Sir G.
Bowen would " accept of a private note " as an answer to questions
raised on Lord Granville's Despatch.

The " private note " is to be found in an English Blue Book 1870
[C.83] p. 39. I regret that it is one of those documents which I
cannot cite *in extenso*.

Mr. Richmond *had* paid £50 for the head of Nikora, and *had* offered
£5 for " every one of the Chatham Island prisoners brought in alive "
—" one of the men so captured *was afterwards killed* "—" a thousand
pounds was on the same day offered for Kooti the ringleader of the
murderers and marauders, and would certainly have been paid for
his body, *dead or alive.*"

The official return that the killed Maoris at Ngatapa were 136,
and that there were *no prisoners*, coupled with Mr. Gudgeons' description of the killing of prisoners *two days after the capture* of Ngatapa,
sheds a lurid light upon Mr. Richmond's " private note " which Sir G.
Bowen transmitted to England with a lengthy despatch dated 25th
June, 1860.

Something more than a " private note " was deemed desirable,
and a still longer despatch of 7th July, 1869, enclosing* an "opinion of
the Honourable the Attorney General," Mr. James Prendergast, was
sent. I wish I could present the whole of it in these pages; but I can
only find room for quotations, and must refer those who would study
the whole paper, to the Blue Book.

" When rebellion has assumed such proportions (Mr. Prendergast
wrote) that those who are in arms against the Sovereign would be
able if forced to do so by the conduct of the Sovereign towards them,
to take such reprisals upon those who adhere to the Sovereign as to
insist upon the observance of the usages of war, then probably those
in rebellion should be treated as enemies with whom the usages of war
should be observed. The adoption of such a course is forced upon
the Sovereign with a view to confining the effects of war to narrower
limits. Acting from such motives, prisoners taken by the Sovereign
would not be put to death as rebels, whether with or without trial,

---

* Blue Book (C. 83.) 1870, p. 54.

lest those prisoners who should be taken by those in rebellion should in reprisal be put to death. The reason for the observance of the usages of war fails (whether the war be a civil war, or between State and State) if those in arms on the opposite side violate the laws of war.

No doubt in such a case the consequences of such violation of the rules of war ought to be confined to those who are responsible for and have taken part in them and ought not to be extended to those who taking no part in them, are nevertheless implicated in the rebellion. The Maoris now in arms have put forward no grievance for which they seek redress. Their object so far as it can be collected from their acts is murder, cannibalism, and rapine. They form themselves into bands, and roam the country seeking a prey.

In punishing the perpetrators of such crimes, is the sovereign to be restrained by the rules which the *laws of nature and of nations* have declared applicable in the wars between civilized nations? *Clearly not.** Even if those now in arms had not been guilty of such enormous atrocities, it does not appear to me that the insurrection or rebellion is of such a character *or has yet reached such proportions* as to enable it to be said that those who having taken part in it, are captured, ought to be treated as prisoners of war. I see no reason why they should not be treated as persons guilty of levying war against the Crown. . . . Unfortunately, however, the revolt has

---

* Lord Chief Justice Cockburn had a short time before Mr. Prendergast wrote this opinion laid down, in a charge printed in 1867, what appears a different doctrine. He denounced (p. 22) "tribunals which are to create the laws which they have to administer, and to determine upon the guilt or innocence of persons brought before them, with a total disregard of all those rules and principles which are of the very essence of justice, and without which there is no security for innocence." Advocates of martial law put forward (p. 23.) "doctrines so repugnant to the genius of our people, to the spirit of our laws and institutions, to all we have been accustomed to revere and hold sacred" that before such doctrines are "countenanced and upheld in an English Court of Justice, we ought to see that there is sufficient authority for the assertion that British subjects can be thus treated." . . (p. 46.) It is true that after the battle of Culloden horrible barbarities were perpetrated—but not by virtue of martial law. . . . I rejoice to think that in respect of cruelties which never can be forgotten while English history lasts, and which outraged and indignant humanity never can forgive—I rejoice, I say to think that these things were done without even the pretence of martial law. I rejoice to think that the name of law, even of martial law, was not profaned and polluted by being associated with such atrocities as these. . . (p. 108.) But it is said that as the necessity of suppressing rebellion is what justifies the exercise of martial law, and as, to this end, the example of immediate punishment is essential, the exhibition of martial law in its most summary and terrible form is indispensable. If by this it is meant that examples are to be made without taking the necessary means to discriminate between guilt and innocence, and that in order that in order to inspire terror, men are to be sacrificed whose guilt remains uncertain, I can only say I trust no Court of Justice will ever entertain *so fearful and odious a doctrine.* There are considerations more important than even the shortening the temporary duration of an insurrection. Among them are the eternal and immutable principles of justice, principles which never can be violated without lasting detriment to the true interests and well-being of a civilized community." Charge, &c., W. Ridgway London, 1867.

been carried on in defiance of all the laws of nature, and there can be no doubt that all who have taken part in it have forfeited all claims for mercy; certainly all title to the observance towards them of the usages of war, if they ever had such title."

Mr. Prendergast referred to Earl Granville's question as to the offer of £1000 "'for the person of the Maori chief Titokowaru, I infer alive or dead, and £5 for the persons of Maori rebels brought in," and alluded to such offers as a "measure."

"This measure does not seem open to any objection in the case of a Government engaged in the suppression of a revolt, accompanied as such revolt has been with all the unrelenting cruelty of savage nature. . . . Even in the case of a foreign enemy who violates the laws of nature and the usages of war, the utmost severities are permitted as a punishment for his crimes."

Thus did Mr. Prendergast justify what had been done, and inform Earl Granville that the powers of the Sovereign of England had been used in New Zealand.

> Upon the king! let us our lives. our souls,
> Our debts, our careful wives, our children, and
> Our sins, lay on the king; we must bear all.
> O hard condition! twin-born with greatness;
> Subjected to the breath of every fool
> Whose sense no more can feel but his own wringing.

There was another hard condition which caused groans amongst the Maoris. By their customs of old time it was incumbent upon a chief (called upon to assist another) either to fight against the demander of aid, or join in his campaign.

Titokowaru when roused to arms (by the wanton seizure of his people as already mentioned) had called on Tauroa to assist him. Colonel Whitmore the Commander of the Colonial forces attributed Tauroa's consent to this custom, and said in the New Zealand Parliament that "it seemed to be a peculiarity in the native character that it never occurred to them to resist or refuse under those circumstances the constraint that was put upon them."

He added that Tauroa had never joined in the barbarities imputed to Titokowaru.

The followers of Tauroa had cause to groan, whichsoever way they turned. Their traditional law compelled them to obey and to act with him. He was compelled to act with Titokowaru. And for so doing he and they, according to Mr. Prendergast, might righteously be brought in, dead or alive, for a money payment offered (in the name of the Queen, O hard condition!) by a colonial Governor at the dictation of a colonial Minister.

Whether Titokowaru really committed the atrocities imputed to him has not perhaps been proved. But it is sometimes difficult to establish the truth even in a court of law.

Such as it was his career has been recorded by me elsewhere.

Without doubt there was much alarm amongst the colonists when

E

having obtained successes in the field, he occupied in November, 1868, a pah at Taurangaika near Nukumaru, not far from Wanganui. On 29th September, 1868, the magistrates at Wanganui met and prayed that two companies of the 18th Regiment might be sent to protect the place.* In October, 1868 the House of Representatives prayed that a Regiment of the line might be retained in the Colony.†

In November, 1868, Titokowaru defeated a colonial force at Moturoa. On 5th December 1868, the Governor transmitted a petition from the wives, mothers and daughters of the inhabitants at Wanganui, praying for Imperial troops.‡ On the 7th, he sent a Despatch reporting "sharp skirmishes on both the East and West coasts," and enclosing the following letter from an officer of the Armed Constabulary to his superior, Colonel Whitmore, with an account of one of these "skirmishes."||

" COPY OF A LETTER FROM SUB-INSPECTOR NEWLAND TO COL. WHITMORE

HEAD QUARTERS, WOODALL'S REDOUBT.

SIR,   27th November, 1868.

I have the honour to inform you that I marched this morning with all the cavalry, being sixty-six of all ranks and corps, three hours before daylight to Wairoa, and remained five or six hours at that place, returning at 11 A.M. with despatches from Captain Hawes.

I reached Nukumaru graveyard at about 1 P.M., and, in accordance with your orders, remained in concealment until an opportunity presented itself to act.

After waiting about an hour and a half, perceiving a considerable number of Hauhaus about Mr. Handley's woolshed, I directed some of the men to advance dismounted, and followed with the rest of the force on horseback. Unfortunately a carbine went off accidentally which gave the alarm, and prevented our being as completely successful as we had hoped; but as soon as possible we mounted the dismounted men and charged, killing eight with sabre, revolver or carbine, besides wounding others.

I wish particularly to mention the extreme gallantry of Sergeant G. Maxwell of the Kai Iwi Cavalry, who himself sabred two and shot one of the enemy, and was conspicuous throughout the affair. Many others of all corps behaved extremely well, but I think it would be invidious to particularize further. The enemy turned out immediately and kept up a sharp fire, following us about three miles.

In accordance with my instructions I did not risk any further engagement, as the horses were tired, and the infantry were still at some distance.

The enemy is encamped in large force in rear of Nukumaru, near the bush, and has six bell tents erected.

I returned to camp at 6 P.M. I must acknowledge the assistance rendered to me by Captain O'Halloran of the Patea Yeomanry Cavalry,

---

and Lieutenant Bryce commanding Kai Iwi and Wanganui Cavalry. These gentlemen were prominent in this affair, and set their men a gallant example.   I have, &c.

"W. NEWLAND, *Sub-Inspector, A.C.*"

THE HON. COLONEL WHITMORE.

One of his ministers sent Newland's letter to the Governor as a report of a "successful attack on a marauding party of the rebels," and there was assuredly nothing in the Governor's Despatch or in his minister's lengthy memorandum which would lead the Secretary of State to believe that the "marauding party of rebels" were unarmed, and that when the Maoris might be afterwards questioned on the subject they would with one voice declare that the "successful attack" had been made by sixty-six troopers on twelve little children, who were not only unarmed, but too small to carry arms.

There was, however, to my knowledge, no publication of the Maori account until 1883. In 1882 a version of it, unhappily incorrect but presumably derived from the Maoris, reached me while I was writing my History of New Zealand.

After applying for and obtaining further written information, I came to the conclusion that the "extreme gallantry" lauded by Newland consisted in attacking unarmed persons, and in running away as soon as armed persons hastened from a pah (1½ mile distant) to rescue their little ones; and I accordingly framed a paragraph on the subject, the inaccuracy of which I have never ceased to regret from the moment that I became acquainted with a statement made by an eyewitness, Uru Te Angina.

In the written information furnished to me, (which purported to have been derived from Dr. Featherston, Superintendent of the Province of Wellington in 1868), it was stated that women were amongst the unarmed persons against whom the act of gallantry was performed.

Though the account given to me stated that several persons were killed (which coincided with Mr. Newland's account), I refrained, or at least endeavoured to refrain, from saying more than that they were "cut down." After the publication of my History (early in 1883) a native chief, Uru Te Angina, supplied a written account which was published in a leading article in the Yeoman, a newspaper at Wanganui, on the 8th June, 1883.

. . . "We publish to-day an account given by Uru Te Angina of the affair at Handley's Woolshed. We may say that Uru was in the Taurangaika pah at the time, and his statement may be accepted as the Native view of the affair. We vouch for the accuracy of the translation of Uru's words :—

" 'The tribes were all gathered at our pah, Taurangaika, waiting for the enemy, the Pakeha, to attack us. . . . One day a number of our children, lads, . . . left our camp unknown to us, and without the leave of their parents. . . About twelve boys made up the party, and away they stole off . . When they reached the house . . they succeeded in catching several geese, and went into the empty house to pluck the feathers off. They had not been long at this when a body of troopers rode over an eminence very suddenly and fired at the boy on the house who was acting as sentry. He slid off at once, and ran into the scrub. Several more shots were fired at the house, but the lads inside thought the boys outside were throwing stones* at the roof and sides, which were of iron; but as the noise increased the boys ran out, and found themselves amongst a body of mounted men, who at once began to slash and cut away at them as they ducked under the horses to avoid the sword-thrusts and the revolver-shots fired at them. The lads ran hither and thither. Two were killed on the spot, and several were more or less wounded; but these, with the others, escaped the slaughter One lad, about ten years old, was killed by a stroke from a sword that cut his head in two halves, one half falling down over his shoulder; he had some revolver-shots in his chest and stomach besides.

"Another lad, about twelve years old, was killed by many strokes of a sword, and was much cut about, and shot with carbines. Neither of these lads had arrived at the age of puberty. Another boy, of about twelve years of age, was cut over the head with a sword, and would have been killed, only that he clasped his hands above and on his head to save himself; but the sword cut off some of his fingers, and he fell at full length under the horse's feet. The trooper then fired his revolver at him, and the ball penetrated his thigh; and then left him for dead. This boy lived, and is alive now. He is a relative of mine . . Another boy hid in some water, like a little crawfish . . None of this young party had guns, pistols, tomahawks, or any weapons; they may have had a pocket-knife or so with them to cut flax. None of us at the pah knew they had gone away hunting, and we did not know of their absence until we saw some of them returning, bleeding and crying . . We at once mustered a strong party and hastened to the scene of action where our children had fallen . . We carried them home to our pah, and buried the two dead lads . . This account is a strictly true one, and can be verified by many hundreds of men and women who saw the bodies. As I said before none of these lads who formed the party had arrived at the age of puberty. Trooper Maxwell was shot soon afterwards in a very foolish attempt to carry off a flag we had attached to our double-partitioned and entrenched pah. He met the fate of a brave man, but it was the act of a lot of fools to ride up as they did, especially after killing our little ones who only went out to catch a few geese."

To those who accept the above version, and as a rule Maori chiefs are scrupulously truthful, it furnishes a singular commentary on Newland's report that after the "killing eight with sabre, &c." Newland "did not risk any further engagement" but fled with his gallant comrades, pursued, "about three miles," by the armed Maoris who issued from the pah to succour the children.

A copy of the '*Yeoman*' was sent to me, and it convinced me that

---

* Subsequent enquiry at Wanganui showed that the shots were fired at a distance—variously guessed at 400 or 350 yards, or less—from the Woolshed (which Uru or his translator called a "house").

the inclusion of women in Dr. Featherston's reported narrative was erroneous.

The fact that I had framed an erroneous statement, even though it was founded on written informatiou, was intensely vexatious to me.

I had already printed one list of errata, and was preparing an enlarged list, as from time to time, any inaccuracy in my History became known to me. Uru Te Angina's statement induced me to add the following correction :—Vol. II., p. 504 in line 28 from top, omit "women and."

In 1884 an action was instituted against me on account of two passages which referred *inter alia* to the transaction described so differently by Newland and Uru Te Angina.

Of the action itself I desire to say nothing here. *Il fatto non si puo disfare ;* and personal affairs are beneath the dignity of history.

As a historian it is proper to show to my readers the manner in which I endeavoured to fulfil my functions.

I do not desire to refer in any other sense to my History—which has been withdrawn from sale by the publishers.

My purpose can be effected without comment upon the trial, which took place in March, 1886. in London.

In 1885, I prepared for my advisers some printed Notes, which were in their hands several months before the trial took place. One passage in those Notes shows the spirit in which I worked :—

" The precision of Uru Te Angina's statement, with regard to the presence of children only among those who were " cut down " at Handley's Woolshed, prompted me at once to add to the errata of my History a correction to the effect that the words " women and " should be omitted from the paragraph (at p. 504, vol. ii.) referring to the transaction. I did in fact prepare, and cause to be printed, an amended list of errata accordingly. But soon after the reception of Uru Te Angina's statement in England, came paragraphs (in New Zealand journals) intimating that (proceedings against me were contemplated.)

Thereupon, I consulted a lawyer, and did not issue an amended list of errata. My advisers will remember that—urging that accuracy at all hazards is the first duty of an historian—I once had a consultation with them and with counsel on the subject, and that in this matter I have acted entirely under advice. It is quite true that the inclusion of the words " women and " was strictly in accordance with information in my hands, the authority for which was Dr. Featherston ; and that therefore I could not be charged with " setting down ought in malice ; " but he who finds that he has been misled, even in a matter of detail, is bound to correct an error, and ought to be glad to do so if he can."

The foregoing sentences, having been in print long before the trial, sufficiently explain my earnestness to be accurate without reference to any outside pressure.

Though I felt myself precluded by advice from formally supplying the new corrections to the publishers, (who had stopped the sale of the work at the time) I did not consider that I was prevented from inserting them in copies to which I had access.

It is of course difficult to remember at what particular time one may have done such things, and I took occasion to refer (in 1886) to three friends who had as I thought, copies of my History.

All three confirmed my recollection, and I am permitted to refer to their letters. One copy was in the Library of the Royal Asiatic Society. Sir Frederick Goldsmid, the Secretary, replied to my enquiry on the subject, thus : —

22, ALBEMARLE STREET,
March 15*th*, 1886.

DEAR MR. RUSDEN,

On receiving your note this morning, I referred to the History of New Zealand, published by you in 1883, and in the first Volume, I find a printed page of errata—clearly intended for inclusion in the book when bound—with the following passage among several others :—

Vol. II p. 14.   *   *   *   *   *

  ,,   ,,   41.   *   *   *   *   *

  ,,   ,,   504, in line 28 from top, omit " women and."

Yours sincerely,   F. J. GOLDSMID.

G. W. RUSDEN, ESQ. Athenæum Club.

Mr. Onslow answered thus :

SEND GROVE, WOKING, SURREY.
May 5*th*, 1886.

MY DEAR RUSDEN,

In answer·to your letter enquiring whether the erratum—Vol. II, p. 504, omit " women and,"—in your History, is inserted in the slip of errata in the copy of your History of New Zealand in my library, I have to inform you that it is so inserted. It was affixed by you on one of your visits to my house but I cannot tell when.

As your last visit was in September 1885, it must have been affixed then or at some earlier date.

Yours sincerely, A. P. ONSLOW.

Receiving a similar letter from a friend in Dorsetshire, I made no enquiry elsewhere. As his letter adverted to the trial (as have many other gracious letters from friends and eminent persons) I abstain from quoting its terms.

It was well known among my friends that I was willing to correct any error. I sent to two friends, one in New Zealand and another in New South Wales, several printed copies of letters which I requested them to show and to publish in the newspapers.

In one, dated September 1st, 1883, I said that if any passage were erroneous "it would be my first duty to make all reparation in my power.   .   .   .   Every writer is bound to examine facts with a desire to make no idle statements, but there are certain persons, such as Dr. Featherston, whose names might make it almost superfluous to go beyond them."

In the other (to the Hon. P. G. King, in Sydney) I said (13th Sept., 1883)—" I appreciate your confidence that I would not make any statement unsupported by good authority, and would readily make amends for any error into which misinformation might lead me. No one ought to write at all who is not ready to retract a statement proved to be baseless."

After this brief allusion to the manner in which I have aboured,* and my readiness to correct any errors, the thread of affairs on the West Coast between Wanganui and Taranaki may be resumed.

Titokowaru was utterly defeated, mainly by the military skill and courage of Rangihiwinui, a friendly chief serving with the Colonial forces.

Colonel Whitmore, who commanded the colonial forces, commended his " gallantry, coolness, and determination to hold the post of honour." His " behaviour was beyond all praise," at Moturoa, when the local forces sustained defeat at the hands of Titokowaru in November 1868. After describing that action, and praising the gallantry of several European officers, Whitmore added—" Lastly Captain Kemp (by which name Rangihiwinui was called in Despatches), brave, modest and generous in all his conduct on this occasion; who never boasted before the fight; who has cast no reproaches after it; who has shown every officer that he is endued with great capacity for military operations; who has exhibited to every man of the force that a Maori chief can manifest a calm deliberate courage in no way inferior to their own ; who has laid up for himself in the hearts of many of the force, the gratitude of the men who received a comrade's help in the moment of need, . . this officer and chief merits a full recognition on my part of his deserts."†

Titokowaru was chased from the district and took refuge in the wilds. Rangihiwinui, commended by the Minister of Defence (Colonel Haultain for " courage and resource as remarkable as his modesty and devotion," went to the East Coast to war against Te Kooti, and the scene of Titokowaru's success and reverses became a desolation in 1869.

A gentleman, who afterwards went to that part of the country to make enquiries, assured me that he was horrified at learning from the lips of those who had lived in the neighbourhood that at one time every Maori creature old or young, " omnis sexus, omnis ætas," was

---

* To a careless person it may signify little if an error be discovered in his work But to one who has seriously laboured to avoid error, the discovery of an error is a pang. The late William Swainson (for many years Attorney General in New Zealand, learned and wise), wrote to me in 1880, " I congratulate you on your success in hunting down *Matahau*, after unheard of perseverance. If all the statements in the forthcoming History have been verified with the same care, what an amount of patient labour you must have bestowed upon it ! " My good friend has now passed to the land of spirits, but it is one of my comforts to remember that he lived to commend my " minute and accurate knowledge of the affairs of New Zealand."

† Blue Book, 1869. (307), p.p. 288, 289, 291.

ruthlessly slain. "I had no idea, (he said) that we had been so wicked." You were not to blame (I replied) for, living at Wellington, you knew nothing about what you now deplore. "We ought all to have prevented it (he said). It was horrible!"*

This of course is but hearsay, after the facts; and too much stress should not be laid upon it. But an officer who led a marauding party through the district, after Titokowaru had fled, formally reported the destruction of *settlements, cultivations, eelweirs,* and of every kind of "*stock we could not eat.*"

Rangihiwinui, in one of his latest excursions saw a few poor creatures dead, or dying of inanition. It may safely be inferred that he slew no child, for when children were killed at Handley's Woolshed in 1868, he declared, "If I knew you were going to kill children I would have nothing more to do with the fighting."

Even if women and children were killed anywhere in the manner reported to the gentleman whose words I have quoted, it would be impossible now to prove it, for who would condemn himself, or plead guilty to having screened such crimes?

Mr. Gudgeon in his Reminiscences of the War in New Zealand,† alludes to the transactions in the district, in 1869, thus: —

(Page 266) "Captain Bryce was sent forward next day and ascended the river ten miles farther, until he came upon three men in a canoe. The men escaped, but the canoe fell into our hands.

By this time the column had penetrated sixty miles up the river, and had destroyed or carried off every thing portable, but the main object of the expedition had failed as the Hauhaus were evidently on their guard and had retired to the Upper Wanganui. Such being the case Major Noake retired to the Weraroa where the loot was sold for the benefit of the men engaged.

On the 20th April, 1869, Captain Hawes . . started with ninety men . . to scour the country inland of the Whenuakura River. No sign of recent occupation was seen. . . The Waitotara and Whenuakura districts had now been searched unsuccessfully, and there only remained the Patea; this was left to Colonel Lyon, who, on the 3rd May, crossed the river at Hukatere and camped at Otauto, where fresh tracks were seen. A party of Ngatiporou scouts under Te Hata were sent in pursuit, and came across three men, two of whom were caught and shot.

On the following day two others were seen, and met the same fate; one of them proved to be a woman dressed in mens' clothes."

These "Reminiscences" may be deemed of doubtful authority by some persons, even though their author was personally engaged in many transactions he describes.

There is, however, a remarkable official description of the district which justifies the most sad reflections. In 1880, a Royal Commission consisting of Sir F. Dillon Bell (now Agent-General for New Zealand in

---

* This gentleman was educated at an English University and a member of a liberal profession.

† Sampson, Low, Marston, Searle, and Rivington, London, 1879.

England), and Sir W. Fox, visited the district to make enquiries as to breaches of faith to the Maori Tribes with regard to land. In their report* (laid before the House of Commons in 1882) they stated : "When the insurrection was suppressed, the country between Waitotara and Cape Egmont had been all but deserted by natives and settlers alike . . . As to rebel natives, they had entirely disappeared. *All their pahs and cultivations had been utterly destroyed.* There was not a native of the rebel tribes to be seen from Waitotara to Waingongoro,"† [Had the lame, the sick, the bed-ridden, suddenly died, or—what had become of them? Was there no Maori Anchises without an Æneas ?]

Before the settlers would return to the farms from which Titokowaru had driven them, the Commissioners reported that, "they exacted from the Minister a promise that if they returned to their homes the Government would forbid the rebel natives coming back. No native fire was to be lighted again by a rebel in the Patea country. *This policy was sternly carried out.* News having come in that small parties of Titokowaru's followers were creeping back to the north bank of Waingongoro, a reconnoitring party *went out and shot* two of the men and captured a woman. At another place, some miles up the Waitotara river, *another native was shot*, and a second woman taken. For a time this severity deterred the insurgents from renewing any attempt to *re-occupy their country* . . . Early in 1870 the settlers still desired that *no native should be suffered to come back.* Perhaps it *was not unnatural that the exasperation to which they had been driven should have tempted* many to distort the promise of the Prime Minister from *rebel native* into *any native.* But the promise could, of course, have no application to men like Hone Pihama . . . who had not only loyally helped us in the war of 1868, suffering jointly with the settlers in life and property, but had often abandoned their private property at the call of the Government. Still less could it apply to such men as Major Kemp (*i.e.* Rangihiwinui) and his warriors who had fought with great bravery by our side."

Commenting on this passage—the admission that it was *their country* to which poor creatures thus lawlessly shot desired to return —the strange statement that it was perhaps not unnatural for the settlers to make *no distinction* between Maoris formerly hostile and Maoris always friendly—the addition that when seen Maoris were shot—I once wrote—"These words reveal how the use which is second nature prevented that which would have been a ghastly phenomenon elsewhere from appearing odious in New Zealand ! "

In thus writing I desired to arouse a keener sense of justice in New Zealand, where many people, living (like my friend in Wellington) far from Waitotara, knew not how the word ' civilization' had been profaned there ;—how indeed the woeful words imputed by

---

* Blue Book, 1882. C. 3382, pp. 50, 51.

† The map will show the great extent of this coast line. Through length and breadth there had once been habitations.

Tacitus to Galgacus were wrought into fact so hideously that a Royal Commission could describe the district as one *from which the natives had disappeared*, in which their dwellings and cultivations *had been destroyed*, to which British subjects demanded that *no native should be allowed to return*, and in which when a poor creature came back to seek for a resting-place he was *shot without enquiry* and apparently without exciting remark until, in later years, a Royal Commission recorded the occurrence without condemnation.

The Commissioners spoke of reported slaughters. How many unreported slaughters were there? They say two women were captured. How many were dealt with as my friend who visited the West Coast was informed?

Who can adequately pourtray the horrors of the time? Who can even faintly imagine, how desperate had been the groans of the Maoris, where in a once populous district, larger than some English counties, not one living soul remained? Strong and feeble,—old and young,—children of both sexes—all were gone.

On the map the district appeared as "confiscated land." What did not appear on the map was the fact that by the proclamation of confiscation peaceful possession of their lands was guaranteed to all loyal natives.

Until Donald McLean appeared on the scene no effort was made to redeem this pledge,—to carry out Mr. Cardwell's instructions,—or the consequent guarantees and Proclamations of the Governor in 1865.

Donald McLean became Native Minister in 1869, after the desolation described by Fox and Bell on the West Coast had been completed. It was he who in 1867 had carried the Bill granting Maori representatives. He had not been a week in office when he drew up a memorandum declaring that the Colony was 'exhausted'* and he strove to prevent a possible junction of the forces of the so-called Maori King with the outlaws, Te Kooti and Titokowaru.

Apprehending such junction, Fox, then Prime Minister, made a piteous appeal to the Governor† about retaining troops and ships of war. He implored the Governor to take such steps, (in concert with General Chute and Australian Governors) as "will avert the fearful loss of life which the removal of the Imperial force, at this perilous juncture, would probably entail."

The Maoris had some confidence in McLean, and to him must be ascribed the better relations which were established with them from 1869 to 1876, when, shortly before his death, he resigned office.

He obtained distinctions for Maori officers who had been eminent in the field against Te Kooti and Titokowaru.

He qualified as soon as he could the grievous condition to which the Waitotara district had been reduced when he took office.

---

* Blue Book, 1870. C. 83. p. 61.

† ib. p. 80. The troops in the Colony at the time consisted of one Regiment, the 18th. Small as was their number the hopes of Sir W. Fox seem to have depended upon them.

As some cruel acts done there at a later date will demand notice, it is well to record here, before passing to other subjects, what McLean did at the West Coast.

Not long after his entering upon office some of the scattered tribes returned to the old haunts in which their homes had been laid waste. A minute (Dec. 1871) by an Under Secretary in McLean's Department shows on what terms the return of the exiles took place—"With regard to the Ngaruahine (*i.e.* Titokowaru's *hapu*) I think it would be politically undesirable, and I fear, practically impossible, to attempt to prevent their re-occupying the country north of Waingongoro, *the confiscation of that country having been abandoned by the Government,* as long as they behave themselves and keep the compact about not crossing the Waingongoro." This minute was approved by Sir Donald McLean,* as now quoted.

On 20th January 1872, McLean issued instructions with regard to the district. In them he said "The lands north of the Waingongoro as far as Stoney River, although nominally confiscated, are with the exception of 1400 acres at Opunake, quite unavailable for settlement, until arrangements are made with the natives for lands sufficient for their own requirements. Mr. (Commissioner) Parris will . . com· pensate the Native owners for all lands . . . they may relinquish . . . at rates not exceeding 5s. per acre."†

In February, 1872, McLean formally reported, and the Governor sent to the Secretary of State, the terms which had been agreed upon.‡

Maclean had seen Te Rangitake who had been so shamefully treated at Waitara in 1860. The chief had visited Taranaki in token of reconciliation, and McLean regarded the visit as "the most significant indication and greatest assurance of future peace."

"Arrangements have also been entered into with a view to a more accurate definition of Native rights within the confiscated territory, and for the acquisition, by purchase, with the good will of the Natives, of such portions of land as they hold within it, but do not require for their own use and which appear desirable for European settlements."

Trusting in the honour of McLean. the Maoris re-entered upon their birth place. He recognized their prior rights, and the qualifying terms of Sir George Grey's Proclamations;* and he engaged to *acquire by purchase any land* required for European settlements in the district. The Governor exulted in McLean's report of his proceedings and the Secretary of State formally approved. Accordingly, in subsequent years, land was purchased from the Maoris under *formal deeds of cession,*† and during McLean's life time the land had rest.

A New Zealand Parliamentary Paper‡ gives a "Return of sums of

---

* Blue Book, 1882, C. 3382, p. 53.
† New Zealand Parliamentary Paper, 1880. G. 2. Appendix A. p. 3. (On 12th April, 1876 (N. Z. P. P., G 2, Appendix A. p. 4.) McLean in writing to Major Brown, Civil Commissioner "authorized him to offer sums amounting "to 2s. 6d. more than the 5s. already mentioned (in Parris' instructions).")
‡ N. Z. Parliamentary Paper, 1872. A. No. 1, p.p. 62, 63.
* Vide supra. pp. 31,32. † Blue Book, C. 3382. p. 58. ‡ 1879. A.—8A. p. 3.

money paid to Natives within the confiscated block on the West Coast, on deeds of conveyance to the Crown." The area of land bought is stated as 434,702 acres, and the amount paid £54,412 5s. 2d., two or three payments being then incomplete.

As it was reported that in 1881 the Government sold land in the district at more than £6 an acre, McLean's bargains cannot be deemed wasteful.

He also maintained peace. How it was broken by others must be told hereafter.

One long standing grievance exists in the Middle or South Island. When the Maoris sold to the New Zealand Company (in 1844) a block of land at Otago, the Governor commissioned a Crown Agent Mr. J. J. Symonds, to control the proceedings, and to inform the natives that none would be sanctioned which were " not honest, equitable, and in every way irreproachable." The deed of sale signed (31st July, 1844) by Maoris and by Symonds, provided for certain reserves, but left the main question of reserves for the Governor's decision.

The Company had bound themselves to the Government in England to secure as reserves for the natives one-tenth of all lands which they were permitted to purchase. In this case Symonds wrote—" I left the further choice of reserves,—namely, *the tenth part of all land sold by the New Zealand Company*—to be decided by His Excellency the Governor."‡

A Proclamation by the Governor in 1844 declared that " of all land purchased from the Aborigines by reason of the Crown's right of pre-emption being waived, one-tenth part, of fair average value as to position and quality, is to be conveyed by the purchaser to Her Majesty for public purposes, especially the future benefit of the Aborigines."*

Will it be believed that for more than forty years, the Maoris have vainly pleaded for fulfilment of these solemn undertakings, and that though a Royal Commission reported favourably to their claims in 1881, the Maoris are vainly pleading still?

The Government was doubly bound to do justice to them; for when the New Zealand Company surrendered its charter in 1850 it was officially declared that " Her Majesty's Government take the lands of the Company subject to existing contracts :"—and the contract to

---

‡ A Compendium of Official Documents relative to Native Affairs in the South Island. Compiled by Alexr. Mackay, Native Commissioner: Wellington, New Zealand, 1873. Vol. I., p. 103. Formal adoption by the Government of Symonds' proceedings; and sanction of the claim for the Maoris of " one tenth of each description of allotment, town, suburban, and rural ;" may be seen in a New Zealand Parliamentary Paper :—Leg. Council, 1885. (Return) No. 15.

* Blue Book, 1845.

assign, as reserves, one-tenth of the land, having been made with the Crown by the Company, the Crown was in a position of double trust, and unimpeded in doing right, if only those who acted in its name in New Zealand desired to act honourably.

In 1848 Mr. H. T. Kemp was commissioned by the Government to purchase for the Government the lands of the Ngaitahu tribe in the Middle Island, and for £2,000, to be paid in four annual payments, he bought land extending over several degrees of longitude from Kaikora to Otago, and embracing the space from sea to sea on east and west. But there was a reservation in the Ngaitahu Deed (or Kemp's Deed).—— "Our places of residence and our cultivations are to be reserved for us and our children after us, and it shall be for the Governor hereafter to set apart some portion for us when the land is surveyed by the surveyors."*

Not only Taiaroa's name but the names of other Maoris, of Mr. Kemp and of two officers of H.M.S. Fly, and of the Principal Surveyor of the New Zealand Company, were duly appended to the Deed.

Subsequently Mr. Mantell was employed as Commissioner for acquiring lands in the Middle Island, and, according to his own letter (5th July, 1856) to the Secretary of State, he acquired 30,000,000 acres, for which "the natives received about £5,000, *and the repudiated promises* which form the subject of this letter." . . By promise of more valuable recompense in schools—in hospitals for their sick—and in constant solicitude for their welfare, and general protection on the part of the Imperial Government—I procured the cession of these lands for small cash payments. The Colonial Government has neglected to fulfil these promises. . . . I trust that Her Majesty's Government will take such steps as will relieve me from the painful position of having been the channel of promises which have been at least forgotten, and secure my Native clients in the possession of advantages which have been so long withheld from them."

Mr. Mantell appealed in vain. The Secretary of State denied him an audience (he was in London), wrote rudely to him, and disparagingly of his appeal for his native clients. Mr. Mantell, after another effort to induce the Secretary to call in the talents and probity of Mr. Justice Martin to adjust the claims, indignantly threw up his office as Commissioner (18th Aug., 1856), on the ground that the Secretary of State had refused to entertain the claims of the Ngaitahu Natives, and that he himself could not approve of the so-called principles and policy of the Local Government towards the Natives.†

To this day are the Maoris groaning for relief from the injustice thus done on the spot, and thus winked at by a Secretary of State.

There are many just and kindly persons in New Zealand, but they have not been able to control the dealings of the Government with the Maoris. Those who desire to study the question of the Middle or

---

* Mackay's Compendium, Vol. I. p. 211.
† Mr. Mackay's Compendium, &c. Vol. II., pp. 81-88.

South Island unfulfilled promises will find ample material in Mr. Mackay's Compendium, and in Parliamentary Papers and Debates.

These cover many thousand pages, however, and for those who have not time for lengthy research, a few lines will present one or two salient cases.

Taiaroa, a chief of high lineage, son of the chief who signed the Ngaitahu Deed, had given notice (in 1872, when Stafford was in office for one month) of his intention to move for a Committee on the Unfulfilled Promises in the Middle Island. Mr. Stafford, the Prime Minister, threw obstacles in the way, but with aid of Donald McLean, Taiaroa carried his motion. Stafford having lost his position, McLean soon returned to office as Native Minister, but did not aid Taiaroa in procuring an enquiry.

In 1874, Taiaroa renewed his demand for a Committee. Mr. Fox admitted that there were unfulfilled promises ; McLean could not deny it. Mr. Mackay, the Commissioner of Native Reserves, reported that the Ngaitahu claims were good on all grounds known in Maori law— " hereditary, conquest, and occupation or possession." But enquiry was refused. In 1879, a Royal Commission was appointed while Mr. Sheehan was Native Minister. Later in that year Mr. Bryce subsequently became Native Minister and informed the House that, while admitting that " no doubt the Natives had a claim," he would urge the Commissioners to " curtail their expenses," and report quickly, Crippled in their action, by refusal of advances from the Treasury to enable them to work, they nevertheless reported in 1881, and recognized the Native claims.

In May, 1882, Taiaroa asked, " what were the intentions of the Government with regard to the Report ? " The Native Minister, Bryce, replied, that " the Government regarded the recommendations of these Commissioners (one of them was a Judge) as being utterly impracticable, and they therefore did not intend to take any action in regard to them."*

A petition on the subject was referred in 1882 to the Native Affairs Committee, which reported upon it. A member moved that the Report be referred " to the Government for consideration." (There are Greek calends in New Zealand.) Taiaroa, alleging that there were " six members on one side, and six on the other " in the Committee, and that the Chairman decided the matter, moved that the Report be referred back to the Committee, " for the purpose of taking further evidence." Sir George Grey supported Taiaroa, and pointed out that " the evidence of Judge Smith was absolutely necessary in the case."

The Report was referred back (Mr. Duncan informing the House that the condition of some of the Natives dependent on the result was " a disgrace to any Government,"† but the Committee " found no reason to alter their report,"‡ and if the House should desire the

---

* New Zealand Hansard, 1882. Vol. XLI., p. 62.
† ib. Vol. XLIII., p. 563.   ‡ ib., p. 800.

Committee to take still further evidence, it was "practically impossible to do so this session." Taiaroa deemed it unfair that he had not been "allowed to give evidence. The proceedings of the Committee had set at nought promises made in former years, and the Committee refused to allow persons to say what they had to say in favour of the natives. I shall not say very much more, because I know the majority of the House will support the Government, as it invariably does in regard to native matters."

Mr. Bryce thereupon said that Taiaroa had "imputed unfairness of conduct in gross terms to the Committee. Let me say one word in reference to the members of that Committee, and let me express a hope that the honourable member will take it to heart. There are four members of the native race on that Committee. . . I warn the native members that if they persist in merely representing the native race, and utterly ignoring considerations in connection with European interests, the House will certainly become impatient of the position. I say that by way of warning; and let me say this also: matters in connection with the Native Affairs Committee are becoming so unsatisfactory, that in my opinion, this House will have to seriously consider whether that Committee ought to continue in existence or not. It is customary in this House to tamely submit to imputations because they come from natives, but I challenge such imputations once and for all, and I warn the honourable members that such imputations will not be tolerated."

Te Wheoro replied with some dignity. Mr. Sheehan, formerly Native Minister, appealed to the sense of fairness in the House. He averred that the Natives no more combined than European members did, and that "anybody can see, on reference to Hansard, that *repeated promises* have been made to the natives by Ministers *none of which have been fulfilled.*"

Mr. Daniel was sorry that the Minister was "putting his foot down on the Native race again. They only want their just rights. . . . I do not see why justice should not be given to them. . . A great injustice has been done to the Natives of the Middle Island. Not only has their land been taken from them, but they have been *deprived of the Reserves* promised to them. . . I am sorry that the Native Minister should make such an attack upon the Native members. I know that on the Committee they give their decisions the same as other honourable gentlemen do, and I have not seen that they have been biassed in the least."

There was a division in the House on the matter, and Taiaroa's prediction of the result was confirmed.

The natives who were left in a condition which Mr. Daniel described as "a disgrace to any Government," are still, so far as I know, left to groan, or to die.

This was the fate of those who made compacts with regard to their lands. Sometimes those who refused to make compacts were haled to prison, as was the case at Parihaka, in 1881.

Sometimes (as in the Waikato country, where the authority of

Tawhiao had been recognized from 1864) slower methods were adopted.

Mr. Ballance, Bryce's successor, read in the New Zealand Parliament a petition received from Waikato by his predecessor. "We have carefully watched the tendency of the laws which you have enacted from the beginning up to the present day. They all tend to deprive us of the privileges secured to us by the 2nd and 3rd Articles of the Treaty of Waitangi, which confirmed to us the exclusive and undisturbed possession of our lands. . . . What possible benefit would we derive from roads, railways, and Land Courts, if they became the means of depriving us of our lands? We can live as we are situated at present, without roads, railways, or Courts, but we could not live without our lands."* This petition was signed by the great chiefs, Rewi and Wahanui, and was more argumentative than groaning; but the plaints of others were alluded to in the same debate, by Sir Julius Vogel, who said that one Minister had "succeeded in securing a very strong dislike to himself on the part of the Natives; and, no doubt, judging from the line of policy that he followed, he is rather proud of having earned such a distinction. It is certain that he is looked upon by the natives as very hard and cruel."†

The manner in which solemn promises made to the Maoris in the Middle Island were broken was not calculated to induce their brethen in the North to abandon their homes and leave the burial-grounds of their ancestors to be desecrated at the command of any Native Minister.

One case may be cited to show the difficulties under which the Maoris laboured, even when their cases went before a Court of law.

The Native Land Court was sitting at Christchurch in April, 1868. A Cabinet Minister, Mr. (now Sir John) Hall, was in attendance; and Mr. Rolleston, then an Under Secretary, but afterwards a Cabinet Minister, was there also.

In giving judgment on one (the Rapaki) case, the Judge said "The court feels that it would be leaving its duty only half discharged if it failed to notice the character of the deeds purporting to extinguish the Native title to this island which have been produced before it. Whether the deed called the "Ngaitahu Deed" can have any effect whatever in law is not a question upon which it is necessary to pronounce any opinion, but having been compelled in the course of these proceedings to consider the terms and stipulations in this and other deeds produced, the Court could not fail to be struck with the remarkable reservation by the vendors of all their "*pahs, residences, cultivations, and burial places, which were to be marked off by surveys, and remain their own property.*"

This provision has not, according to the evidence, been effectually and finally carried out to the present day, nor has any release been sought for by the Crown. . . Conflicting instructions from the

---

* New Zealand Hansard, 1885. Vol. LI., p. 277.　　† ib., p. 405.

Government seem to have reached Mr. Mantell with a curious rapidity, and finally, his most useful powers were withdrawn before he had been able effectually to operate under them. The Court feels very strongly that it would be greatly to the honour and advantage of the Crown that the stipulations and reservations of these Deeds of Purchase should, without further delay, be perfectly observed and provided for."*

This was in 1868—and as the unfulfilled promises of the Crown in the Middle Island provoked the scene (just alluded to) in the New Zealand Parliament (in 1882) and are yet repudiated or postponed, it does not seem that the honour and advantage of the Crown have been taken to heart by those whose duty it was to respect them.

The Judge had another notable case before him at Christchurch in 1868 Heremaia Mautai and others claimed land "from ancestorship and occupation." He still lived on a part of it, but the government claimed it by virtue of the Ngaitahu Deed.

Evidence was taken, on 28th April, and "after some conversation with the Honourable John Hall and the counsel on both sides,"†the case was adjourned "in order to see whether any arrangement could be made."

In the morning no settlement had been made, and counsel for the Crown proposed to "hand in a document signed by Mr. Hall, on behalf of the Crown, referring this case under section 38 of the Native Lands Act, 1867,‡ for decision by the Court." Mr. Williams, Counsel for the Crown, understood that Mr. Cowlishaw (who was counsel for the Maoris) "would object to the order of reference being admitted, and he regretted this."

Mr. Williams handed in a document referring to the Ngaitahu Deed of 1848, and concluding thus:—" Now, therefore, the said agreement is hereby referred in accordance with the above mentioned Acts to the Native Lands Court.

By command,

Christchurch, April 28, 1868."   John Hall."

Every one knew that the Governor (Sir G. Bowen) was not in the same island with Mr. Hall. He was in the North Island, and an English Blue Book, of 1869 (307), p. 136, furnishes a singular commentary upon the use to which Sir G. Bowen's functions were applied at Christchurch in his absence. The Governor met some Maoris at Ngaruawahia on the Waikato River in May, 1868. One of them asked if they were to understand that the Treaty of Waitangi was

---

* Compendium of official Documents, &c.   Compiled by Alexander Mackay. Native Commissioner, Vol. 2, p. 203.   Heremaia Mautai's case is at page 204 and subsequent pages of the same Volume.

† Mackay's Compendium, Vol. 2, p. 205.

‡ The Native Lands Act of 1867, provided that lands referred to in Sec. 83, of the Native Lands Act, 1865 should, unless otherwise directed, be excluded from the operation of the Act of 1865; but it left power to "*the Governor*" to refer agreements about land to the Land Court.

" still in force," The Governor replied (through an official interpreter).—" The faith of the Queen will be preserved inviolate. . . The Treaty of Waitangi is still in force ; the only difference of late years is that the disposal of their lands is *now placed more entirely at the discretion of the Maori owners.*"

Such was Sir G. Bowen's florid account of what was going on. But such was not Heremaia Mautai's experience. His counsel, Mr. Cowlishaw, objected to Mr. Hall's order of reference. " He did not see how the Crown could step in in this summary way and stop a case now under adjudication. The case was now before the Court and he submitted that neither the Crown nor anybody else could step in the middle of it, and say—you are to proceed no further. . . It was never contemplated that the Governor should have such a power as this—that after the case had proceeded to a certain stage the Government could step in, and *because it was going unfavourably to them,* tell the Court that it must not proceed further with it. Such a proceeding would be an act of the greatest injustice."[*] Counsel for the Crown objected to Mr. Cowlishaw's statement. and the Judge thought he could not " allow the objection raised by Mr. Cowlishaw," who still contended that " although the power to make it a matter of reference was given to the Governor, the Legislature never intended to make it *ex post facto.* . . There was "*nothing to prove that the Order of Reference was authorized by the Governor.* He would propose *putting it in evidence that the Governor had never authorized* Mr. Hall to refer the matter to the Court. . . The order of reference was merely signed 'John Hall,' and the Court must therefore have evidence before it that the Governor delegated his authority to that gentleman. Mr. Hall did not even sign as being connected with the Government." Here (continues Mr. Mackay's official compendium), " Mr. Hall added the words after his signature," " A member of the Executive Council of the Colony of New Zealand."

" The Chief Judge said the Court was *bound to presume* that the order of reference was duly authorized by the Governor. The Governor's signature was not necessary; and it was presumed that Mr. Hall acted on his authority until the contrary was shown." Parenthetically one may remark that it is rather violent to *presume* what is known not to be the fact ; but when a Maori is in the case, strange presumptions take place].

" The order of reference was admitted, Mr. Cowlishaw objecting. The Chief Judge said he would proceed with the case with *increased powers.*" The hearing of the case was soon concluded, but it did not tend to confirm Sir George Bowen's idea that the disposal of their lands had recently been " placed more entirely at the discretion of the Maori owners." Mr. Hall appears not to have been examined; for a Maori member of Parliament said (N.Z. Hansard, 21st July, 1881, vol. xxxviii , p. 622) that when Cowlishaw " rose in his legal apparel " he " failed to find the Honourable John Hall, because that honourable

---

[*] Mackay Vol. 2. p. 206.

gentleman had got on his horse and gone to his own place fifty miles off." Mr. Mackay's official documents do not mention at what point of time Hall left the scene where he had played so conspicuous a part.

The judgment given for the Crown was a notable instance of neglect of those principles which Lord Derby had insisted upon in dealing with the Treaty of Waitangi.

The efficacy of Mr. Halls "order of reference" in the Court was apparently doubted afterwards, but not, perhaps, on account of injustice to Heremaia Mautai.

In 1868, the Legislature passed a "Ngaitahu Reference Validation Act" to "remove doubts as to the sufficiency of a certain order of reference" signed "as by command and on behalf of the Governor," and enacted that the order should be deemed as "valid and effectual to all intents and purposes *as if the same had been made* by and given under the hand of the Governor"; and "to have been a valid agreement for the extinguishment of the Native title . . ."

And yet this same John Hall (now, by grace of the Colonial office under Mr. Gladstone's and Lord Kimberley's guidance, Sir John Hall) has been heard to assert that the Maoris have always been kindly treated. And he, and such as he, object when the truth is placed before the public.

One more instance of denial of justice in the Middle Island must suffice for these pages, which will not hold a thousandth part of those which are calculated to cause groans among the Maoris.

A few large cases find their way into Courts and Parliaments. Unnumbered cases which involve the misery of the poor are usually unrecorded. It is fortunate that amongst the settlers in New Zealand there has been more kindness than has been displayed by some of those who, dressed in a little brief authority, have brought their acts within the scope of these pages.

In Dec. 1852, Mr. Mantell requested that small portions of land might be granted to Maoris who were in the habit of visiting the towns of Dunedin and Port Chalmers, and needed accommodation there for their boats, &c.* The Governor acquiesced and Mr. Mantell selected the sites. The site at Dunedin was at Prince's Street, and according to Mr. Mantell was the "only suitable piece of land now vacant." Its extent was three acres.

There is much to be said about both reserves, but that at Dunedin is a sufficient sample for these pages.

On the 6th June, 1853, the Governor, Sir G. Grey, formally approved of the reserve "as recommended."

It might have been thought that the small remnant of their lands

---

* Most of the facts about the Prince's Street Reserve for the Maoris at Dunedin are in Mr. Mackay's Compendium of official Documents relative to Native Affairs, in Vol. I. pp., 107 to 195, and unless otherwise mentioned, the text is generally quoted from his book.

thus set apart for them would be permanently secured for the Maoris; but local envy was early at work to wrest it from them.

In 1853, the colony was divided into Provinces under an Imperial Constitution Act * (15 and 16 Vict. Cap. 72), and the Province of Otago obtained a Provincial Legislature, and a Superintendent, or quasi-Governor.

The General Assembly, or Parliament of New Zealand, was not convened under the Constitution Act until 1854. It was, of course, paramount to the Provincial Legislatures, and the Governor of New Zealand being still Governor over the Provinces was resorted to for certain purposes by the Superintendents of the Provinces.

In June, 1855, Mr. Cargill, Superintendent of the Otago Province, applied to the Governor for a grant to himself officially of all the Public Reserves in Dunedin. He abstained from describing them. His net was so large and his terms were so vague that Governor Browne informed him (Nov., 1855) that grants should be "of a specific piece of land and for a specific purpose."

Mr. Cargill renewed his assault in 1856, still keeping back particulars, and the Governor (Feb., 1856) still required them.

In this year, Mr. Mantell was in England, and was not within reach of the Maoris for whom he obtained the reserve thus jeopardized by Mr. Cargill's demand for control over all reserves.

Particulars having been obtained at last, certain grants were issued in 1858.

In 1858, Mr. Cutten, a Commissioner of Crown Lands at Otago, gave a significant intimation of the covetousness with which the Maori Reserve at Prince's Street was eyed. He thought the Governor had "exceeded his powers" in setting it apart for the Natives. His reason was so quaint, if not absurd, as to deserve notice. He seemed to think the claims of the Otago settlers anterior to those of the Maoris to their native soil.

In 1862, he supported a petition from persons desirous to rent the Reserve, and Sir George Grey (who had become Governor for a second time) acceded to the request.

The rent of frontages varied from £6 16s. to £3 19s. per foot, and amounted to £2525 16s. a year.

The rent was not handed to the Maoris, but (Cutten wrote) "paid into a separate account to be dealt with according to instructions."

He applied for leave to pay £604 to the Town Board of Dunedin for "making a footpath along the front of the Reserve on the East side of Prince's St. Dunedin."

The suspicions of an Assistant Law Officer were aroused, and he

---

* Vide supra. p. 7. In this statute Lord Derby's ministry did its work thoroughly. The Provinces of New Zealand were to have local legislative bodies. Subsections of clause 19 of the Constitution Act (1852) enacted that it should "not be lawful" for such local legislatures "to make or ordain any law . . . affecting lands of the Crown or lands to which the title of the aboriginal native owners has never been extinguished," or "inflicting any disabilities or restrictions on persons of the Native Race to which persons of European birth or descent would not also be subjected."

wrote (22nd Dec., 1862): " The information given by Mr. Cutten does not enable me to see either what the Reserve he alludes to actually is, or the Ordinance under which the rate is imposed. . . . I suspect it is a Native Reserve. Mr. Cutten should be requested to give further information and meantime to refuse payment of the rate."

Mr. Cutten after some weeks furnished information, and still cast doubts upon the power of the Governor to grant to the natives of the soil the use of the small patch of land which (in consequence of the discovery of gold in Otago in 1861) had acquired commercial value.

The Superintendent of the Province, and Mr. Cutten, availed themselves of a visit by Mr. (now Sir) F. Dillon Bell to ply him with arguments about the hardship they endured while the Maori rights were respected.

The Prime Minister, Mr. Fox, moved by Mr. Bell, directed that full enquiries should be made by Mr. H. T. Clarke, resident magistrate at Invercargill.

Mr. Clarke without delay "waited upon His Honour the Superintendent, and Mr. Cutten, but could not obtain any positive information on the subject."

To a formal request in writing, he received no reply. He reported (Oct., 1864) that as the original Deed of Otago specially provided for the making of such Reserves for the Maoris he presumed that it should " set the question at rest."

Mr. Fox vacated office as Premier, in November, 1864, and was succeeded by Mr. Weld. The Postmaster General in the new administration was Mr. J. L. C. Richardson, who had formerly been Superintendent of the Otago province.

The new Native Minister was Mr. Mantell, who had, in 1852, induced the Governor to grant the Princes Street site to the Maoris.

In January, 1865, Mr. Mantell asked for the opinion of the Attorney General upon the matter. "After Sir G. Grey's departure in 1854 (Mr. Mantell wrote) the Provincial authorities seem to have questioned the power of the Governor to make these Reserves, and in 1861 when I spoke with the Superintendent of Otago, and Commissioner of Crown Lands on the subject, it was urged that they were too valuable for the Natives. There is now no reason why the title to these Reserves should not be distinctly recorded. How can that be done?"

Obstruction in the Province was going on, and (29th March, 1865) Mr. Weld himself requested the Superintendent of Otago to furnish a statement of the claims made by the Provincial Government.

Action and not evasion had become necessary to deprive the Maoris of the Reserve. The Postmaster General, Richardson, who had formerly been Superintendent of the Province, conferred with the Superintendent of the day, Mr. J. Hyde Harris.

Richardson wrote him a letter on the 13th April, 1865, which was answered by Harris on the same day. Richardson movingly told Harris that the failure of " a Mr. Clarke" to extract information from the Provincial Government in 1864 had led the General Government to conclude that the claims of the Province were unfounded, and that "in the meantime steps are being taken to vest the property in the hands of Trustees for the natives of the province, and to apply the rents which have been received."

"It will be evident to your Honour that should any claim exist in the part of the Provincial Government not a mail should be lost in making it known to the Hon. the Colonial Secretary."

No time was lost. On the day that Richardson wrote to Harris, Harris answered Richardson lengthily, and sent the correspondence to Mr. Weld. Richardson also forwarded copies of the correspondence to the Prime Minister, but complained to Harris that the latter's silence at the time of Mr. Clarke's visit had justified "the conclusion arrived at by the Government."

Mr. Harris wrote a long reply, which he may have thought a justification, and which is contained in Mr. Mackay's Compendium. He brought before Richardson a new fact, viz. : that £6031 18s. 9d. accumulated rents for the Reserve, had been by order of the Government, transferred from a special account to the "General Goverment account."

Richardson was soon at Wellington, interchanging memoranda with Mr. Mantell whose replies will repay perusal.

In June, 1865 the Attorney General (Sewell)gave his opinion that the land had been " duly reserved as a Native Reserve"and that he did not " see any ground upon which either the Provincial Government of Otago, or any municipal body constituted in Dunedin, or any private individual could impugn " the appropriation.

The Attorney General was then a Cabinet Minister, and in most countries such an opinion from such a man would have been decisive.

But Maori lands have been subject to influences not common in other countries.

There were two cogent reasons for struggle. The land, and the thousands of pounds of accumulated rent.

The Superintendent of Otago begged that the Prime Minister would "let the question rest" till the Provincial Government of Otago could appeal to the Parliament, or General Assembly, of New Zealand.

The Government did not promise to comply with the request, but in effect nothing was done.

The assembly met on the 26th July ; and Mr. Mantell, the advocate of justice, left the ministry on the following day.

A select committee in which Mr. Stafford sat, recommended, 25th August, 1865, that a Crown grant of the Reserve should be " *issued in favour of the Municipality of Dunedin.*"

In the House, Mr. Mantell strove to avert the adoption of such a report by moving (13 Sept.) that as the land was claimed as a Native Reserve the claim should be decided upon by the Supreme Court, and the Government should facilitate the trial.

Mr. Mantell might almost as well have "used question with the wolf." But sixteen other members voted with him against twenty nine. With bitter irony he afterwards wrote (1866) that though he was willing to believe the proceedings perfectly parliamentary, they warned all who took an interest in Maori rights that the "time might not be far distant when by precisely similar and equally parliamentary action there may remain in the whole Middle Island, and in any part of the Northern Island in which our perceptions of justice are not strengthened by our fears, not one acre of Maori land or Maori reserve which shall not have been appropriated to provincial uses."

There may have been persons for whom such a consummation had attractions. But there seemed some hesitancy about openly consummating the wrong recommended by the Select Committee. The highly respected Mr. Fitzgerald became Native Minister in the place of Mr. Mantell, and his censure may have been feared.

Be that as it may, Mr. Weld's ministry came to an end on the 16th October, and Mr. Stafford became Prime Minister. The session was closed in October, and the way was open for departmental action without risk of unpleasant questions in the House.

But the mode of action adopted seemed like that of a man who thinks that by wearing a mask he qualifies his acts for the better.

On the 4th November 1865, a Crown Grant Clerk at Dunedin, sent by order, " for His Excellency's signature two Crown Grants to the Superintendent of Otago " " as per accompanying Schedule." Without being specified one of these was the Maori Reserve at Dunedin. Its description in the Schedule was, " Piece of land situate in Prince's Street, Dunedin." " Public utility " was assigned as the " Nature of Reserve." (Mackay, vol. i., p. 142).

Mr. Stafford, on 21st November, wrote to Mr. Dick, the Superintendent of Otago that " As it is the invariable rule and requirement of the Act that the specific purpose for which a grant is asked should be stated, I have to request your Honour to be good enough to specify more particularly the object of the trust." " His Honour " complied (28th December) by suggesting the words " As a reserve for wharves and quays."

At this period of the transaction, events occurred which none of the actors have been able to explain, though an examination conducted in 1877 before the Native Affairs Committee sheds some light upon them.

What is clear, is that the Crown Grant was put before the Governor for signature on the 11th January, 1866.

Sir George Grey's evidence proves that the subject of the Grant had been previously discussed and that it was deemed wrong to sign it.

He said (in 1877) " Discussions had taken place between myself and law officers and I had resolved that I *ought not to sign the Grant* until the matter had been fully discussed. A number of Grants were presented. . . I believed that one of them. . . was the Grant for this land, but I could not positively identify it ; and as the Colonial Secretary (Stafford) *who presented the Grant to me* was perfectly satisfied that it was *not the Grant for this reserve,* I signed it. Subsequently it turned out that the grant had been signed. It was done under a mistake. . . It was discovered the same day that the Grant had been signed improperly, and the Government tried to recover possession of the Grant, but it was found that the Grant had been *sent off that day* in a vessel going to Otago, and in that way the land passed. . . Mr. Stafford found out that the mistake arose from the negligence of a clerk in the Crown Lands Office. Mr. Domett, then Commissioner of Crown Lands, whom I sent for, told me how the error had occurred."

Mr. Stafford testified in 1877, " As far as I can recollect, I think it probable that neither the Governor nor myself were aware when that particular Grant was signed. . . I think is *very probable* that this Grant *may have come up* inadvertently with a number of others, and in the same way *may have been* sent on by me to the Governor for his signature. I use the word *inadvertently* because I have some recollection, I will not be quite positive about it, that I had given a *special instruction* that that Grant should *not* be sent on for signature without my attention being called to the fact. . . I believe although I will not be absolutely positive at this length of time, that I gave such instructions. . . I have been informed that Sir George Grey who was then Governor has stated that he put some questions to me with regard to this Grant. I have no recollection (that he) ever put questions to me about any Grant whatever at any time. But if Sir George Grey says he is perfectly certain he did put such questions to me, I am not at this length of time prepared to say that he did not, but I have certainly no recollection of (his) having at any time questioned me as to a Grant, and I think if such an occurrence had taken place I should have recollected it." Two things are proved by these statements. Mr. Stafford had thought it right to give a *special instruction* to prevent a surprise, and the Governor had come to a conclusion, *after consultation with advisers*, that the Grant *ought not to be signed*.

Another thing is clear, viz. : that when the Governor's signature had been surreptitiously procured it was the duty of Mr. Stafford who had suspected that the Grant might be sent on without his attention being called to the fact, to take immediate steps to rescind the Grant, not at the expense of the Maoris, but by direct action on the part of the Government.

Another thing which is not so clear may be inferred from the swiftness with which the Grant was hurried away when signed. A hearsay rumour has reached me that it was this part of the transaction which gave the greatest pleasure to the actors in it, and that they were proud of having thus obtained the honoured name of the Queen to crown their proceedings.

It was then thought safe to drop the mask. Until January, 1866, the Dunedin plotters had usually spoken of the Maori Reserve, as " a Reserve in Prince's Street " or " on the east side of Prince's Street," or " a piece of land situate in Prince's Street : " but having obtained the Governor's signature they seem to have thought it safe to use the language adopted by others.

On the 29th January, 1866 the Town Clerk boldly applied for the back-rents, or "certain monies in the hands of the General Government on account of the Reserve *lately known as the Maori Reserve*,* Prince's Street South, Dunedin.

This seems to have been at first thought audacious. Mr. Under-Secretary Gisborne replied, by direction of Stafford the Prime Minister, "There appears to be no power to transfer rents accruing on account of this land, previously to the issue of the Grant either to the Grantee or the City Council of Dunedin.

A Bill will be submitted to the General Assembly next session for determining doubts as to the appropriation of the land and the funds arising out of it."

English readers may be inclined to ask why the Maoris were not asked what they wished to say upon the subject before their Reserve was thus shuffled out of their possession. Mr. Fitzgerald's and Donald McLean's efforts had not then given them seats in the Legislature, and the conduct of the actors in the Prince's Street drama does not suggest a hope that the Maoris were called upon to express an opinion. Moreover, Mr. Stafford's ministry was re-constructed, and Mr. J. L. C. Richardson, so active about the Reserve in 1865, became Stafford's colleague in 1866. According to Mr. Mackay's compendium,—quoting a report of a Select Committee,—Mr. Stafford performed a remarkable feat in the matter of the Reserve in 1866. He introduced in the Lower House, and *carried through important stages in one day* a Bill "to declare the Superintendent of the Province of Otago to be entitled to certain Rents received on account of a Reserve situate in Prince's Street in the city of Dunedin." (Vol. i., p. 162).

There were, fortunately, two Houses of Legislature; and on the 28th September, the Legislative Council ordered the Bill to be "read a second time, this day six months."

If there had been a plot to ratify by a law in September the abstraction from the Maoris of the land (for which both the Governor and the Prime Minister testified, that "*by mistake*" a Grant had been procured for the Otago Superintendent in January of the same year) the plot had failed. But it is to be hoped that the attempt to pass the Bill was but another mistake—of the same kind.

The first note of the Maori feelings on the subject which Mr. Mackay's Compendium affords us, shows (Vol. I. p. 143) that Mr. Stafford had means of knowing what those feelings were, before he carried his Bill through one House in so rapid a manner. But public men are very busy during a session, and we may hope that as he testified that the "Grant may have come up inadvertently" for the

---

* Mr. Mantell was blamed for *disrespect to the Provincial Government* in advising the original Reserve. He advised it, in 1852, before there was any Provincial Government, before indeed the boundaries of the Provinces had been proclaimed by the Governor; (as they were in 1853.)

Governor's signature, so the Bill may have come inadvertently before the House in September, 1866.

Be that as it may, we find in Mr. Mackay's Official Documents, (Vol. I. p. 143) a letter from the Chief Taiaroa, dated 5th August, 1866, to the Governor. " . . . I have a word to say to you about our reserve here in the Town. I request you to make clear to us the case in respect of it. I have heard that it is being taken away by the Pakehas of the Town, that land is. It is very wrong thus to take our land away without a cause. Friend, Governor—with you is the disposal of that land. Do you, in replying to us, make clear its position. If any Pakehas importune for that land, do not let them have it without paying for it. Friend, give heed. . ." The Prime Minister waited apparently more than two months before writing to " His Honour, the Superintendent, Otago " (Dick), about taking away of the land " without a cause " ; having in the meantime made his abortive attempt to deprive the Maoris of the accumulated rent by a special Act. On the 16th October, 1866, Stafford sent, to Dick, Taiaroa's letter and said—" After a careful consideration of all circumstances connected with the Native claim to this reserve, and with the Crown Grant referred to, the Government is of opinion that the question of the validity of the Grant should be submitted to a proper judicial tribunal." (He proposed to test the matter by a writ of Intrusion). " The expenses attending the process will be chargeable on the contingencies of the Native Department, or on the proceeds of the reserve, according as the issue may be." (Mackay, Vol. I. p. 143).

But trials, especially fair trials, were never palatable to that section of the Colonists, which deemed the Maoris fit objects for pillage or maltreatment. Dick replied, 30th October, 1866, " on behalf of this Government (i.e. the Government of the Province Otago) I decline to try the validity of the Crown Grant by the course proposed, on the ground that the Provincial Government cannot recognize any Maori right or title to the reserve in question, which point it was understood, had already been definitely decided by the General Assembly."

To any one ignorant of the curious way in which people can persuade themselves that their conduct is right, when they set aside in their own favour the weightier matters of the law—judgment and faith—it may appear unaccountable that such letters could pass at such a time between Stafford and Dick :—but they stand printed in Mr. Mackay's valuable " Compendium of Official Documents " (of which I may remark that I found it difficult to obtain a copy, but of which I have taken great care, and which I am prepared to show to any one desircus to consult it).

The next important document contained in it, is a letter addressed by no less than sixteen Members of Parliament to the Prime Minister on the 12th July, 1867. Mr. Macandrew was one of them. They tell him that in accordance with his own " request " made " on the 9th inst." they apply to him for the rents, and that in their " humble opinion " it " would be an act of injustice on the part of the General Government any longer to withold them " from the Province of Otago.

Stafford informed them (23rd July) that "the Government after a careful review of all the circumstances of the case is of opinion that the payment requested should be made, and will consider in what manner this *can be legally effected*." On the 24th July he wrote to Mr. Macandrew (who had become Superintendent of Otago) and who was conveniently in Wellington. Stafford had been advised that the Superintendent of Otago must be "recognised as the recipient of the rents."

But proceedings were threatened with a view to obtain a declaration of the invalidity and cancellation of the Crown Grant" and Stafford required, before paying the money to Macandrew, an undertaking for the return of the money, if the proceedings should be successful, or any other person than Macandrew should be found entitled to the money. On the 25th July Macandrew declined such a responsibility :—
"however improbable it may be that the Supreme Court will give other than an equitable decision in this case, yet I am not warranted in committing the Province to the chances of such a contingency." Macandrew added that after consultation with other members it was thought desirable that Mr. (now Sir) Francis Dillon Bell should re introduce in 1867 the Bill thrown out by the Council in 1866, the object of which was to enable the Otago Province to receive the Maori rents.

But an obstacle had already intervened. A Maori Chief, J. T. Patuki, had, 15th July, prayed that the Governor would "permit and enable" the Ngaitahu and Ngatimamoe tribes to try in the Supreme Court their right "to this reserve and these funds"; and on the 22nd July, Patuki had been informed that his petition had been assented to.

Mr. Mantell was courteously informed accordingly by a Minister, Mr. J. C. Richmond, 25th July, and was invited to interest himself as a friend in the matter as the Government wished "to afford these Natives every facility to test the validity of their claim, and will guarantee a payment to their legal advisers of a sum not exceeding £200 on account of expenses incurred by you on their behalf."

The sum was not large, and it would have to be paid from funds derived from the patrimony of the Maoris, but the tone of the letter was kindly.

Mr. Mantell agreed to act in accordance with it. But when application was made to the Attorney General, Mr. James Prendergast, for a Writ of *scire facias* in the case he replied, 6th August, "Upon the usual bond being given to the Registrar of the Supreme Court, let the Writ issue."

Mr. Mantell (7th August) promptly requested his gracious correspondent, Mr. Richmond, "to indicate the mode in which the demands of the Attorney General are to be acceded to, and to appoint bondsmen to undertake the responsibility on behalf of the Government."

Mr. Richmond's reply was neither prompt nor gracious. On the 19th August, 1867, he wrote :—(Mackay p. 149).

"Sir, referring to my letter of the 25th July last, agreeing to guarantee up to a certain amount the costs of a suit as to the ownership of the Prince's Street Reserves, Dunedin, I regret to be under the necessity of informing you that the Government having at or near the time of *my promise* entered into *an arrangement altogether inconsistent therewith,* have considered it proper to *withdraw* the guarantee in question so far as the future is concerned. . ." (They would however pay costs already incurred).

J. C. RICHMOND."

THE HON. W. B. D. MANTELL, M.L.C.,
Wellington.

After brief interlocutions, Mr. Mantell replied formally on the 26th August. Meanwhile, Mr Dillon Bell had, on the 30th July, introduced his Bill to enable Otago to receive the Maori rents, and on the 6th August had withdrawn it, on the plea that "the Government had taken the matter up;"* and on the 7th August Stafford had re-introduced a similar Bill †

On the 10th September it was passed in the Lower House, and was sent to the Upper, where, in technical phrase, it "lapsed."

A Select Committee of the Lower House reported in 1868 thus :‡ "The loss of the Bill appears to be attributable to the following circumstances :—On the 22nd August a petition from a native chief, named John Topi Patuki, claiming to be interested in the reserve, was presented to the Legislative Council. Its prayer as described in the journal was that the Dunedin Princes Street Reserve Bill be not passed, but that 'the whole question be dealt with by a judicial tribunal.'" (Similar had been Bishop Selwyn's and Sir W. Martin's prayer in 1860, about the land at Waitara and the Chief Te Rangitake.) The Legislative Council resolved 17th September to accede to Patuki's prayer, on the ground that the matter "could only be equitably and satisfactorily decided by the Supreme Court."

The significance of Mr. Richmond's abandonment of the promise made by the Government to the Maoris is more easily understood by observing that after the promise was made on the 25th July by Richmond, his colleague, Mr. Stafford, as Premier, introduced his Bill to sanction the payment of the accrued rents to the Province of Otago.

It was while the Bill was before the Lower House, that Mr. Mantell formally replied, 26th August, to Mr. Richmond's astounding announcement that a promise not so old as "one revolving moon" would be repudiated. Some warmth of expression was perhaps natural. . . "I cannot understand the mode in which the Govern-

---

* Mackay's Compendium, Vol. I., p. 172.

† It appears that on its introduction the Bill was framed, so as to validate the grant; but on the 23rd August amendments were made to avoid such an interpretation. But on what ground could the accrued rents be paid over to the quasi grantees if the grant was vicious ? ib. pp. 152-172.

‡ ib. p. 172.

ment can reconcile with any reputable idea of honour and good faith the limitation and withdrawal of the guarantee of 25th July, intimated in your letter of 19th August. (Amongst other details, Mr. Mantell mentioned that he had recommended Mr. Izard, the Maori legal adviser, to tender Patuki's bond for £500 to satisfy the demand of the Attorney General.)

"Whether that unfortunate chief can 'withdraw' this guarantee with the facility which you appear to believe attends a similar but far less justifiable act on the part of the Government, the Attorney General can inform you..... It seems scarcely necessary to inform you that after this experience of the ways of your Government towards the weak, I decline to take any further action in this matter on behalf of the Government. You will, of course, address any further communication to Mr. Izard, who, with Mr. Allan, on your letter and guarantee, undertook the conduct and charges of the case —my correspondence with you ending, I trust, here.

"To me the case is but too clear; on the one hand the Natives require from you, out of the funds received by you as their self-constituted guardians, sufficient to enable them, as encouraged by the Queen's Representative and by yourselves to try in the Courts of the Colony to recover property long recognized as theirs, ... on the other, a demand for these funds is made on behalf of the body which now holds that grant, supported by no argument that has not yet been fairly met, but preferred by sixteen members having votes in the Legislature. . . . And in this dilemma the Government proposes now to assume a position of absolute passiveness, withholding from suitors of its own creation enough of their own money to pay their expenses. . . Of the choice thus made by the Government there is, I fear, but one opinion open to any man who cares for the reputation of the Colony and his own honour." Mr. Richmond retorted that some of the "topics" in Mr. Mantell's letter were of "a purely personal kind, and call for no official reply; although the injurious character of some of your remarks and insinuations will require notice when time shall enable a more temperate view to be taken on the subject."

The manipulation of the matter required almost the art of a Joseph Surface, and it is well that Mr. Mackay's "Official Documents" reveal the facts.

On the 25th July, Macandrew refused to enter into an obligation to refund the rents if the Supreme Court should decide that he ought not to have received them.

On the 27th August he proposed to hand over another piece of land to the Maoris instead of the Princes' Street Reserve, and Mr. J. C. Richmond was the go-between he made use of.*

In September the Bill to enable him to receive the accrued rents was arrested in the Upper House.

On the 12th September a Committee reported to the Legislative

---

* Mackay's Official Documents, p. 156, Vol. I.

Council that Patuki's "petition (against the Bill for handing the accrued rents to Macandrew) should be acceded to."

On the same day Mr. Richmond wrote to Macandrew that another member of Parliament had suggested "in conversation" with Richmond, that Macandrew would probably accept the rents, and give (what he had formerly refused) a guarantee "to refund the same if the result of proceedings at law or in equity should be to upset the Grant." (Mackay, Vol I. p. 157.

On that same day, and apparently in a hurry, Macandrew informed Richmond "officially" that he was "prepared to give the necessary undertaking to refund the accrued rents," and naturally enough suggested that if he could thus obtain possession of the funds, there would be "no object in pressing the Bill now before the Legislative Council." If pressed, it might have been defeated in accordance with the determination to accede to the prayer of Patuki ; and as its object was to put the money into Macandrew's hands, he did not require the Bill if Richmond would give him the money without it.

Accordingly, on the 24th September, 1867, the accrued rents (£6,031 18s. 9d.) were paid to the Superintendent of Otago, he giving the required guarantee.*

If Banquo had been in New Zealand, he might have said to the successful Province :—

> " ' Thou hast it now ! ' land, rents, and favouring aid
> From sublunary powers ; and should Heaven grant
> That no historic eye shall spy the matter,
> The Maori wrongs shall vanish in the past,
> As Maori lives in present.   They depart
> Like mist-wreaths of the morning ; but a book
> Which graves the stubborn facts on winged leaves ;
> Guard thou 'gainst that ! for it shall tell the tale
> To countless generations, and 'twere better
> To do no wrong than let the wrong be proved
> In the eternal blazon of the truth."

But there was no Banquo at hand.

Patuki's petition to the Queen was presented by Mr. Mantell to the Governor on the 19th August, 1867.

It was not until the 5th October that Mr. Richmond furnished a memorandum to be forwarded with it to the Secretary of State.

Both Sir George Grey and Mr. Richmond alluded to the manner of the Grant.   Sir George Grey said : " My responsible advisers at a meeting of the Executive Council inadvertently advised me to sign a Crown Grant dated 11th January, 1866."   Mr. Richmond said : " In the meantime inadvertently as regards His Excellency and the Colonial Secretary (Stafford) a Grant which had been prepared on the authority of the resolution of the House of Representatives was presented for signature and issued."

---

* In 1868 a Select Committee of the Lower House reported that they had "not been able to satisfy themselves that this undertaking would be a security in the absence of an appropriation for the purpose by the Provincial Council of Otago. Mackay, Vol. I. p. 172 . But the hurry of Messrs. Richmond and Macandrew made it impossible for them to allow reference to Otago functionaries.

Mr. Richmond's memorandum obscured the facts. The Governor wrote that he had " sincerely desired " that the case should have been " compromised in a generous spirit towards the natives of the Middle Island, who parted with large tracts of land to this Government for an almost nominal consideration." The Secretary of State dismissed Patuki's petition by saying he was " unable to advise Her Majesty to take any steps in relation to it."

Sir George Grey encountered difficulty in endeavouring to arrange the matter before quitting his post as Governor.

He told Mr. J. C. Richmond that he "thought the expenses of a suit for testing the validity of the Grant should be borne out of the accrued rents of the reserve," and Richmond replied : " That fund is no longer in the Treasury," * but suggested that proceeds might be abstracted from other native reserve funds, and on the 26th October, 1867, a formal order was made, in the Executive Council, to take £400 from Ngaitahu Reserve Funds to enable the Ngaitahu tribe to contend against the injustice done to them by " inadvertently " taking their land, and very " advertently " sequestering their rents.

Mr. Mantell was persuaded in November to watch the case, and the disbursement of funds on behalf of the Maoris.

Soon after these arrangements were made in 1867 the Native Lands Court sat (April, 1868) at Christchurch, and Mr. Hall (a colleague of Stafford, J. C. Richmond, and J. L. C. Richardson, in the ministry,) made that singular Order of Reference which the New Zealand Parliament was fain to validate by a special Act, with regard to the Ngaitahu Deed, and *the extinction of Maori titles.*

From Christchurch the judge proceeded to Otago, and there the question of the Maori Reserve at Prince's Street was raised before the Court.

An official return † states briefly how it was dealt with.

Name of Claim.	Name of Claimant.	Date of Hearing.	How disposed of.
Prince's Street, Dunedin.	Kerei Taiaroa, and others.	May 23rd, 1868.	Application dismissed, evidence having been given that the land had been granted to the Superintendent of Otago. Applicants were instructed that they would have to go to the Supreme Court.

It was not unnatural that the Maoris should think the Native Lands Court the proper tribunal to resort to, with regard to their land; but they are not the only persons who have formed erroneous notions as to the redress obtainable in a court of law.

* Memorandum by Mr. Richmond. Mackay's Compendium, vol. i., p. 155.

† Mackay's Compendium, vol. ii. p. 243.

They did not understand the law, but they knew something about equity and about human nature. They collected, as best they could, funds with which to sustain their cause; and the account was called "The Naboth's Vineyard Account."

After a time the case went before the Supreme Court at Dunedin, and Judge Ward decided on technical grounds against the Maoris.

They were not allowed to put the merits of their case before the Court, and therefore none of their champions could complain of being treated more shabbily than they were. There were the usual technical proceedings; and Judge Ward decided that the Maori "declaration" was bad.

There was an appeal to the Court of Appeal sitting at Wellington, on the 2nd, 3rd, and 4th November, 1869. The declaration had set out a writ in form of a *scire facias*, and long arguments were used on both sides. Much mint and cummin were expended, but some weightier matters were not dwelt upon. The case was called THE QUEEN, Plaintiff in error *v.* James Macandrew, Defendant in error:— but the solemn act to which the Queen had been a party in New Zealand—The Treaty of Waitangi—morally conclusive as to Maori rights, was not allowed to be the measure of their claims. The Judges decided that the declaration was bad ; and, on application of counsel for the Queen, reserved leave for him to apply to amend the declaration before the close of the sittings.

The proceedings occupy a score of pages in Mr. Mackay's copious compendium, where those who do not shrink from the unsavoury task can read them.

Mr. Mantell and Mr. Izard, a legal adviser, petitioned for a hearing before the Privy Council. Taiaroa journeyed to Wellington to consult about the necessary funds; others assisted, and the "Naboth's Vineyard Account" increased.

The appeal was in progress in 1872, and it may be that an exposure of the facts in England was not deemed desirable. It may have been thought that an English tribunal would closely investigate the Maori case ; and deal with its merits, rather than stifle it in the wrappings of technicalities.

Messrs. Stafford, Richmond, and Richardson, were not at this time in office. Mr. Fox with Mr. Vogel and others acceded to office in 1869, and with them Donald McLean for the first time became Native Minister.

Mr. Stafford expelled the Fox ministry in September 1872, but was himself driven from office in the next month. McLean again became Native Minister in a Waterhouse Ministry in which Mr. Vogel was Treasurer and for the first time, Maoris were made Executive Councillors.

Mr. Vogel informed Mr. Izard that "the Government were desirous that the action should be stopped," and that the Provincial Government of Otago shared the desire and "wanted possession of the land."

Mr. Izard had "every hope of succeeding" in the appeal, but consented to compromise, and after sketching terms with Mr. Vogel, consulted Mr. Mantell. The result was that a telegram was sent to England to stop the appeal on payment by the Province of Otago of £4,560 and £500, which would provide, after certain deductions, £5,000 for division among the Maori claimants and leave the Province in quiet possession of the land which it had coveted so long.

Mr. Izard wrote to Patuki that though he did "not think the Maoris entitled to anything less, in strict justice, than the whole of the land," —the chances of success must be considered, and he had made the best bargain he could with Mr. Vogel

Mr. Mantell also wrote to Patuki that the compromise represented not the Maori rights, but their prospect of obtaining them. He believed the rights unquestionable. " On considerations of public policy (he wrote) in the true interests of the colony, I should and do desire that the case should go on before the Privy Council whatever the result; for I am not absolutely without hope. . . . that an authentic exposure of all the facts relating to this case might at last arouse some English statesman to a sense, that in delegating powers to colonists the Imperial Government is bound in honour and duty to insist upon the honest fulfilment of every engagement made by Her Majesty's representatives on behalf of Her Majesty, and in Her Majesty's name, prior to such delegation; and that of this duty the Imperial Government cannot divest itself before God, though it may succeed in doing so before man—as man goes. But you will say . . . what is the best in a pecuniary point of view, that I can do for myself and my tribe in this matter? In this view I conscientiously believe that by accepting the proposed compromise you will obtain the full value of your chances, as far as I can see them. The law is always uncertain . . . no proper care has been taken when promises have been made to your tribe, or benefits guaranteed, so to bind the Crown as to give you a claim irrefragable against it in the Courts of Law. . . . The decision of the Privy Council may be adverse, or may not be final, and the case may have to be begun again, if you can go on with it; and whence are the funds to be derived? "

Whence indeed when there is a powerful syndicate leagued together to wage war with combined funds against the Maoris and their friends?

Mr. Mantell wrote also to Taiaroa, who told Mr. Izard that he could not say the compromise was bad, although it was known that the land was rightfully the property of the Maoris.—"However I will consent in order to save my property and that of all my people—lest we lose the case in England as we have lost it in the Supreme Court of New Zealand."

Thus the title to the land passed away—at a time when its value was estimated at £100,000, and when a member of the New Zealand Parliament said that the condition of the Maori victims of " unfulfilled promises " in the Middle Island was a disgrace to any Government.

In the absence of some apprehension that an English tribunal would do justice without fear or favour, it may even be doubted whether the Maoris would have received any compensation at all.

G

When Taiaroa afterwards moved for a Select Committe on "Unfulfilled Promises," Mr. Macandrew complained that the composition of the claim to the Reserve for £5,000 " seemed only to have had the effect of giving a taste for blood."

What, then, must have been the appetite of the Province of Otago which had swallowed almost all the land of which the Reserve was but a fragment, and sought that sweet morsel in the manner by which Sir George Grey's signature was obtained for the grant?

Is it to be wondered at, that, seeing how his people groaned, Taiaroa sometimes used strong language? There was a report by Judge Fenton upon a petition from the Ngaitahu about the failure of the Government to afford the hospitals and schools promised when they parted with their land.

The Report said that "even failure in this respect cannot be the subject of pecuniary compensation. Such compensation would be as incapable of calculation as the consequential damages in the Alabama claims." It quoted a legal maxim to support the rejection of the groans of the Ngaitahu people.

Taiaora obtained leave to lay a written comment on the report upon the table. He criticized it as "confused." "You refer to the Europeans having brought peace. I reply to that, I would be rather dead than live to witness the distress and pain which my people suffer through the deceitful and unfulfilled words of the false-speaking race the Europeans. You say *qui sentit commodum, sentire debet et onus*; but I have not seen any benefit derived by myself and my people from the Europeans. . . . The words of the report are merely grumbling words ; they have no force. They are deceitful and delusive ; (Kahore e pono) they are not true. Mr. Fenton refers to that vessel "the Alabama." Is the same course to be taken with the Middle Island as with that vessel? What was done about her? Did not England pay on her account to the American Government, because she was built on English soil?" Sensitive people may blame such language, but can they wonder at it?

Having obtained for his suffering people the money paid by the Otago Province to stay the appeal to the Privy Council about the title, Taiaroa naturally applied for the arrears of rent which had accrued before the "inadvertent" grant of the Reserve to the Province.

In 1874, Donald McLean and Mr. Vogel gave no answer to his appeals.

In 1875 Mr. Mantell supported him, but McLean was uncompliant.

In 1876 Taiaroa asked in the House whether McLean would restore to the Maoris the rents "due before the issue of the Crown Grant." They exceeded £6000, McLean postponed his reply in order to consult his colleagues ; and, when again questioned, refused to recommend the restoration "inasmuch as it was understood that the claim was settled or compromised by the payment" in 1872.

If that had been the case it would have been easy to say so in the first instance ; and in that case also it would have been supererogatory to endeavour to procure Taiaroa's signature to a document which had not been shown to Mr. Izard. This was proved in 1877, when the persevering Chief renewed his efforts, and the matter was examined by the Native Affairs Committee.

Donald McLean, so powerful in the House on Maori questions, had then retired. The intricate methods resorted to in previous years to deprive the Maoris of the Reserve, and withhold from them the rents, were discussed before the Committee, but need not be mentioned here. Taiaroa gave cogent evidence. Mr. Fox and Mr. Macandrew warmly opposed the restoration of the arrears of rent. But the Committee nevertheless recommended it. Fox and Macandrew protested. Sir George Grey had become Prime Minister in October 1877, Mr. Sheehan was Native Minister. Mr. Macandrew was their colleague.

A sum of £5,000 was put on the Estimates as "Final settlement of Native Claims to the Dunedin Prince's Street Reserve," and was passed on the 6th December by 28 votes against 23.

Taiaroa, though present during the evening, did not vote. The three Maori members for the North Island voted for the grant. Mr. Macandrew, consistently with his former opinions voted against it. So did Mr. Bryce a North Island member, who was Chairman of the Native Affairs Committee which had recommended the vote. Sir George Grey supported it. His ministry had only recently been formed, and it is possible that some votes were given on party grounds and without much enquiry.

Numerous avocations,—public and private,—prevent large numbers of persons from examining closely all the questions on which they are called upon to vote, and the duty of making no unfair demands upon their supporters ought to weigh heavily upon ministries.

Such was the end of the Maori Reserve at Dunedin, so small, so coveted and—to use Pistol's language—so conveyed.

Speaking of the proposal of certain theorists "to confiscate, either openly, or under the thin disguise of a predatory use of the taxing power, every man's freehold, Professor Goldwin Smith remarks:— "That the State has, by the most solemn and repeated guarantees, "ratified private proprietorship, and undertaken to protect it, matters "nothing; nor even that it has itself recently sold the land to the "proprietor, signed the deed of sale, and received the payment. That "such views can be propounded anywhere but in a robber's den or a "lunatic asylum, still more, that they can find respectful hearers, is a "proof that the economical world is in a state of curious perturbation."*

What language would the learned Professor have used about the Maori Reserve at Dunedin, if the facts had come within his knowledge? There, not only the ordinary obligation to do right existed. England had only obtained a footing in New Zealand by a Treaty in which she guaranteed to the Maoris all the rights of British subjects, and acquired a power of pre-emption by the Crown of such lands as the Maoris might wish to sell. Under that Treaty the Crown acquired by Deeds of cession all the land in the Middle Island at a nominal cost,

*False Hopes. By Goldwin Smith, D.C.L. Cassell & Company, London, 1886.

guaranteeing at the same time large reserves to the Maoris by promises which are admitted to be "unfulfilled."*

The Prince's Street Reserve, however, was specially allotted to the Maoris.

It cannot be denied that the elaborate and curious manner in which it was wrested from them after "solemn and repeated guarantees" and pledges of protection from the Crown, deserves exposure in these pages. It has caused many groans, some pathetic, and some indignant.

The exposure of wrongs done is easy when circumstances have caused them to be officially recorded. A chief like Taiaroa having a seat in Parliament could drag the question of the Dunedin Reserve into light.

Some Reserves were lost in gloom; but those who should have been the beneficiaries were no less pillaged and had no less cause for grief than the Ngaitahu of Otago.

In 1882 in debate on a Native Reserves Bill, Captain Fraser (New Z. Hansard, Vol. 43 p. 637) said in the Upper House that "four Native Reserves were totally lost in Hawkes' Bay; nobody knew what had become of them." And a newspaper remarked, "In spite of trustees, laws, regulations, red tape .... they have been blotted from the map Not a creature from the Native Minister (Mr. Bryce) down ...... has the faintest notion of where they are."

And yet some people are willing to swear that the Maoris are under great obligations for the justice and kindness with which they have always been treated! and some other people without further enquiry, believe them.

Well might the old chief Parore say in a petition to the Queen in "1882:—These things, and many of the laws which are being carried "into effect, are, according to Maori ideas, very unjust, creating "disorder amongst us, giving *heart pangs and sadness of spirit* to your "Maori children, who are ever looking towards you, Most Gra- "cious Queen; and it is averred by men of wisdom that these "matters, which weigh so heavily upon us, are in opposition to the "great and excellent principles of the Treaty of Waitangi."

Lord Kimberley, forgetful of, or vilipending the Treaty, and the oft-repeated and solemn assurances of his predecessors that it should be religiously and scrupulously respected,—arrested the course of their petition, and told its bearers that "it was not the duty of the Colonial Office to advise the Queen in reference to local matters like the present."†

---

* When Taiaora moved for a Select Committee on the unfulfilled promises, a member was shocked. The motion "might cover a claim for two millions of acres in the Middle Island." In other words the largeness of an obligation is a reason for setting it aside altogether!

† Blue Book 1882. C 3382. p.291. The Earl's ideas about the honour and good faith of England and England's Queen on this occasion, help us to understand how it was that he was willing to sever Ireland from the United Kingdom and to abandon the Queen's loyal subjects to the yoke of those whom Mr. Gladstone had described as seeking to "march through rapine to disintegration and dismemberment of the Empire."

The seizure of the Maori Reserve at Dunedin was special, and the arts of a Provincial, aided by the powers of a General, Government succeeded in abstracting from the Maoris, under the forms but against the spirit of law, the coveted vineyard of Naboth.

But even the forms of law were not always respected ; and the time came in 1881, when deeds were done for which it was not even pretended that there was any legal sanction.

When my censure of those deeds provoked indignation against me, I hoped that by showing how unlawful they were, I should justify a certain portion of what I had written ; but, the contention of my counsel on this point was overruled in 1886, in a court of law, on the ground that though the seizure of dwellings at Parihaka might have "been a very arbitrary act" the Judge thought (counsel on the other side) "quite justified in saying 'I will not go into that question.'" In another part of the summing up, the learned Judge said : "No doubt that Parihaka affair would open, and did open, a strong observation about the position of the Natives and about the repressive measures which were to be taken against them. With reference to that I think it would be advisable as far as we can, to keep clear of all that discussion."*

It is the manifest duty of all loyal subjects to obey the law, and I do not desire to complain here, of the manner in which the law was laid down by the learned Judge in 1886.

Accepting implicitly the condition that the arbitrariness or unlawfulness of acts done at Parihaka in 1881 could not be represented on my behalf before an English jury in 1886 as I wished,I may still present the facts historically to that tribunal—public opinion—for which these pages. are written.

If critical censure were prohibited there would be practically no check upon brutal or unlawful acts; for there is no process of Impeachment possible in a colony.

The far-seeing William Wentworth did indeed urge in a petition from New South Wales in 1844 that a tribunal for Impeachment ought to be created ; and he cited in proof of the necessity, the judgment of the Privy Council in 1842,† which pronounced that, as to a Colonial Assembly, the right of Impeachment was "a claim for which there is not any colour of foundation."

The colonial office saw no way to comply with Wentworth's demand, and no such way has since been found.

To the wider court of public opinion, therefore, must all friends of their fellow-creatures resort when they seek to denounce, and thereby to prevent, oppression.

In previous pages (31, 32) I have shown under what circumstances, in 1865, a Proclamation of Confiscation—saving the rights of loyal holders—was issued with regard to the West Coast, and simultaneously with it another Proclamation guaranteeing to " at

---

* I quote these words from a printed report of the case which has been sold in New Zealand, but I know not who authorized the publication.

† Keiley & Carson. Moore's Privy Council Reports, vol. 4, p. 89.

once restore considerable quantities of land to those of the Natives who wish to settle down *upon their lands.*"

The desolation of the district in 1869, as described by Sir William Fox and Sir F. Dillon Bell in 1880, and the resumption of the duties of humanity under Donald McLean, have also been recorded. McLean's instructions, and arrangements recognizing Maori possessory rights at the West Coast, and his purchasing their lands there, under deeds of cession, and the exultation of Governor Sir George Bowen, and the approval of the Secretary of State of Mc Lean's proceedings have also been mentioned.

It is necessary to explain briefly now in what way the Government, with armed men, invaded the peaceful homes thus seemingly secured for the Maoris, trampled over tilled fields, destroyed stores of food, haled away women and children; imprisoned their beloved chief (or, as they deemed him, prophet) ; denied him a trial; and, when they nominally released him under a special Act, retained under it the power of re-arresting him and imprisoning him without even an allegation of his having in any way offended.

The story of Te Whiti is too long to be repeated in these pages. It is sufficient to say here that he had established such a reputation amongst his countrymen that those who were gathered round him at Parihaka on the West Coast, within the territory on which Maori possession had been so completely recognized by the Government, religiously accepted his advice.

Their numbers increased so much, that it was stated that at no part of New Zealand had there ever been, within European knowledge, so large and compact an area of land cultivated by Maoris.

The Governor, Sir Arthur Gordon, described Te Whiti, in a Despatch to Lord Kimberley (February, 1881),* as having at all times refused to join in fighting against the Government, as " deeply versed in the Scriptures," and while " professing not to have abandoned the Christian faith preaching a vague and mystical religion of which he is himself the prophet. Eloquent and subtle, and animated by an unquestionably earnest patriotism, he has for many years exercised a powerful, and for the most part beneficial, sway over the hearts and lives, not only of his own tribe, but of a large section of the Maori population. Where his influence extends drunkenness is unknown, industry is exacted, and peace sedulously inculcated."

Two Royal Commissioners, Sir W. Fox and Sir F. Dillon Bell, formally reported in 1880 much to the same effect, *e.g.* " The influence of Te Whiti has always been exercised against war ; " † "in his addresses at the Parihaka meetings he has frequently lamented the mischief that has ensued among his people from the drink which they can get in the European settlements; and according to Major Brown he has been successful in doing what neither the wisdom of the Colonial Parliament, nor the vigilance of the Executive Government

---

* Blue Book, 1882, C. 3382, p. 118.

† Ib. p. 45.

have done elsewhere, he has prevented the sale (and to a great extent the use) of intoxicating liquors within his own particular district." *

The Governor, Sir Arthur Gordon, told the Secretary of State at a later date (13th February, 1882) † "In any general estimate of Te Whiti's character and career, the salient points should never be overlooked that he has, with unvarying consistency, for a long course of years, advocated peace and non-resistance, that morally and materially he has benefited those for whom he has worked, and that his main offence has been, I believe, disclosed by Mr. Bryce, viz., that he is opposed to the passing of land from Natives into European hands. That he is so, there can be no doubt; but this is not unnatural, nor indeed from his point of view can I pronounce him wrong; for, that the alienation of their land, the introduction among them of public-houses, hitherto proscribed, and the cessation of regular industry, hitherto exacted of them, will produce injurious effects in the Maoris of Parihaka, cannot be doubted."

Testimony as to the industrious character of Te Whiti's people is abundant.

When, by advice of his Ministers, Governor Sir Arthur Gordon despatched his aide-de-camp, Captain Knollys, with a letter to Te Whiti in December, 1880, Captain Knollys reported : "At a distance of three or four miles from Parihaka we passed through some large and good fields of potatoes, maize, tobacco, &c. These had the appearance of being well looked after, were carefully fenced, and the crops were looking very promising. . . . *These fields, I was informed, are in the land proposed to be put up for sale by the Government.* . . . Parihaka shows no sign of fortification" (p. 109). "Te Whiti also prohibits any spirits to be taken to Parihaka" (p. 113, Blue Book, 1882, C. 3382). The same Blue Book (at page 226) contains the report of a newspaper correspondent that "the slur cast upon the Maoris by their rabid foes, that they do not cultivate the land they hold, proceeds from deep ignorance of the facts. There are square miles of potato, melon and cabbage fields around Parihaka; they stretch on every side, and acres and acres of the land show the results of great industry and care."

Parihaka was therefore situated thus :—in compliance with Mr. Cardwell's injunctions the Governor in his Proclamation of 2nd September, 1865,‡ declared that "no land of any loyal inhabitant" within the district would "be taken," (except such as might be needed for) "security of the country, compensation being given for all land so

---

* Ib. p. 69. At page 68 they said : "In the case of a chief like Te Whiti, who has so often shown a strong moral sense . . . and who has ever laboured to elevate the character of his people, and to restrain them from the vices so fatal to a savage race, the spectacle of a Government allied with spies and seeking to profit by their intrigues, cannot but degrade us in his estimation, and justify his aversion from our rule."

† Ib. p. 277.
‡ N. Z. Parl. Paper, 1879. A.—8A.

taken," and that the rebels who might come in within a reasonable time and submit would receive "land in the said district under grant from the Crown."

Construing this Proclamation, Sir F. Dillon Bell publicly declared in Parliament in 1879 that the land "never had been confiscated.[*]

"It was untrue to say that the whole of the land between the Waitotara and the White Cliffs had been confiscated. It never had been confiscated. The only instrument by which the claim of confiscation was ever set up, was the proclamation bearing the signatures of Sir George Grey as Governor, and of Mr. Fitzgerald as Native Minister, in Mr. Weld's Government What did that say? It confiscated the land of those in rebellion: but it not only did not confiscate the land of those who remained loyal, it conserved their rights, and made the express promise to them that their land should not be taken. That was an undeniable fact. He could not conceive how any one acquainted with the history of the country could deny that these promises existed from the very inception of the confiscation. And it was equally true that none of the promises had been kept. They remained to this day in the same state in which they were in 1865, and the natives who were at that time in loyal obedience to the Crown, and had never been in rebellion since, had never had their land given to them yet."

After other Native ministers had done more or less mischief, Sir Donald McLean encouraged the Maoris (not only the loyal like Te Whiti, but others who had been in arms) to occupy the country, and he so completely recognized their title that he paid money on behalf of the Government in purchasing lands from those who were called returned rebels.

The Governor reported McLean's arrangements "for the *acquisition by purchase, with the goodwill of the Natives,* of such portion of land as they hold within it, but do not require for their own use, and which appear desirable for European settlements.[†]

McLean's "arrangements" were approved by the Secretary of State. The district was largely occupied; and especially under Te Whiti's moral control at Parihaka, industry and sobriety were remarked.

How it came to pass that in 1881 a notable tragedy was enacted and his village was laid waste by the New Zealand Government must now be briefly told.

---

[*] N. Z. Hansard, 1879. Vol. xxxiv., p. 864. Sir Dillon Bell was no ordinary person. He had been Speaker of the Lower House, was in 1879 a member of the Upper House, was in 1880 selected with Sir W. Fox to act as a Royal Commissioner to report upon the state of affairs on the West Coast, and has now been for years Agent General in London for the colony of New Zealand.

[†] New Zaland Parl. Paper, 1872. A. No. 1, pp. 62, 63.

After McLean's retirement and death the district to which he had restored peace underwent rapid change.

In 1877, Major Atkinson being Premier, Whitaker Attorney General, and Dr. Pollen Native Minister, preparations were made to survey the lands for sale, with little regard for, if not in contempt of, Maori rights and occupancy. The preparations were continued after Sir G. Grey became Premier in 1877, with Mr. Sheehan as Native Minister.

It was certified by a public officer (Mr. Brown, Civil Commissioner) * that in 1879 " one road was surveyed through cultivated and fenced land belonging to Titokowaru." The Royal Commissioners, Sir W. Fox and Sir F. Dillon Bell, declared that "this unlucky step alienated Titokowaru, and lost us the benefit of his friendly influence,"† and without doubt similar steps caused groans among many Maoris.

Te Whiti's people at once, but without violence, deported the trespassers across the Waingongoro River, and the Government of the day (Sir G. Grey's) instituted inquiry. Mr. Sheehan, the Native Minister, said afterwards in Parliament (N.Z. Hansard, 1879, Vol. 31, p. 185): "I was not aware in 1878, nor was the country aware, nor do I believe the House knows as a fact, what the exact position of those lands on the West Coast was. It has only been made clear to us by the interruption of the surveys. It turns out that from the White Cliffs down to Waitotara *the whole country is strewn with unfulfilled promises.*"

In May, 1879, Te Whiti's people ploughed up lands in various places. It was alleged by some persons that this step was taken to raise the question of confiscation, and of title, in the courts of law, and Te Whiti appears to have given colour to the allegation. The West Coast Royal Commissioners reported somewhat to the same effect. ‡

The ploughmen were arrested, and submitted to imprisonment without murmuring. Te Whiti said:—"Go, put your hands to the plough. Look not back. If any come with guns and swords, be not afraid. If they smite you, smite not in return. If they rend you, be not discouraged."

Before many weeks had elapsed nearly 200 captives had been sent to various prisons.

When the Parliament assembled in July, 1879, a vote of censure was carried against the Government on the motion of Sir W. Fox;

* West Coast Commission Report. N.Z. Parl. Paper, 1880. Evidence in Appendix. Answer 671. Another witness, the surveyor employed, said (Answer 1016) "it was very unfortunate that this line should run through their cultivations, as Titokowaru had said the day before that they would resist any lines being cut through their cultivations. The meridian line is right into one the first thing, and is likely to go into several." Can a historian commend such acts, or keep silence about them ?
† Blue Book, 1882. C 3382. p. 62.
‡ Ib. p. 67. "Te Whiti's followers expressly said that (the ploughing) was done to force a settlement." . . . Te Whiti and his people declared that it was done to test the right of confiscation " (*ib.*)

and a dissolution was resolved upon. Before it took place Mr. Sheehan, the Native Minister, in concert with some members of the opposition, brought forward two Bills bearing upon the Maoris.

Mr. Swanson declared that Mr. Sheehan was obeying the behest of Major Atkinson in the matter : "I am ashamed of such a measure . . I never thought I should live to see such Bills introduced."*

One empowered the Governor " to fix the date and trial of certain Maori prisoners," and thus delayed if it did not deny justice.

This Bill was passed by both Houses, and was called a law. Mr Macfarlane protested against it as "abominable." Mr. Stewart called it a gross infraction of the Great Charter.

The other Bill was called a Peace Preservation Bill. It belied its title. It enabled the Government—to issue Proclamations ordering Maoris to withdraw from their abodes ; to imprison the non-compliant with or without hard labour ; it denied bail ; it denied trial without an order from the Governor ; and specially suspended the Habeas Corpus Act. The lower House passed the Bill without delay.

When it reached the Upper House, Sir F. Dillon Bell declared, "We are asked to pass an Act such as no Legislature in the world I believe, has ever been asked to pass. We are not only to create a new offence but to enact that a native who commits that offence is not bailable. . . . Sir, I can hardly trust myself to speak upon such a measure. . . . I say you are absolutely mad to think of proposing an Act like this. I warn you that so surely as you are guilty of so *great an outrage on our civilization, so perfidious a reversal of the promises of the Crown,* so gross and unwarrantable an injustice to those who have never committed a crime as to pass such an act as this, so surely will you have bloodshed the moment you try to enforce it. I will not say, as members of the other House have said, that I shall wash my hands of it, but I shall record my protest against so *utterly shameless* an Act. . . . Until I hear the statement made (that the Governor had promised his assent) I shall not hesitate to say that under the Royal Instructions he cannot give his assent to the Bill. It is of a nature expressly violating all former Royal Instructions." †

Mr. Waterhouse declared the Bill to be " the most monstrous, the most iniquitous proposal that was ever submitted to the Legislature of any country. Hundreds, even thousands, of people occupying a large tract of country under the assurance conveyed by a Proclamation of the Governor (would under the Bill be made) liable to a year's imprisonment. I would sooner submit to have my right arm cut off than be a party to it."

By sixteen votes against six, the Upper House supported these noble protests, and for a time the honour of the country was saved.

The Parliament was prorogued on the 11th August, with a view to immediate dissolution ; and as Te Whiti's followers were still plough-

---

* N. Z. Hansard 1879. Vol 31. p. 553.
† N. Z. Hansard, 1879, Vol. 31, p. 544.

ing and being arrested,* several leading Maori chiefs, members of Parliament and others, sent an urgent manifesto to the tribes on the West Coast, urging Te Whiti and all others to abstain from all causes of offence, and to leave all disputed questions about lands to be decided by the Supreme Court, from which there was an "appeal to the great Court of the Queen in England." They had formed a committee which would " take steps for bringing all questions touching your claims to the confiscated lands before the Supreme Court."†

This Panui, or manifesto, was not only sent to Te Whiti and the tribes, but printed in Maori and English, and sent to every member of the Parliament. The Royal Commissioners of 1880, Fox and Bell, reported that the ploughing "entirely ceased at the end of August."‖

If, therefore, there had been a desire to test the legal position of the Government and of the Maoris, no difficulty was to be apprehended.

But some persons prefer making new laws to obeying those which exist.

---

* It is difficult for those who have not seen a Maori chief of ancient lineage and high character, to appreciate the Maori race, in which there is a large range from the highest to the lowest. The testimony of Sir W. Fitzherbert, Speaker of the Upper House in New Zealand, and recently delegated to represent the Colony in the great Conference at the Colonial Office (1887) may fairly be cited.

Speaking at a meeting of the Royal Colonial Institute, on the 10th May, 1887, Sir William said : " I have the honour to preside over what is called the Legislative Council—an Upper House—and in that Council there are three members of the Native race, and I can assure you that those gentlemen behave *just as well as any of their English colleagues.*"

One of the gentlemen thus characterized by Sir W. Fitzherbert was Taiaroa, Chairman of the Committee which strove by the Panui mentioned in the text, to avert violence from Parihaka.

I heard Sir W. Fitzherbert speak as above, but I copy the words from the " Proceedings of the Royal Colonial Institute, 1886-87."

Sir W. Fitzherbert had in former days recognised the nobler qualities of the Maori race.

After the wanton seizure of the Waitara block in 1860, and the war which ensued, it was felt by some persons that the settlers in other districts were completely at the mercy of the Maoris; and many distrustful and uncomplimentary expressions were hurled at the Maoris, coupled with confidence that " British Troops will throw themselves between us and the merciless savages not yet satiated with blood and murder."

Sir W. Fitzherbert rebuked such language by retorting—" The remark that we were living at the mercy of the aboriginal race was true, and reflected the greatest credit upon them. What greater panegyric could be pronounced on the Native race than was contained in the statement of fact that for the past twelve months we had been living among them with the knowledge in their possession that we were in their power, and yet that they forbore to use that power ? It was a fact unparalleled in history. Seeing, therefore, that we owed so much to the forbearance of the Native. . . ." New Zealand Hansard, 1861, June 11th, p . 24.

To some minds it is more congenial, when much is owing, to cancel rather than redeem.

† Vide the manifesto in the Appendix. Taiaroa was Chairman, and Wi Parata was Secretary of the Committee which drew it up.

‖ Blue Book, 1882. C. 3382, p. 63.

After the elections, Sir George Grey's ministry encountered an adverse vote, and a new ministry was formed in October, 1879. Mr. John Hall was Prime Minister. Mr. F. Whitaker, the Attorney General, was the person who in the same capacity had supported the Suppression and Confiscation Bills of 1863. Mr. Bryce was Native Minister, and Major Atkinson was Treasurer. Mr. Rolleston and Mr. Oliver filled other offices.

In December, 1879—the Maori prisoners not having been tried— a "Confiscated Lands Enquiry and Maori Prisoners' Trial Bill" was passed.* It enabled the Government to keep the Maoris indefinitely in prison without trial. It was opposed in the House. One member, Mr. Stewart, said that the Government "were afraid, apparently, to go to trial to ascertain whether the Maoris were guilty." Another, Mr. Turnbull, denounced the treatment of the prisoners as "not only barbarous, but cowardly." Another, Mr. Tole, declared that the Bill "took away all the rights held dear by British subjects."† As that was the object of the Bill, his protest was in vain. Mr. Bryce said that "If the House declared that these trials were to come off in due course, that was next month, he would not like to take the responsibility of remaining in office." The Bill was passed.

(By various Proclamations the trials were postponed to April, June and July), 1880, and were then further denied by a new and singular measure).

The Confiscated Lands Inquiry part of the Bill of 1879, enabled the Governor to appoint three Commissioners to conduct an enquiry on the West Coast.

One was to be a Maori. Sir W. Fox, Sir F. Dillon Bell and Tawhai were accordingly appointed. When the latter saw the terms of the Commission he declined to act, feeling that he would be powerless. He liked not (he wrote) to be driven by two Commissioners sitting in a conveyance heavy laden with Maori grievances; and no good could be expected from a Commission which did not authorize enquiry as to the root of the matter—the unjust Waitara war.

Fox and Bell were therefore the only Commissioners and they with the full knowledge of the Governor, Sir Hercules Robinson, stipulated, before accepting the task, that pending their enquiry and report the status quo should be maintained as regards titles, reserves, claims &c. This the government agreed to. ‡

This stipulation appears to have been broken almost as soon as made. The Commissioners commenced their labours in January 1880, and in that month the Native Minister sent a large armed force into the district. The newspapers commented upon the action as a direct provocation to disturbance or war.

No official remonstrance against it by the Commissioners has, so far as I know, been published.

---

* Ib. p. 41.   † N.Z. Hansard. Vol. xxxiv. p 621, 784, 787, 798.
‡ M. S. letter to the author at the time,

One can only surmise that some objections must have been made. Sir F. Dillon Bell had clear views as to the condition of the district, for on the 23rd Dec. 1879 he had said in his place in Parliament,* "It was untrue to say that the whole of the land between the Waitotara and the White Cliffs had been confiscated. It never had been confiscated. The only instrument by which the claim of confiscation was ever set up, was the proclamation bearing the signatures of Sir George Grey as Governor, and of Mr Fitzgerald as Native Minister, in Mr. Weld's Government. What did that say? It confiscated the land of those in rebellion; but it not only did not confiscate the land of those who remained loyal, it conserved their rights, and made the express promise to them that their land should not be taken. That was an undeniable fact. He could not conceive how any one acquainted with the history of the country could deny that these promises existed from the very inception of the confiscation. And it was equally true that none of the promises had been kept. They remained to this day in the same state in which they were in 1865, and the natives who were at that time in loyal obedience to the Crown, and had never been in rebellion since, had never had their land given to them yet."

The Native Minister's conduct must have jarred against these views. Describing the affair subsequently to his constituents he said—

"I moved the Armed Constabulary across the Waingongoro River . . . People felt convinced that it meant war, and from various influential quarters the government were urged not to advance the Constabulary across the River until the Royal Commission had completed its labours . . . One may not regard it so now but at that time it was very generally regarded as a most important step, a step which would not improbably lead to war . . I settled my plans in anxiety . . . I, acting of course for the government, moved the Constabulary across the river; I made roads, and I made them without the consent of the Maoris; I completed the telegraph line which Te Whiti had resented; I caused the light-house to be begun to which Te Whiti had refused his consent; I falsified all his predictions and put the camp within two miles of Parihaka . . . The fencers who were sent down to obstruct the road-making (the reader must bear in mind that some roads were made through Maori cultivation fields) were captured and put in prison." †

Thus,—in spite of the stipulation made by the Commissioners Fox and Bell, in spite of the understanding made known to the Governor Sir Hercules Robinson,—the toils were closing around the peaceful Te Whiti, and the demon of war or violence menaced the territory.

Madman as some called Te Whiti, enthusiast as all deemed him, he was not deterred, even at this moment, from his resolve to repress all tendency among his people to acts of resistance.

Still he preached, and still they hung upon his words, though there was apprehension, if not belief in some minds, that if his patience

* N. Z. Hansard 1879. Vol. xxxiv. p. 864.
† Blue Book 1882. C. 3382. pp 127, 128.

should be exhausted, he would sanction an appeal to physical force which Maori traditions rendered probable.

In February the Commissioners were busy in the district. They announced to the Maoris who appeared before them that promises made by the government would be fulfilled, and reserves would be made for the Maoris; but they did not say that all existing holdings occupied by Maoris would be secured to them.

On the general question they reported—"We of course knew from the first that the legality of the confiscation would be contested before us by the adherents of Te Whiti, and we had to make up our minds very early as to the right course for us to take. . . . We therefore refused to hear counsel who wished to question the validity of the confiscation, and we told the natives from the very outset that we were not there so discuss such questions with them, . . " *

This decision of course frustrated the intention of Taiaroa and his friends when in August 1879 they sent their manifesto entreating the tribes to leave their " rights to be settled by the law."

The marching of an armed force to the threshold of Te Whiti's peaceful village could not but seem to the tribes an intimation that the government relied upon force and not upon law.

Te Whiti addressed his people in March—"I speak of the bayonet that has glittered this day in my face . . I talk of the flash of the gun before my eyes and the bayonet pointed at my heart. Who can deny it? O Maori, O Pakeha can you say that I am wrong? . . . Although some of you in the darkness of your hearts. seeing your land taken from you, might wish to take up arms and kill the aggressors I say unto you *it must not be.* . . . I do not want war, but the Pakehas want war. The flashes of their guns have singed our eyelashes, and they say they do not want war· . . . Referring to me what do they say? They say I am a fanatic, a fool, and a madman; but I am neither. The land is yours, but what I have seen lately is enough to turn the brains within my head into the brains of a fanatic. Still we must cause no more trouble to come upon the land by any action of our own."

The Royal Commissioners made Reports on 15 March, 14 July, and 5 August 1880. It seems that when Sir Hercules Robinson left the Colony in September 1880 the time was deemed suitable for further trial of Te Whiti's long suffering. A speech by the Native Minister tells how he desired to march upon Parihaka with "two thousand concentrated men." If Te Whiti had resisted† . . I should have arrested him, . . I have been accused in the public press of a great many things. I have been told that I was going to make a desperate advance, and occupy Parihaka, violently arrest Te Whiti, and bring on a war. In fact I have been represented as a bloodthirsty wretch who only wanted an opportunity to have his name handed down as the perpetrator of another massacre of Glencoe."

Mr. Bryce's colleagues did not agree with him, and he "sent in his

---

* Blue Book. 1882. **C.** 3382. p. 79.
† Blue Book 1882. C 3382. p. 128.

resignation" in September but withdrew it. "hoping that he might get his "own way on the essential point.* In January 1881 he retired, however, and the foregoing account is borrowed from his own explanations.

Sir Arthur Gordon having been called upon by Lord Kimberley for a Report on affairs at the West Coast, furnished it on 26 Feb. 1881; but it was not laid before Parliament in that year.

The delay is explained by a Paper *not presented to the House of Commons*, but to the New Zealand Parliament† after delay of more than a year.

The Despatch itself was presented to the House of Commons late in 1882, but not the secret cause of delay, which was thus explained in New Zealand :—

On the 13th July 1881 Mr. (now Sir) John Hall, head of the Ministry, entreated the Governor to telegraph to the Secretary of State their " request that the Despatch may not be published at present, and the expression of their hope that any intended publication of the document will be so made known to them that their opinion as to such publication may reach and be considered by the Imperial Government."

The Governor complied, and the answer of Lord Kimberley is thus given in the New Zealand Parliamentary Papers:—

"The Secretary of State replied that he would delay publication if possible; but that, as the papers had been promised, they must be published, if pressed for."

It was more than a year before the Despatch was produced in England, and then only after Sir Michael Hicks Beach had publicly asked for it.

Such was the concert of Lord Kimberley with the New Zealand Ministers. They were intent on suppressing Te Whiti, and the Secretary of State aided them in suppressing Despatches.

They proceeded with their work of carving out the land for sale, and laying out roads with disregard of Maori occupants.

The Commissioners, Fox and Bell, made three Reports, which are contained in an English Blue Book (1882, C. 3382), the last being dated 5th August, 1880.

In the Session of 1880 several measures were passed which must have caused groans among the Maoris, and were denounced in the New Zealand Parliament.

On July 15th, 1880, when already two Reports (of March 15th and July 14th) had been signed by Fox and Bell, with regard to their labours on the West Coast Commission, and had shown the manifest injustice under which the Maoris had laboured, the Native Minister's "Maori Prisoners' Bill‡, 1880," was introduced.

Some of the prisoners had been sent by him to the Dunedin gaol; and as Dunedin was colder than their native place, Taiaroa

---

* ib. 129. † N.Z. Par. Pap. 1882 A 8. p 16.
‡ New Zealand Hansard, Vol. XXXVI., p. 251.

had asked in the Upper House why they were not tried, and if the Government would hold themselves responsible in the case of the death of any of the prisoners. The Attorney-General, replied that the Native Minister would explain the whole policy of the Government, that it had been thought inexpedient to try the prisoners, and he was not aware that "if any of the natives died" any responsibility would "rest upon the Government or anybody else." In the Lower House Tawhai remarked: "These men were taken from this island, where the climate is warm, to the other island where the climate is severe; and I cannot help thinking that they must have been taken there in order that they might be got rid of, and that they might perish there."

On July 16th, the Native Minister* in moving the second reading of the Bill (introduced) by himself as a Maori Prisoners' Bill said : "This is not a Maori Prisoners' Bill that I am now proposing. The truth is, it was a mere farce to talk of trying these prisoners for the offences with which they were charged. . . If they had been convicted, in all probability they would not have got more than twenty-four hours imprisonment, if so much, in addition to the term of imprisonment they had already served. . . Now in this Bill we drop that provision in regard to the trial altogether We consider that to be a mere sham; and what we ask for now is that the Government shall have the power to say whether these men are to be detained in captivity or to be released."

The Maori members of the house pathetically implored that a trial might be vouchsafed to their countrymen and boldly denounced the Bill.

Tomoana said† the proposed imprisonment was "the worst way of killing anybody. It is making perfect slaves of these men."

Mr. Stewart denounced the deprivation of the right to a writ of *habeas corpus*.

Mr. Turnbull declared that Sir W. Fox and Sir D. Bell had proved "the grave injustice" done to the prisoners and their friends. The Report "teems with evidence of the manner in which we have endeavoured to destroy a noble race. . . We have ill-treated these people for years, and let us now determine to deal fairly and justly with them."

Sir George Grey regarded the Bill as "a cruel measure, and as an unnecessary measure. It violates almost every principle of the law."

Tawhai demanded trial for the prisoners "before the Supreme Court."

Mr. Montgomery declared that in passing a Bill to place some of "Her Majesty's subjects outside the pale of the law," the Government would commit "an act of great injustice."

---

* Ib. 285.

† *N. Z.* Hansard 1880, vol. xxxvi. p. 288. The succeeding quotations are from the same Volume, extending as far as page 363 as regards "the Maori Prisoners' Bill, 1880."

Mr. Pyke denounced that "policy of wrong, that policy of expediency, that policy of dishonour, which ministers are striving in this case to induce the House to adopt."

Mr. Reeves considered the measure "one of the most iniquitous Bills ever discussed in any British Colony. It is a Bill that would be scouted out of any civilised community. . . It is a disgrace to the colony to pass such a Bill as this."

With dim consciousness of the truth to which the New Zealand Government was doing violence, Captain Russell, a supporter of the Bill, declared—" In days to come, when historians write the annals of this country, they will view the struggle which has taken place from a very different standpoint from that which we can take who are mixed up in its turmoil and disagreements. The men whom we look upon as rebels will to my mind occupy a brighter page of history than many of those men whom we look upon as faithful . . "

Mr. Hutchison said he was "irresistibly driven to the conclusion that the Bill is an outrage upon both law and justice;" and he wondered how the Governor could reconcile with the terms of his commission the sanction of such a measure.

Mr. Ireland could not vote for the Bill " without violating his conscience."

Mr. Speight declared that in the " unjust form " of the Bill, " cuting as it does at the root of all our liberties," he must vote against it.

Mr. Tole (who afterwards became a Cabinet Minister in New Zealand) entered his " most serious and solemn protest against the Bill."

Major Harris thought the Bill " the most wanton piece of cruelty that ever was proposed in any part of the country."

Tawhai sorrowfully stated that during the imprisonment of his countrymen, five of their children, who might not have perished unless deprived of their parents' care, had died.

The prisoners should be tried, and " if innocent taken back to the land."

Mr. Andrews delared that the treatment of the prisoners was "most severe, most harsh, most unjust, and cruel. I do not know that in my reading of history I have ever come across a parallel case. Certainly in English history there is nothing like a parallel case. . . I never knew a Maori to break faith."

The Bill was supported by many adherents of the Ministry, and was carried by fifty votes against thirty-four, including pairs.

On the following day the Bill was passed through committee and read a third time, the Native Minister and his friends resisting successfully an amendment, providing that before discharge from custody a native should have lawful trial.

The Upper House passed the Bill, and it obtained the Royal assent on July 23rd, 1880.*

It was to remain in force till Oct. 31st, 1880, but power was given

---

* The Act is in the Blue Book, 1882. C. 3382, p. 28.

H

to the Governor to "extend" its operation for periods "not exceeding three months at one time."

All captive natives were to be "deemed and taken to have been lawfully arrested, and to be in lawful custody." (Sec. 3.)

No court, judge, justice, or other person was to discharge or bail a captive without an order from the Governor in Council and in that Council the Native Minister was the authority on native affairs. (Sec. 4.)

Not content with these powers, the Ministry introduced, through that functionary, on July 30th, 1880, a "Maori Prisoners' Detention Bill," which he hoped the House would pass "without discussion through all its stages."*

He had thought it necessary to make some arrests, "and might have to continue making more arrests in the same way." The prisoners taken or to be taken in this manner were to be "deemed to have been and to be detained under the provisions of the (previous) Maori Prisoners' Act, as effectually as if such natives were included within the terms of that Act."

Major Te Wheoro having opposed the Bill, Mr. Hutchison said, "he did not think there was any other free country in the world where a Minister of the Crown could have announced that he had arrested individuals unlawfully and without any charge of crime being brought against them."†

The Native Minister replied that the Government accepted the fullest responsibility, and it must be evident that they "had no intention of shrinking from responsibility because they had *already taken these prisoners without any form of law.*"

They were, in fact, at the time arresting Maoris whom they found fencing in plots of ground within that territory to which Sir Donald McLean had invited them to return, and within which the Governor (Sir G. Bowen) had informed the Secretary of State in 1872, that arrangements had been made by Sir D. McLean "for the *acquisition by purchase with the goodwill of the natives, of such portions of land as they hold within it, but do not require for their own use. . .*"‡

This was the land on which armed men were seizing the Maoris, and the Native Minister informed the House that seizures were made *without any form of law.*" ‖

Mr. Speight said "he knew of nothing which would bring the blush of shame to their cheeks in after days so much as the passing of this Bill would, unless they were past feeling shame altogether"

Mr. Pyke said the Bill was "cruel, tyrannous, unjust. If those natives had done no wrong, why arrest them? If they had done wrong why not punish them? He demanded justice for these natives from the House—from the country." "He believed that the

---

* *N. Z.* Hansard, 1880, Vol. XXXVII. p. 16.
† *N. Z.* Hansard, Vol. XXXVII. p. 19.
‡ *N. Z. P. P.* 1872, A. No. 1. p. 63.
‖ *N. Z.* Hansard. Vol. XXXVII. p. 19.

Imperial Government would refuse to advise the Queen to assent to such a measure." For the treatment of the Maoris "there was no precedent in the history of the British people," and it could "bring nothing but disgrace and humiliation" on its perpetrators. Mr. Turnbull was so indignant that he "could scarcely trust himself to speak on this occasion."

Tawhai pointed out that contrary to the rule with regard to Bills affecting Maoris, the Bill had "not been translated" into Maori.

Major Harris said that the "West Coast Commissioners (Sir W. Fox and Sir D. Bell), in their report acknowledged that the land belonged to the natives. It was very hard that the Government should entrap the natives and then pass a law to justify their action. This was a shameful act which they had been guilty of. . ."

Mr. Seddon said that the Bill was "unconstitutional and vicious in the extreme."

Sir G. Grey pointed out that women and children might be arrested —"without any charge made"—under the Bill. "In the worst days of the French Revolution such a power was never sought, never given, and never attempted to be taken. . . This measure would be a constant reproach to the Assembly of New Zealand if it were passed in its present form. . . It was too much to ask that the lives of many women and children and men should be dependent on the will of one man. He would still ask the hon. member to consider what he was doing. He asked him not to compel the House to pass a Bill which must reflect disgrace upon it."

The Native Minister "could only say now that he felt ashamed of the action* of the Opposition on this occasion;" and the Speaker having regretted "that there had been an infraction of the Standing Orders which prescribed that Bills specially affecting the Maori people should be translated and printed in the Maori language, and that this Bill had not been translated," the Bill was passed and was assented to on August 6th, 1880.

But further powers were demanded by the Ministry. What was called a "West Coast Settlement Bill" was introduced on the 10th August.

It contained four clauses under the heading of "offences." These clauses gave almost absolute power to the Government.

Any orders which might "seem necessary, or fit to preserve the public peace," might be given.

Breaking or removing fences, buildings, pegs, &c., digging, ploughing or disturbing surface of land, whereby (what a Native Minister might call) lawful occupation of land might be obstructed; erecting fences on land, breaking up the surface of land which might be declared to be a highway; persons assembling together "armed or unarmed," "with or without tools or implements," "for the purpose of aiding, assisting, or countenancing the commission of any such" acts, or who

---

* N. Z. Hansard, ib. p. 26.

" being present may reasonably be SUSPECTED to be present for all or any of such purposes or objects "—all these were acts, or conditions, or *suspicions,* which were to enable a Native Minister to harry the inhabitants in a district to which, in the name of the Government, a previous Native Minister (Sir D. McLean) had invited them to return, and in which the Government had given pledges that they would be unmolested.

Offenders, or suspected persons, might be arrested " without warrant."

A curious clause enacted that " Natives who have been arrested or shall hereafter be arrested (under) 'the Maori Prisoners' Detention Act, 1880,' shall be deemed and taken to be in custody under ' the Maori Prisoners' Act, 1880,' and shall be detained accordingly."

Thus, men arrested under one of these persecuting Acts were to be deemed arrested under another, in accordance with the terms of a third —and all three Acts were passed in a few weeks in one session.

Yet, while advocating the last of them, the Native Minister bore witness, that "however perplexing the tactics of the natives on the coast have been, I do say that those tactics indicate that they do not wish to proceed to hostilities."*

Mr. Pyke said " A more arbitrary, despotic, or unconstitutional measure than this West Coast Settlement Bill—except the Maori Prisoners' Trials Bill and the one that succeeded it—never disgraced a Parliament of free men. . . Illegal arrests have been made of these natives for a considerable time ; and this very Bill proves that they were illegal arrests, for it is a Bill to justify the arrests made. . . . I believe that the Armed Constabulary, in a violent and hostile manner, entered upon this land, destroyed the fences, ruined the cultivations of the Maoris, either allowing the cattle of native owners to wander unchecked over the country, or cattle belonging to other persons to enter thereupon. *All the crime the natives were guilty of was the re-erection of fences around that which they believed to be their own property based on their own usage from time immemorial* which is to them as sacred as any number of parchment deeds that all the lawyers in New Zealand could draw up. . . I should lose my respect for the colonists of New Zealand, and for the country from which we came, if they sanctioned the enforcement by the Government of such an abominable and despotic Act as this I hold in my hand."

Mr. Moss " ventured to say " that the Act would be disgrace to the Statute Book of New Zealand; "it was one of a series of which the House will yet feel ashamed."

Mr. Macandrew said : "I believe the future historian of New Zealand will refer to the Bill as something quite as bad as anything that ever took place in the worst times of the Star Chamber. I look upon it as being inspired by pretty much the same feeling as that which led up to the massacre of Glencoe. . . I enter my protest against the Bill as being unworthy of Englishmen and free men."†

---

* N.Z. Hansard, 1880. Vol. XXXVII., p. 482.
† N.Z. Hansard, 1880. Vol. XXXVII., p. 487.

The Native Minister (in reply) said, " I have always taken up the position that these Maoris do not intend to provoke hostilities. . . (but) if these Maoris went on private lands and began ploughing, and *induced armed men with guns in their hands*, and those guns in many instances at full cock, to drive them off by violence, those acts would lead to hostilities whether they were so intended or not."*

One who read these speeches in 1880 was reminded of the fable of the wolf and the lamb.

The Bill did not pass through the Upper House without eliciting from the Honourable Captain Fraser the statement that its " second part " (as to offences) " breathed the harsh and hostile spirit of the Native Minister towards the native race."†

The reader may judge whether a harsh and hostile spirit existed in some minds, by the following remarks of Mr. Scotland in the Council in debate on native claims at the West Coast.

He quoted the following phrases from a West Coast newspaper of June 14th, 1879 (N.Z. Hansard, 1880. Vol. XXXV., p. 308.):—

"Perhaps all things considered, the present difficulty will be one of the greatest blessings ever New Zealand experienced, for without doubt it will be a war of extermination. . .

" The time has come in our minds when New Zealand must strike for freedom, and this means a death-blow to the Maori race." " Good Heavens " (exclaimed Mr. Scotland, himself from Taranaki), " a war of extermination a blessing ! . . . That is only a specimen of the Taranaki press."

The West Coast Settlement Bill became law on September 1st, 1880, and is printed in the Blue Book, 1882 (C. 3382), p. 29.

During the Parliamentary Session of 1880, many Maoris were arrested for fencing in the Parihaka district. The armed road party pulled down a fence on 15th July, and their commander Colonel Roberts reported,‡ "Two natives came to put it up, stating that they did not want to stop the road, only to protect their crops. . . "They are willing to put up a swing gate. . Please let me know if you will authorize such being done." On the following day the gallant Colonel told the invaded farmers that the Native Minister " would only approve of a gate as a temporary measure until they had fenced the road off."

Day by day, until more than 200 had been arrested and despatched to various prisons, the vain attempt to save crops was persisted in. But, on the 12th November, the "Maoris instead of as usual erecting a solid fence . . put up slip rails, which of course sufficed to keep animals out of the growing corn, yet which could be taken down to allow the passage of any horse or waggon using the road. Colonel Roberts telegraphed for instructions, and was very wisely told to allow the slip-rails to remain."§

Thus Governor Sir Arthur Gordon reported in February 1881, being apparently ready to give credit when he could to his ministers.

* Ib. p. 524.   † Ib. p. 652.   ‡ Blue Book, 1882. Despatch of the Governor. C. 3382. p. 123.   § Ib. p. 124.

But they were so discontented with his temperate report, that, as has been seen, they implored the Secretary of State to withhold it from the House of Commons, and it was withheld from the House until late in 1882, when Te Whiti had been seized and his village laid waste, and a measure, misnamed a law, had been passed to deny him those rights which belong to all subjects of the Crown.

Governor Sir Hercules Robinson left New Zealand on the 8th September 1880, and the Chief Justice Prendergast became administrator. (It was he, who had given in 1869 the legal opinion already quoted as to the claims of Maoris to rights of British subjects, &c.) During his administration in 1880 it appears that some of the Maoris arrested at Parihaka were tried. Their counsel raised an objection that the area within which arrests might be made was undefined in the West Coast Settlements Act under which they were alleged to have been made, and that his clients were entitled to strict construction.

The objection was over-ruled, and the judge sentenced the prisoners to two years' imprisonment with hard labour, in Lyttelton gaol, and to find a surety in £50 each, to keep the peace for six months after the expiration of the sentence. He also told the interpreter to tell the prisoners that whether they would serve the full term of their sentences depended* on the conduct of their countrymen whom they left behind them. (Blue Book 1882. C. 3382, p. 27.)

Is it a daring supposition that as the prisoners had always desired to be at peace, and were nevertheless imprisoned, they uttered groans when transported from their native island, under a sentence of which the duration was contingent not upon their own conduct, but on that of others?

Yet according to Sir Frederick Whitaker, no "reasonable objection can be taken" to the treatment of the Maoris. (*supra* p. 27.)

Whether reasonably or unreasonably there is no doubt that they often groaned, and their grievances deserve to be recorded.

While Prendergast was Administrator, in September 1880, it appears that the Native Minister desired to march upon Te Whiti's settlement.

In the same speech to his constituents which has been already quoted with regard to sending an armed force into Te Whiti's district he explained that "Everything went on well until September last . . I ought to have gone and seen Te Whiti with such a force at my back . . . If he had resisted . I should have arrested him. . . . I have been accused in the public press of a great many things. . . In fact I have been represented as a bloodthirsty wretch, who only wanted an opportunity to have his name handed down as the perpetrator of another massacre of Glencoe. . . As a matter of fact I did resign last September . . . but I withdrew that resignation. . . ."†

The scruples of the ministry gave a qualified breathing time to Te Whiti's people; but "settlement," as it was called, was pushed forward in the district.

---

* *New Zealand Herald*, 24th September, 1880.
† The speech is fully reported in the English Blue Book. 1882. C. 3382. pp 127-129.

The *New Zealand Herald* reported in November 1880 that "a large portion of the Waimate Plain has been sold at high prices,"—some at £6 an acre "for cash, and £7 on deferred payments."

Who the extruded Maori proprietors were, and how they groaned, no newspaper told.

Sir W. Fox and Sir F. Dillon Bell had concluded their labours, and had recommended the reservation of 212,520 acres for the Maoris—*to fulfil the promises of former governments*—besides 25,000 acres at the Waimate Plains, and 25,000 acres of Parihaka for Te Whiti and his people. Sir F. D. Bell went to England as Agent General for the Colony, and Sir W. Fox was made sole Commissioner to determine the allocation of the lands in terms of the Report of the previous Commission.

The award of that Commission must have surprised some persons. Mr. Bryce himself after he became Native Minister had said, in Parliament, that there were "*probably no grievances* to speak of on what is known as the Waimate Plains proper;"* and yet much of his life had been spent on the West Coast; he was at the time the member for Wanganui, and he said in Parliament, 26th May, 1882, "I was in the way of being acquainted with the natives on that coast."

In 1880 the Commissioners found many grievances and said "the story ought to fill us all with shame." †

When the new Governor, Sir Arthur Gordon, arrived in November 1880 and found that he had been called upon to furnish a Report to the Secretary of State, he received statements from the ministry. Among them was a memorandum from the Native Minister, about Te Whiti, whose tribe, the writer said, had "formerly engaged in hostilities, but so far from Te Whiti joining in such acts *himself* he *has always preached peace*." (Blue Book. 1882. C. 3382. p. 103).

The Ministry advised the Governor to send a letter to Te Whiti; and accordingly Captain Knollys, C.M.G., A.D.C., took one in December, 1880.

Captain Knollys described how roads had been forced through cultivated grounds—how Te Whiti appeared peaceful—and how he prohibited the introduction of intoxicating liquors in his settlement. "If the chiefs struggle to suppress the evil among their people, cannot some assistance be given them in their good object?" Captain Knollys asked. Not such assistance, but active interference of another kind was advocated at this time by the Native Minister, for on the 12th January, 1881, the Governor told the Secretary of State—"Mr. Bryce was desirous that measures of active hostility against Te Whiti and the natives of Parihaka should be at once undertaken by the Government, but has been unable to induce his colleagues to share his views, and has consequently retired from the cabinet." ‡

A newspaper remarked at the time that Mr. Bryce's "retirement is a public benefit. Of narrow views, ignorant of the native history,

---

* New Zealand, Hansard, 1879. Vol XXXII. p 358.
† Blue Book, 1882. C. 3382, p 72.   ‡ ib. p. 113.

and insight into a native's character or customs, Mr. Bryce with the best intentions, was totally unfit for the responsible position of Native Minister."

Sir Arthur Gordon sent to England on 26th February, 1881, his report on the affairs of the West Coast, and as has been seen, was induced in July, 1881, to telegraph to the Secretary of State the earnest desire of the ministry that the report might be kept back from the public.

In September, 1881, while the Houses were in session, Sir Arthur Gordon, who was High Commissioner in the Pacific as well as Governor of New Zealand. sailed for Fiji. Sir James Prendergast (recently knighted) became Administrator of the Government. He had not been gone many days before Mr. Rolleston, the Native Minister, obtained a vote (in the House) of £100,000 for " Contingent Defence additional," on the last night of the session. A Maori member said afterwards in the House that the vote was " brought up suddenly after most of the members had gone on board the steamers to depart for their homes."

Some persons had said that Te Whiti had made a warlike speech in September, but the Government received official telegrams to the effect that the speech was not warlike, and that Te Whiti had taken care to say so. But if he was not warlike, it was soon rumoured that the ministry were.

The *New Zealand Herald* of 26th September, placed the words, " The sudden increase of the Armed Constabulary Force "—at the head of an article.

Another paragraph mentioned that Maoris were ploughing " on land bought at the late sale by Mr. Hunter. *It is one of their old cultivations."*

Mr. Rolleston went to Parihaka and, according to the newspapers, sent " long telegrams " to the effect that "neither in Parihaka nor elsewhere is there the slightest indication of any intention to fight. On the contrary, the whole attitude of the natives is thoroughly pacific and good-tempered, while they are engaged to an unusually large large extent in cultivation and other peaceful employments."

Nevertheless the military body, the Armed Constabulary, was largely increased.

At the end of August it was returned as 678 in number.

At the end of September the number was 802.

On the 31st October it was 1074.*

On the 5th October Mr. Hall and another minister, Major Atkinson, were reported as having visited Mr. Rolleston at the West Coast, and it was stated that Mr. Bryce, who had left the ministry in January, had been invited to rejoin it in order to carry out what was called his " native policy," *i.e.,* making a raid upon Parihaka.

Meantime Te Whiti, on the 17th October, preached mystically, but peacefully, as usual.

" Every year I have been saying—Be patient. . . The gun will not be a protection for man in these days. Man must not look to the

---

* New Zealand, Hansard 1886. Vol. L., p. 372.

gun, the sword, or the spear, for safety. . . We are like a brood of chickens left in the nest by the parents. We have no one to assist us, but though the Almighty has permitted trouble to pervade the land do not fear. . . Though the land be overrun by a multitude they shall vanish. My heart is sad. The people are dead, and the land is gone. There is no quietness, no peace of mind in these days. I always counselled you to be manawanui, (full of courage, fortitude, and patience). We will in time overcome all difficulties. . . Guns and powder shall no longer be the protection for man. . . God has protected and will protect the people and the land—not guns and powder. . . I alone know how to guide you all."

Peaceful as the speech was,, it did not deter the New Zealand ministry from their intended raid.

The newspapers reported that Mr. Bryce was " in conference with ministers" for two or three days before their plan took formal shape. Meanwhile, Sir Arthur Gordon's Private Secretary, Mr. F. P. Murray (who had remained in New Zealand) had, with the full knowledge of the Ministry, written to Sir Arthur Gordon.*

He had told him, 26th September, of the augmentation of the Armed Constabulary Force; that settlers were being enrolled and armed, that a vote for £100,000 had been taken, and that "war with the Maoris .was regarded as almost inevitable."† But no communication had been received from Sir Arthur.

He, however, on receipt of Mr. Murray's letter, determined to return at once to New Zealand, and as a vessel was sailing from Fiji to Sydney he sent thither a telegram to be forwarded thence to Lady Gordon at Wellington.

It arrived there on the 16th October, announcing the Governor's "immediate return." On the morning of the 19th Mr. Hall, the head of the ministry, conversed with Mr. Murray about the Governor's movements. Mr. Murray told him that the Governor " might be looked for at any moment." " My intention (Mr. Murray wrote) was to convey to Mr. Hall without quoting a private telegram, the strong probability there was of the immediate return of the Governor."‡

That this information quickened the movements of the Government cannot be demonstrated, but they could hardly have been quicker or more irregular than they were.

At half-past five in the afternoon, when *official hours were past*, Mr. Murray received a note from Sir J. Prendergast, the Administrator, desiring him to " summon a meeting of the Executive Council for *eight o'clock the same evening*." " I sent out the summons as directed, and then went to see Sir J. Prendergast to ask what was the business for which the Council was to meet. He told me, as a secret, that Mr. Bryce was to be appointed a member of the Executive Council. I told him that I had heard rumours of a Proclamation of wa. The

---

* Blue Book, 1883. C 3689, p. 47, where Sir J. Prendergast himself stated that he and the Native Minister had such knowledge.

† Blue Book 1882. C. 3382. p. 165.

‡ Mr. Murray's memorandum is set out in full in the Blue Book. 1883. C. 3689. pp. 56—57.

Administrator replied that that was all nonsense. . . I said that I supposed before any 'active hostilities could be undertaken the consent of the Governor or Administrator must be in some form obtained.' Sir James Prendergast said 'not at all'—'it was a matter the whole responsibility for which rested with Ministers.' I said that I thought it at any rate right to say that the Governor might return at at any moment; that I knew from what he had told me when he would close his work at Fiji; that I was sure he would come direct thence to Wellington, and that allowing eight or nine days for the passage I was surprised he had not arrived the day before. . . I thought I had spoken sufficiently clearly to show the Administrator that I had good reason to expect the immediate return, and no reason to expect any more delay than might be caused by wind and weather in the return of his Excellency; nor was I justified in saying more. I gave my opinion strongly, as was natural with my knowledge of Lady Gordon's telegram in the background, and I considered that the certainty of the Fiji mail, which was already overdue, arriving very speedily, together with the strong expression of my belief that the Governor would be in the Colony within a few hours, should be sufficient, if anything could be sufficient, to delay any measures of great importance at any rate till the arrival at Auckland of the 'Southern Cross' the (Fijian mail steamer)."

Did Mr. Murray expect too much? Would he have expected so much if he had known some earlier events in the history of New Zealand as to the applicability of the laws of nature and of nations in dealing with the Maoris?

The nocturnal council was held. Hall submitted a memorandum imputing blame to Te Whiti (who only desired to be left in peace) and Prendergast signed a Proclamation denouncing Te Whiti and declaring that if within fourteen days Te Whiti should not submit to its dictates, all "previous promises will then have passed away. . . ." Such "passing away" was too common to have any special terrors for Te Whiti's followers.

The haste of the nocturnal council spread to the departments. That night the Proclamation of war (as some called it) was printed and furnished to the newspapers. Telegrams scattered it abroad, and on the morrow it was widely disseminated.

But something else was done at night by Sir J. Prendergast and his advisers. Mr. Rolleston signed the Proclamation, but immediately resigned office; Mr. Bryce was appointed Native Minister—and it was arranged that he should start at daylight with the Proclamation signed by his predecessor and by the Administrator.

And where, meanwhile, was the Queen's Representative? Mr. Murray had truly warned Prendergast and Hall that Sir Arthur Gordon might arrive at any moment; and while the secret conclave was busy—before their Proclamation was hastily issued,—H.M.S. 'Emerald," with the Governor on board, was at anchor in the harbour of Wellington. . He did not land that night, and when he went on shore in the morning the new Native Minister was on his way to Parihaka.

Not only on the spot but in Australia the electric telegraph on the 20th October described the nocturnal deeds of the New Zealand Ministers. Knowing of Mr. Bryce's resignation early in the year, and its causes, I apprehended the significance of his return to office: though of himself I knew nothing except from his public acts and speeches. But I had conversed with Mr. Rolleston, and I wrote the following note immediately :—

" MELBOURNE CLUB, MELBOURNE,
October 21st, 1881.

" MY DEAR MR. ROLLESTON,

" I cannot express to you the pang which it gave me to see that you had resigned the post of Native Minister, and had been succeeded by Mr. Bryce.

" It would be impertinent in me to advise, but I may entreat you to reflect upon what must be the judgment of posterity if the marauding schemes of the New Zealand Company—the robbery at the Waitara, the persistent sharping at the Dunedin Prince's Street reserve, the confessed broken promises on the West Coast—are wound up by an attack on Te Whiti because he preaches peace, and preaches it with more eloquence than his enemies, or some of them, can advocate war. Had I but a trumpet tongue, I would cry to the world ; but I have not, and I appeal to you as one who has, until now, maintained the manners of an English gentleman, though brought into contact with strange Englishmen or civilized savages abroad, as well as with 'naked savages'—as the New Zealand Company called the Maoris.

" I have been intending to write to you for some weeks to ask you to let me have any fresh printed papers about the West Coast ; but I have now little heart in the matter. I trusted in your supervision : ὄμμα γαρ δωματος δεσποτου παρουσια—but if you shut your eye, and brutal force is used, woe be to the reputation of New Zealand !

" Yours sincerely and sadly,
" G. W. RUSDEN.*

"THE HON. W. ROLLESTON,
    WELLINGTON, NEW ZEALAND."

I received no answer, nor did I expect one after I saw an account of Mr. Rolleston's subsequent proceedings.

When Sir Arthur Gordon landed, after 9 a.m. on the 20th October, he asked Mr. Hall for a " statement of the causes which had led to so great a change of policy and action. "

The haste of the mid-night council seems to have exhausted the

---

* I wrote on the same day to Mr. Swainson, and urged him to let his voice ring out against the contemplated enormity. I reminded him how he had formerly raised it against wrong, and as an advocate of right. " I can only think of you. Th sound of your voice, or the dictates of your pen, would engrave themselves mor[e] readily than if the public were daily familiar with them. For Heaven's sake launch a bolt in favour of the right, so that at least it may be said that there was one righteous man among you." Mr. Swainson, who was old and infirm, did not comply with my request ; but he lived to write to me in 1884, and congratulate me upon my " minute and accurate knowledge of the affairs of New Zealand."

activity of Hall, for though he at once promised the statement he had not furnished it on the 22nd.*

It was rumoured that there was difference between the Governor and his advisers, and a Wellington newspaper, opposed to what it called "pandering to Maori idiosyncrasies," said—"The Governor will interfere at his peril."

Peculiar "Idiosyncrasies" had once made the *Wellington Independent* say (21st July, 1868) "no mercy should be shown. No prisoner should be taken. Let a price be put upon the head of every rebel, and let them be slain without scruple wherever the opportunity is afforded. We must smite and spare not. . . . We must treat them as a species of savage beasts which must be exterminated to render the colonization of New Zealand possible."

Between such an "idiosyncrasy," and the feelings of honourable Englishmen there was necessarily a wide gulf.

It must not be supposed that only the Governor respected the claims of humanity and duty. On the 26th October, 1881, Mr. Lautour, a member of the N. Z. Parliament, wrote to a newspaper:—"No pious uplifting of the hands and committal of the Maoris to the help of God amidst the plaudits of the multitude can wash our hands in innocency, and put the sin we contemplate upon the few ignorant and foolish men whose blood Taranaki means to have if their living bodies are not continuously confined in Southern gaols. . . . What is the South to gain by the extermination of the natives on the West Coast? Extermination is not my word. Major Atkinson† speaking at Hawera, about two years ago, is reported to have said : 'he hoped if war did come the Maoris would be exterminated.' . . . It is the exclusion of enquiry into confiscation that has mainly induced the natives to withhold recognition of the West Coast Commission. The refusal of one of the parties to recognize and accept the decisions of a tribunal of appeal created by the other, when that tribunal is forbidden so much as to lift the veil which hangs over the original confiscation, is no sufficient cause of war.

"Every Maori or European shot, and every European woman and child subsequently massacred in revenge for such shooting, in consequence of the injudicious and unreasonable ultimatum of October 19th, if indeed it be carried out, will be a human soul murdered for no better reason than this : that successive Ministries have been as fruitful to promise as they have been slow to perform their promises."

Mr. (now Sir) Robert Stout, who had been, but was not in October 1881, a member of Parliament, but was afterwards elected, and became for three years Attorney General and Prime Minister in New Zealand wrote also to a newspaper, thus:—

"I suppose, amidst the general rejoicings at the prospect of a Maori war, it is useless for any one to raise his voice against

---

* Blue Book, 1882. C. 3382, p, 166,

† Major Atkinson was a Minister in October, 1881. It is fair to add that at a later date, 10th June, 1882, he denied the accuracy of the newspaper report (7th June, 1879) of his speech. Blue Book, 1882. C. 3382, p. 285.

the present native policy. I do so more as a protest than with any hope that any one colonist can ever aid in preventing the murder of the Maoris, on which it seems we, as a colony, are bent. I call it murder, for we know that the Maoris are, as compared with us, helpless, and I am not aware of anything they have done to make us commence hostilities. The race is dying, and if we were at all affected with the love of humanity we should strive to preserve it, or to make its dying moments as happy as possible. To this end, I think, we ought to have given Te Whiti and his people a Crown grant of the Parihaka block, and allowed them to live there unmolested. If they disturbed settlers on other lands, why not treat them as we treat European disturbers of the peace—bring them before our courts of justice for trial and punishment? Instead of thus acting we have had most unconstitutional Acts passed, depriving them of liberty without trial. And we have had them punished for fencing a road—the proclamation of which was not known to them, and which it is questionable whether the Crown had the right to issue. We are powerful, they are weak, and that is the only explanation that the future historian will give of our conduct."*

All that occurred when violent hands were laid upon Te Whiti and his people, need not be told here. But some of the events which caused the Maoris to groan may be touched upon.

An advocate of the Government measures had written (9th September) to the *London Times* that in spite of Te Whiti's preachings, "the Government has sold the confiscated territory up to the very gates of his fortress." Te Whiti had no fortress;—but putting aside that mistatement (*vide Times*, 25th October, 1881) the sale of their cultivated fields was calculated to cause many groans among the dispossessed.

What was to be done at Parihaka would appear to have been left to the Native Minister's discretion, or indiscretion. When the Governor asked Mr. Hall, the Premier, what instructions had been given to guide Mr. Bryce, Mr. Hall answered, "It has not been considered necessary to furnish written instructions to Mr. Bryce. He has discussed the whole situation. . . , and as the Minister to whom it specially belongs to deal with the question . . . a large amount of discretion must necessarily be vested in him . . . Where special circumstances or sudden emergency render immediate action necessary Mr. Bryce will act on his own responsibility."†

Armed forces were collected under the Native Minister's orders.

Te Whiti nevertheless preached peace. On the 17th October he said "Guns and powder shall no longer be the protection for man." On

---

* Sir R. Stout, when afterwards Prime Minister, resorted to the ordinary law in dealing with the Maoris on the West Coast.

† I have not been successful in my search for this document in the English Blue Books. It is to be found at page 2 of a New Zd. Parliamentary Paper, 1883, A. 4. The ministry which gave this *carte noire* to Mr. Bryce, consisted of John Hall; F. Whitaker ; H. A. Atkinson; W. Rolleston ; Richard Oliver; T. Dick ; and W. W. Johnston.

the 1st November he said—"God said to Moses, Do not strive against me or you will die. By faith only can this tribe be saved. . . . Our salvation to day is stout-heartedness and patience . . . Do not think I am fighting against men, but rather against the devil and all wickedness that he may be destroyed; let us not use carnal weapons. The ark by which we are to be saved to day is stout-heartedness, and flight is death. Let this sink into the ears of all—even the children. . . . Obey God and glorify him. . . . All fighting is now to cease. Do not follow your own desires, lest God's sword fall upon you. Forbearance is our ark of safety to day. . . God will not be pleased with fighting but with praising His name. Be forbearing to the utmost against all temptations. . . By forbearance alone shall we be saved."*

Te Whiti was looked upon as a prophet by his people, and he seems clearly to have divined the meaning of the gathering of 2,000 armed men around his village.

Early in November the *Wanganui Chronicle* reported that Te Whiti said :—"I am still for peace. I will go into captivity, and the lions will dwell upon the land ; then there will be no more war.

"What matters it ? My object is accomplished; peace reigns. I am willing to become a sacrifice for my object. . . . Oh, hardhearted people ! I am here to be taken. Take me for the sins of the island ! Why hesitate ? Am I not here ? Though I am killed, I yet shall live; and, though dead, will yet live in my object—which is peace. The future is mine, and little children will answer in the future when questioned as to the author of peace; they will say, Te Whiti, and I will bless them."

On November 4th the Native Minister issued an order prohibiting civilians from being present with his army on the 5th.

A few newspaper correspondents † disregarded the order, and were with Te Whiti early on that day, but secreted themselves while they watched the proceedings. When they explained their object Maoris said to them—"We quite understand why the government is ashamed that the country should know what it is doing; but we have nothing to be ashamed of and you are welcome."†

The army arrived. Te Whiti sat unmoved with his people. "Whatever he might direct would inevitably be done. The whole assemblage sat with eyes fixed on Te Whiti. His slightest variation of countenance was reflected in the faces of all, and any words

---

* Blue Book, 1882. C. 3382. p.p, 191—193.

† The interest excited in the minds of the correspondents may be inferred from the fact that one of them wrote—"Of the Taranaki contingent (of the colonial forces) it was said with a frankness that made the blood run cold, that twenty men were *sworn to shoot down the first Maori* that chance placed it within their power to kill." Blue Book, 1882. C. 3382, p. 225.

‡ Ib. p. 227. In the same page the writer says " The whole spectacle was saddening in the extreme ; it was an industrious, law-abiding, moral and hospitable community, calmly awaiting the approach of the men sent to rob them of everything dear to them."

that he addressed to those close to him were whispered from one to to another till they reached the uttermost circle of the densely packed meeting."*

> Watching their leader's beck and will
> All silent there they sate, and still.

Te Whiti and his lieutenant Tohu were heard to enjoin forbearance : " Even if the bayonet be put to your breasts, do not resist.†

The Riot Act was read, the bugle sounded an advance ; an officer was reported to have told his men " if any Maori flashed a tomahawk to shoot him down instantly."‡

Te Whiti was ordered to go to his visitors, but answered that he " would remain with his people. . . . he had nothing but good words to say to Mr. Bryce. Mr. Bryce replied in a tone that those who heard considered harsh that he would not come to him unless he made a path among his people through which Mr. Bryce could ride. The natives, it must be remembered, were so compactly packed that to do this was an impossibility. Te Whiti replied quite calmly that the horse's feet might hurt some of the children." (The interpreter for Mr. Bryce said) " the horse was a quiet one." Te Whiti replied that if Mr. Bryce wanted to speak with him, he must come on foot.¶

Some of an " arresting party," of about one hundred armed men marched through the men, women and children and laid hands on Te Whiti, who " quietly awaited their approach. The moment they laid their hands on him he rose. . . He came away in a very dignified manner, his wife following closely. . . . Te Whiti said to his people— Be of good heart and patient . . . Be steadfast in all that is peaceful."‖

I refrain from characterizing these proceedings in these pages. Criticism might offend any, if such there be, who, having been enriched at the expense of the Maoris, would not only wrongly win, but would enjoy their gains unchallenged.

I may, however, quote what was written by a gentleman who had observed the conduct of "the army" as it tramped among women and children, and laid hands on their peaceful chief.

The reporters emerged after Te Whiti's seizure, and one of them wrote : — " If anything in connection with one of the saddest and most painful spectacles I have witnessed could be ludicrous, it was the expression of the faces of the authorities, when they saw that their grand scheme for preventing the colony from knowing what was done in the name of the Queen at Parihaka had been completely frustrated. Not an action escaped observation. Not an order given was unheard or unrecorded." §

The newspapers published narratives ; but the local government still withheld information in New Zealand, and Lord Kimberley still obeyed their behests, and kept back information from the Imperial Parliament. I must be brief, and refrain from comment here. Those who wish to trace the proceedings in detail, will find them in the English

---

* Ib. p. 228. † Ib. 228. ‡ Ib. p. 228. ¶ Ib. 228.
‖ Ib. p. 229. § Ib. p. 229.

Blue Book, which, at last, on demand of Sir M. Hicks Beach, was yielded to the House of Commons late in 1882 (C. 3382), and in the supplementary Blue Book produced in 1883 (C. 3689).

A few extracts from those documents, and from newspapers, will sufficiently describe the treatment of Te Whiti and of his people. Besides newspaper information, the Blue Book of 1882 contains official telegrams from the Native Minister to his colleagues, and the public are greatly beholden to the Governor for the copious materials he sent to the Secretary of State, to enable that functionary, if inclined, to guard the honour of his country.

Te Whiti was carried to prison.

" Comment is freely being made, both among the troops and civilians, upon the fact that on the day of taking possession of Parihaka, Colonel Roberts was placed simply in the position of an aide-de-camp to Mr. Bryce, who personally gave all orders, taking care however to keep himself clear of any possible danger." *

The Maoris were described on the 6th November, as sitting disconsolate, in sad contrast to the gaiety and light-heartedness that usually reigned in Parihaka. " Still they are as polite in demeanour as ever." †

Newspapers commented openly upon what their activity had exposed. The *Lyttelton Times* (8th November) said :—" The Native Minister organizes a demonstration against a native village, and he contrives to attain to a pinnacle of absurdity which no one has even imagined in dreams. After carefully collecting a huge force of soldiery from all parts of the colony he has to read the Riot Act to a peaceful population, calmly seated in their own market place . . . . Every one is aware of the discreditable trick which the ministers played off upon the Governor, taking advantage of his absence to hurry out a most ill-advised Proclamation. That Proclamation was, probably, illegal. In it the name of the Queen's Representative was made to endorse one statement so disingenuous as to be dangerously near to falsehood, and another of which the truth never has been, and never will be evident to any candidly reasonable capacity. . . . If the consequence should be the taking of a single acre of the lands in cultivation at Parihaka, as threatened in the Proclamation, that taking will be an act of simple spoliation." ‡

On the 9th November, the same paper declared that a statement in a ministerial organ was " tantamount to an official admission that ministers conspired to play Sir Arthur Gordon a dirty trick. Feeling assured that the Governor would raise difficulties, they rushed the Proclamation through the hands of the Administrator of the Government, when they knew—and had been informed—that Sir Arthur Gordon might return at any moment. The low cunning, characteristic of the whole proceeding leads us to suppose that its conception must

---

* ib. p. 231.   † ib. ib.
‡ Ib. p. 214—215.

have originated in the mind of the Attorney General."* . . "how long will the people tolerate the buffoonery at Parihaka?† . . . Was it intended in the event of even slight resistance to the arrest of Te Whiti, to make that quiet marae a human shambles." ‡

On the 8th November the Native Minister told the Maoris "to disperse." Assuming that *they* were trespassers, and that their only lawful abodes were such as he might appoint, he issued a proclamation ordering them to "return to their own settlement, there to await the instructions of the Government concerning them." (Blue Book, 1882, c. 3382, p. 235.) His verbal order was reported in these words :—"Go away, all of you ; pack up your belongings. Go and leave the place." (ib. p. 234.)

Parihaka was then subjected to a curious and perhaps unexampled process, "Mr. Bryce personally directing every movement." (ib.) The Blue Book furnishes the names of a colonel, and of captains, who figured on the scene. Two of the latter were ordered to search the village. Armed men entered dwelling-places, and property was dragged out and laid "at Mr. Bryce's feet." (ib.)

While the pillage went on, one or other chief implored the woeful Maoris to "remember the advice of Te Whiti and Tohu, and to preserve the peace and maintain order." (ib. p. 234.)

It was "truly pitiable to see the Maoris calmly and patiently looking on while their homes were being rifled" (ib.) . . "the feeling of sympathy for Te Whiti and his followers, which I mentioned in a previous telegram as having recently sprung up here, is extending, while Mr. Bryce is going proportionately down in the scale of popularity." (ib. p. 236.) A telegram to the *New Zealand Herald* (6th November), said :—

"I saw Te Whiti this morning . . his influence seems to be felt by all who approach him, and the roughest men say, with curious unanimity, that he is a gentleman."

On the 8th November, while Te Whiti was thus comporting himself in gaol, Mr. Justice Gillies, of the Supreme Court, was reported by a Press Association telegram to have said, in addressing a Grand Jury in the immediate neighbourhood (at Taranaki, *i.e.*, New Plymouth) "that he would be wanting in his duty if he ignored the circumstances of the position of the district in which large bodies of armed men were assembled on active service, and he took leave to remind them of the *constitutional principle* that the employment of an armed force was only justifiable either under the authority of Parliament in repelling armed aggression, or in aid of the civil arm of the law, when that arm had proved powerless to enforce the law's mandates ; *in any other case the use of armed force was illegal, and a menace, if not an outrage, upon the liberties of the people.*"¶

---

* ib. p. 217.　　　† ib. p. 218.　　　‡ ib. 218

¶ This charge appeared at once in the New Zealand press. Judge Gillies' last remark (in the text) is quoted in the Blue Book, 1882, C. 3382, p. 220.

Commenting on the Judge's dictum, the *Lyttelton Times* said, 10th November:—"The behaviour of the Maoris at Parihaka is the most striking feature of the story of the last few days. Such a feat of dignified, passive resistance has never been performed by a savage race. Such completeness of good temper under circumstances of great provocation has never been paralleled in history." (Blue Book, 1882, C. 3382, p. 219.)

The demeanour of the Maoris and the censure of a Judge worked no change upon the Government. Various neighbouring settlements were "ransacked" on the 9th November (ib. p. 237).

On the 11th November, "arresting operations were resumed . . under the immediate supervision of Mr. Bryce" (ib. p. 239), and the Blue Book (p. 240) contains the following official telegram:—

"Bryce to Hall, November 11th, 1881.

"The danger of retaliation in the case of burning whares [dwellings] must have occurred to every one, because retaliation would be easy. I never intended to burn, although I have thought and *think that it may be necessary to destroy every whare in the village* if the Maoris hold out. It would be very difficult to distinguish between the whares of the different tribes. This is the so-called Waikato quarters, and the Wanganui quarters, but of the 350 huts in the village I *could not have ten identified with certainty* as belonging to any particular tribe. Then again we are told that the Wanganui, &c., should be ordered to their homes. Well, I have ordered them to their homes emphatically enough, and apparently I might as well called from the vasty deep [*sic*].

"Then as for their apprehension and selection into tribes, people seem to think that each one has the name of his tribe written on his forehead. To show the difficulty, I may mention that yesterday I wanted to arrest Taputepeora, a Ngaruaun [*sic*] chief of note, and there was not a man in camp could identify him. If there is difficulty in such a case as that, consider what it must be with the 2,000 men, and women, and children, who are nobodies. . . . I am pointing out these difficulties, not because I think them insuperable, but that you may be aware of them and consider them when you hear of my doing things which do not altogether recommend themselves to your mind. I may be forced into a choice of objectionable courses. Consider, here are 2,000 people sitting still, absolutely declining to give me any indication of where they belong to, or who they belong to, they will sit still where they are, and do nothing else. . . . If I take the whole lot prisoners, as Atkinson recommends, the operation *per se* will be difficult, and in that case the unfortunate result will happen that the whole of their personal properties, such as drays, ploughs, &c., cattle and so forth, will be lost to them. Moreover, it is *extremely probable that wives would be separated from their husbands, children from parents, and so on.* Notwithstanding these difficulties, this thing has to be settled, and I am confident I can do it if I am not stopped. *That the manner in which I do it will be free from objections is more than I can promise,* but I hope that you and my colleagues will put the most favourable construction on things. I send copy of this to Whitaker."

On the 12th, he telegraphed to another colleague (ib. 241) :—" I have great difficulty in selecting them, although I have the services of a half-caste belonging to the Alexander troop. . . Mete King, if he comes, may be able to assist in this. The question is between going with their property and going without, but go they must."

Will any reader picture to himself the aspect of an English village, recognized as the most sober and industrious of its kind, dealt with in such a manner?

On the 13th (p. 247) "I shall to-morrow complete the apprehension of the Wanganui tribe, and begin marching them down to Wanganui. I do not propose, unless their own conduct compels me, to place these prisoners on their trial. I intend to send them to Wanganui with an escort . . . and to release them unless they intimate an intention of returning In that case I shall, I suppose, indict them for a breach of the West Coast Act."

On the 14th (ib.) he telegraphed :—"*Probably we have made a few mistakes*, but the number of these tribes now arrested is certainly over eighty. A great difficulty now remains, for it is impossible to identify women and children as we have done the men, and they, like the men, remain impassible. After the men had dinner, I directed Mr. Booth to tell the women to go and take their things out of the Wanganui quarters, as we were about to pull it down. [On the 11th it has been seen that the Native Minister admitted that he could not have identified ten out of 350 dwellings *with certainty as belonging to any particular tribe.*] They, however, made no sign. We have pulled down the whole of the Wanganui quarters, just removing the things belonging to the natives, and placing them in piles in front of each hut. . . . If the women go for the things as the Waikatos did, we may identify most of them by that means. . . . I suppose if I cannot get the women, I shall have to indict the men under the West Coast Act. I may add that I ascertained with considerable [!] certainty that the whole of the huts destroyed belonged to the Wanganuis."

On November 15th (ib.) he telegraphed: "The Wanganui Maori women have not brought away the things from the whares we pulled down yesterday, and they evidently intend to prevent us from making them join their husbands. I am now going to see what can be done, but there is more difficulty in identifying women than men."

On November 15th (ib. 248) he telegraphed that "I have succeeded beyond my expectations, by the aid of Utiko, in selecting the Wanganui women and children. . . . It was a curious scene. We brought out into rows about 650 women and three or four hundred children, and then proceeded to separate them, the Wanganuis being put one by one in a corner." The writer of a telegram for the Press Association said (Nov. 14th), (ib. 249) "Mr. Bryce informed me that beyond about a dozen women who are known to belong to the Wanganuis, the others cannot be identified."

The same authority vouched, (ib. 251) on Nov. 16th, that, after arresting some Ngatiawa men, "attention was then directed to the women and children, and during the afternoon the whole tribe was placed in confinement. The number taken was 250 men, 109 women, and fifty children. Nine of the women, and between forty and fifty men were released this afternoon, as they had been taken in mistake. No resistance whatever was offered by the Maoris. . . . Several of the natives brought out from the pah refused to give their names. These were immediately handcuffed. . . . Unless the prisoners agree to select their property, it will, along with the whares, be destroyed by the Armed Constabulary, as Mr. Bryce is of opinion that on their release at Waitara they would immediately *return to their property*."

The *Lyttelton Times* correspondent telegraphed on November 15th: (ib. 249) "The measures taken for turning away strange (*i.e.*, supposed to be strange) Maoris are still being carried out. The process is strangely like drafting sheep. To-day the Wanganui ewes were culled." Another telegram declared that "there was much discussion last night about the way in which sixty-two Maoris were mustered like sheep from the pahs near Parapara, and driven up to Parihaka that the Wanganui ewes might be culled out."

On November 18th the special correspondent of the *New Zealand Herald* (a paper friendly to the ministry) telegraphed that he found at Parihaka "a mob of about 200 prisoners—men, women, and children . . . all being escorted to Opunake. . . .

It seems very doubtful whether Mr. Bryce knows *who these people are, or where they really belong to. Some of the women cried, and had to be forcibly put in the drays*."

Force applied to women, weeping of mothers, and sobs of children scattered to all quarters of the compass! Are these events to be washed in Lethe and forgotten?

On the 15th (p. 250) we read in the Blue Book :—* "Mr. Bryce expects a difficulty in identifying the Natives who have come from districts between the Waikato and Mokau, no Europeans having visited these. However, he is determined to disperse them, and, if necessary, by force. Mr. Bryce mentioned that he was afraid the larger portion of the crops (principally potatoes) now under cultivation by the natives, would have to be destroyed. He gave it as his opinion that if this was carried out, there would be no attraction to Parihaka, and the alien tribes would thus be prevented from assembling there."

To destroy food certainly deprives a locality of some attractions, but as the Courts of the Colony had solemnly recognized the Maori law of adoption, there were no alien tribes at Parihaka, and all the Maoris there were British subjects, to whom the Queen had guaranteed

---

* Press Association Telegram.

all British rights, in addition to the special safe-guard of their lands by the Treaty of Waitangi; moreover, Donald McLean, on behalf of the Local Government, had recognized their right of residence on the spot.

At page 254 we read (18th November) "The Maoris are being arrested indiscriminately in many instances, *neither their names nor that of the tribes to which they belong, being known.* To-morrow a novel experiment is to be tried with a view to identifying male prisoners. They are to be paraded close to Parihaka, in the anticipation that their wives and other female relatives will come out and speak to them. If I understand the arrangement aright the object is not only to identify the male prisoners, but to trap the women and children, and thus render their wholesale arrest more easy. It is due to the armed constabulary to say that in private conversation most of them express themselves thoroughly disgusted with the work they are called upon to perform. . . Parihaka presents a most melancholy appearance. A large portion of the village has been torn down, without the slightest regard as to whether the owners had committed any offence, and *homeless Maoris* may be seen *searching among the ruins* for such of their household goods as have not been ruthlessly destroyed or stolen."

At page 256 the same correspondent describes the rifling of houses far distant from Parihaka. A chief Motu, the door of whose store-house for food was broken open, complained bitterly. Sir Donald McLean, when Native Minister, had presented a Union Jack to him (in 1875) " in acknowledgment of his loyalty." When the armed force had completed their work Motu invited the commanding officer into the house, and, seizing the Union Jack, threw it at the officer's feet, exclaiming angrily " you had better take that too ! " " And this," said Motu, to the correspondent, " is the treatment I receive for my loyalty."

At page 259 we read that " Tom Preston's " house was " broken open " (he being at work in his field), " and the axes applied to his boxes, and everything in the house was tossed about and smashed. Besides (guns, powder, &c.) he lost £5 4s. and two greenstone ornaments. . . He was very grieved, he declared that he had always been loyal to the core. He must give up the Government; he could follow them no longer. They might just as well burn his house over his head, and have done with it."

George Kukapo was in like distress. Governor Gore Browne had presented a gun to him, to be kept as an heir-loom. " It was a reward for his valour, and he prized it. This had been taken from him and his whare damaged."

The correspondent wrote sadly what he saw.

On the 18th November (Blue Book, 1882, C. 3382, p. 261) the Native Minister telegraphed—" Have taken nearly 400 prisoners in all to-day. . . I am going to mark the empty whares (houses) *to-night a mid-night for destruction* " (ib. p. 261).

On the 20th (ib.) " I intend to *pull down a number of whares* around the marae to-morrow, and shall put them into the marae so as to deprive it of its sacred character and break the magic spell."

On the 21st November (ib. p. 262) he telegraphed to his colleague— (Mr. Rolleston) "Forty-seven more Maoris brought up from the fences, twenty resident, twenty-seven strangers; this makes total 2,200. . . Pulled down some whares this afternoon, *amongst the rest the sacred medicine-house*, where people had to take off their shoes before entering. It was *a great job to get it demolished*, as it was very substantially built." *

Food was destroyed at Parihaka, and the subject was mentioned in the New Zealand Parliament by the Native Minister on 26th May, 1882, thus—(N.Z. Hansard, 1882, Vol. XLI., p. 116) "A great deal was said in the papers and elsewhere, about the pulling up of the Maori potatoes by the Constabulary. Now, Sir, if I had done what perhaps I ought to have done, I should have pulled up a great many more potatoes, so as to reduce the supply of food. . . . "

In the same session, a question having been asked as to the pulling down of some houses remaining at Parihaka, in April, 1882, the same functionary admitted (ib. p. 438) that his "orders were then carried out in respect to pulling down certain whares. About a dozen whares were pulled down. . . He was not aware whether Te Whiti's whare was one of those pulled down, but, if so, it was a very good thing for Mrs. Te Whiti, because the whare she resided in was one of the oldest, smallest and most unwholesome in the whole village."

When these words were spoken Te Whiti, lawlessly rent from his home and imprisoned, was denied a trial; and despatches concerning him were kept from the public in England and in New Zealand, by concert of Lord Kimberley with the New Zealand Ministry!

On such events it would seem that some persons demand that history should be silent; but silence which might in some cases become a commendation of crime, would be a reproach to the historian. We have seen that (in the Native Minister's own language) the total number of peaceful Maoris "brought up," and haled away, amidst wailing and weeping, was two thousand, two hundred.

That, bereft of their prophet, they should groan under the inflictions they endured was natural; but that they rigidly obeyed his mandate to abstain from resentment extorted wonder from friend and foe.

It was said that some persons were disappointed because the absence of resistance deprived the Government of the occasion of sweeping Te Whiti's followers from the earth.

Soon after the raid upon Parihaka, the Native Minister was himself reported as having said at a banquet in his honour that if he had been shot, it "meant the death of the *whole of the natives* assembled there." How many women and children would thus have fallen it is impossible to say, but one of the Native Minister's own telegrams (15th November) already quoted speaks of "about six hundred and fifty

---

* Their place of worship, built by common effort, was, of course, more substantial than the private houses of the Maoris. I know not how a historian could refrain from commenting upon its wanton destruction.

women and three or four hundred children" dragged before him. It is satisfactory to know that he was not shot at and that no such were-gild was extorted, as his estimate implied.

Having seen the Maoris scattered, it is necessary to observe the treatment of Te Whiti.

The charge of Judge Gillies on the 8th November to the Grand Jury at Taranaki already quoted, warned the public that the proceedings at Parihaka might be deemed "illegal and a menace to, if not an outrage upon, the liberties of the people."

Nevertheless Te Whiti and Tohu were brought before the magistrates on the 12th November.

An information against them had been sworn to by an interpreter, who, when reminded by a magistrate of some expressions contained in the information, replied (Blue Book 1882, C. 3382, p. 243) "I cannot swear to expressions I did not hear. . . I was not aware that I was responsible for all that appeared in the information or I would not have sworn it."

It was asserted by Te Whiti's persecutors that Te Whiti had refused to accept their arbitrary proffer of reserves of land. The proclamation promulgated so hastily at night by Prendergast after the conversations with Mr. Murray about the Governor's expected return, accused Te Whiti of having "repeatedly rejected proposals made with the hope of a settlement."*

Tohu asked the interpreter if that functionary himself knew what was the proposed division of the land (ib. 244).

"Yes, I know it. "Did you tell us where it was?" "No."

Mr. Parris (well known to readers of New Zealand history in the period preceding the unjust war at the Waitara in 1860) was on the bench, and questioned another interpreter, Carrington, thus :— (ib.)

" Were you not supplied with a plan showing the land that had been reserved for the natives, and were you not instructed to show the boundaries to the natives ? "

"Certainly not."

" *Mr. Parris.* Remember you are on your oath.

" *Mr. Carrington.* I know that. You need not remind me of it.

" *Mr. Parris.* A plan was made out by Mr. Humphries, the chief surveyor, showing the reserves, and given to you.

" *Mr. Carrington.* I received a plan of the reserves, but it was given me for the purpose of finding what natives were cultivating portions of the land coloured on the plan,† and I did so. I did not understand that I was to point out the boundaries of the reserves to the natives, or I should have done so.

" *Mr. Parris.* Have the 25,000 acres ever been defined or pointed out ?

" *Mr. Carrington.* Not that I know of.

---

* Blue Book 1882, C. 3382 p. 164.

† This statement proves that the Government were well aware that cultivation was going on upon the lands about to be seized.

"*Mr. Parris.* Were you not aware by the map that a portion of land seaward of Pungarehu was reserved for the natives?

"*Mr. Carrington.* I understood that without the map.

"*Mr. Parris.* And yet you never explained?

"*Mr. Carrington.* Certainly not.

"*Mr. Parris.* Well, I recollect giving you those instructions. myself.*

"*Mr. Carrington.* I never was told to point out the boundaries to the natives. It was altogether out of my line."

When Te Whiti was told that he might ask questions he exposed another of the methods by which the Government endeavoured to damage or entrap Te Whiti. Maori speech is enigmatic,—full of allusions to ancient proverbs,—and Te Whiti's was more mystical than that of many of his countrymen. Few Europeans have acquired such consummate knowledge of the Maori language as to be trusted in defining the meaning of the words they hear from a fluent orator

Many Europeans have a smattering of the language. It has been seen that there were often doubts as to the meaning of Te Whiti's orations, various reports of which were sent to the newspapers and to the Government.

He asked Carrington: "Did I not tell you not to write down what I said at the meeting because you did not understand me?" And Carrington replied: "I remember you telling me not to write down your speech."

Whatever might be the evidence, the committal of the chiefs was looked upon as a foregone conclusion. Te Whiti briefly said that the Maoris had been cultivating their lands, that they had not raised food to cause a quarrel, but to procure the means of living; that it was not his wish that evil should come to either of the races: "my wish is for the whole of us to live happy on the land. I have never wished to do evil, or to kill any one up to the present time. My desire is for the whole of us to live happy on the land. Such is my desire, and such is the manner in which I have addressed the Maori people. I have no more to say." The magistrate told him: "You are committed to the common gaol of New Plymouth, there to be safely kept until you shall be thence delivered by due course of law·"

In that "due course," Te Whiti would have been tried in May, 1882, The *Lyttelton Times*, of 17th November, 1881, remarked on the committal, "Every provocation has been given to the natives. The absence of bloodshed is owing to the very remarkable restraint, —unparalleled we believe—which at the bidding of Te Whiti they have exercised on themselves in most exceptional and aggravating circumstances. It is fortunate for the good name, and for the welfare

---

* I find in a scrap book a leading article of the *Lyttelton Times*, November 16th, 1881, which says that Parris having been an agent for the Government in approaching Te Whiti, his conduct in going on the bench as "magistrate, prosecutor and unsworn witness for the prosecution" was such that he "ought to be struck off the roll of justices."

of the colony, that the selfish and aggressive instincts of Messrs. . . . and Atkinson have been over-ruled, for a time at least, by Te Whiti's higher and nobler qualities. . . .

"The error throughout was to ignore the Supreme Court, which Te Whiti evidently has wished all along to try his case. He knew that once before that court the whole question of confiscation must be raised, and that he could if he wished, appeal against an adverse decision on points of law to the Judicial Committee of the Privy Council. He has tried by peaceful means to bring the question before the Supreme Court, and he has been persistently baffled by the perversity of the Government, who believe more in royal commissioners and big battalions than in high and independent courts of law. What hollow hypocrisy it must sound in Te Whiti's ears, to hear the ministerial parrot-cry of the rule of law, when resort to the highest and purest source of law and justice is studiously forbidden to him! . . . We were lately told by a contemporary . . . that about two thousand natives at Parihaka, though not arrested, tried, or convicted, were actually in prison and in the armed custody of Mr. . . . and his myrmidons. What law, we ask, has made Mr. . . . the controller of human liberties and lives? What right, human or divine, has he to imprison, break into houses, and to take away other men's goods? . . . There is one hope, that if Te Whiti . . . is tried in the Supreme Court, and is properly defended, his whole case may be thoroughly sifted, and an opportunity given for the vindication of law, in spite of Mr. . . . and Major Atkinson."

The appeal of the Editor on behalf of the "noble qualities," of Te Whiti failed to persuade the Ministry, for in the month of February, 1882, the *New Zealand Herald* reported the Native Minister as declaring to a great chief in the Waikato district—"I say that as the representative of the Government of the Colony, and as the representative of Her Majesty the Queen."

Can it be deemed strange that some of Her Majesty's lieges failed to recognize in such language the accents of a beloved Queen? might not, to use Chief Justice Cockburn's words, an "honest indignation" be aroused in loyal breasts if they believed the report?

Before the time arrived for the trial of Te Whiti and Tohu, (which would, by "due course of law," have taken place at Taranaki (*i.e.* New Plymouth) in May, 1882, before Judge Gillies) the Attorney General (who had become Premier on the retirement of Mr. Hall, in April,) had removed Te Whiti and Tohu from Taranaki to the Middle Island where their trial could not be brought on for some time; and the removal was commented upon by public men.

Mr. (now Sir) Robert Stout (who became in 1884 the Prime Minister of New Zealand, and Attorney General) wrote that he believed "the removal was made for no other purpose than to stave off the trial till after the meeting of Parliament, to allow if necessary one of those disgraces to New Zealand legislation—a special Act—to be passed."

The *Lyttelton Times* (19th April 1882) thought that the " new Parliament will refuse to be a party to anything *so thoroughly disgraceful;*"—but Mr. Stouts' prophecy was correct.

When the Special Bill (which some persons called an Attainder Bill) was brought in, in May 1882, many members denounced it, and Mr. Hutchison said:—"It appears to me that when the Attorney General . . . obtained leave to change the venue from New Plymouth to Christchurch, he must have been cognizant of the fact that there was no intention to try Te Whiti and Tohu, and the Supreme Court was consequently made a mere machine to carry out the purposes of the Government. I am speaking now in the presence of gentlemen of the legal profession, and I venture to say that if the English Attorney General had done the same thing before any of the Courts of Judicature in England, he would have stood the chance of being struck off the rolls. * "

However, though Te Whiti and Tohu were not allowed to appear before Judge Gillies, other Maoris were arraigned at New Plymouth in May; and the Judge explained the law as to the nature of the raid upon Parihaka.

Among the Maoris arraigned, was Titokowaru. After his arrest the old chief was described in a newspaper, as "crouching hand-cuffed like a large dog in a low whare like a kennel. He is said to have refused food for a long time." †

It was not said, but it may be inferred, that the old man groaned under this treatment.

On the following day, (21st November) two events happened which may have caused exultation in some minds.

The Native Minister "demolished" Te Whiti's "sacred" building and the Blue Book(1882. C. 3382. p. 260)informs us that "Titokowaru who has obstinately refused to accept any food during the last two days, gave in to day, and gladly accepted that offered him.

Dr. O'Carrol visited him this morning, and found him in tears, (Te Whiti had then been committed for trial.) . . he is still kept hand-cuffed, and in a separate whare from the other prisoners."

On the 25th November, the old man was taken before the magistrates on a charge of using threats (some time before his seizure at Parihaka) but as a witness, called against him, said:—"He was only joking. Titokowaru had been offended by Europeans, and was chaffing in return" (ib. p. 264),—the magistrates (singularly in accordance with a newspaper prediction as to the ministerial intentions, ib. p. 260) ordered him "to find two sureties in £500 each," . . and to be "kept in the common gaol" until he could find sureties.

This was deemed by some persons equivalent to permanent imprisonment, unless the Supreme Court should intervene.

---

* New Zealand Hansard. 1882. Vol. XLI., p. 120.

† *New Zealand Herald.*

On the 1st May, 1882, Titokowaru and Rangi were to be brought before Judge Gillies, and the Blue Book (p.p. 282, 283) informs us how they fared.

They were to be tried on "charges of obstruction," under "the West Coast Settlements Act, 1880," which made an offender of "any person who wilfully and unlawfully obstructs any person authorized by the Governor to do or perform any act or thing in pursuance of this Act, or for the purpose of carrying out the provisions thereof." "In the present case" (the judge said) "the natives merely sat still, and did not go away when ordered to do so. This may, or may not, according to the circumstances, amount to the crime of obstruction. It would at most be a passive obstruction, if there is proof that a person authorized by the Governor had ordered them to move. To make this act a crime it is necessary that the order to remove should be given by a person authorized by the Governor. It would not be sufficient for some Minister verbally to give such an authority. It must be *the official act of the Governor*, through a minister, authorizing some special person to do some particular act in pursuance of the provisions of the statute. So far as the depositions show, there appears to have been no special authority from the Governor to Mr. Hursthouse to do any special act or thing—merely a general verbal authority to disperse certain natives, given by a Minister. . . . If this be so, then these natives have been taken into custody for disobeying the order of a person who had no authority from the Governor, though a Minister, to do any special act or thing under the provisions of this statute. . . . When the Government come into a court of law alleging their action to be legal, it must be shown that the provisions of the Act have been strictly complied with. You must say whether the accused, when sitting quietly, were committing an obstruction within the meaning of the Act, and whether, when told to go away, it was by a person authorized by the Governor. No Minister can personally, of his own mere will, authorize any person to do any act or thing for the purpose of carrying out the provisions of the Act—it must be a formal and official authority. I commend this to your special attention, and again ask you to remember that you have nothing to do with the policy of the Government. . . . It may have been a right thing to do, to disperse the natives, and the Legislature may approve of all that has been done; but when the matter comes before you, it is for you to say whether, in accordance with the provisions of this Act, the Governor authorized Mr. Hursthouse to do that act of dispersing the natives, and whether they by their inaction obstructed him in the performance of that duty. If you are satisfied that he was duly authorized, and that he was obstructed, you will bring in a true bill; but, on the other hand, should you find that he had no authority, it will be your duty to find no bill."

The Grand Jury found true Bills, and the Judge was publicly railed at in newspapers for his Charge.

But there must have been a foregone conclusion that he was right in law, and would be upright in doing his duty.

No such "official act of the Governor," as was needful to warrant the arrest of Te Whiti or any of his people was ever produced. *

Failing to produce the needed authority the Ministry ordered the Crown Prosecutor to take such steps as would elude a decision, and a *nolle prosequi* was entered.

On the 8th May, Judge Gillies said from the Bench, (Blue Book, p. 2?3) "I understand the Attorney General (Whitaker, the Premier) has ordered the Crown Prosecutor to enter a *nolle prosequi* in the two native cases under the West Coast Settlements Act. I have no right to interfere in the matter in any way, except to express my surprise at such a course being taken. That prisoners should be brought up on a serious charge under a special Act, that they should be kept in prison for six months on that grave charge, and that the Crown Prosecutor should then apply to enter a *nolle prosequi*, seems a very extraordinary proceeding on the part of the Government, more especially when I see that two of the indictments have been quashed on account of insufficiency in the face of them." (Then, addressing Rangi, he said) "The Government have determined not to bring you to be tried on the charge. You have already been in prison six months, waiting for trial, nor does the Government offer any evidence. You are therefore free to go where you will." † The native did not seem *to understand the situation,* but left the box."

The situation was not easy for any one to understand without careful watching. But by collating various reports at the time, it was possible to comprehend why it was that Lord Kimberley in England, and the Ministry in New Zealand, strove to withhold from the public the despatches which would have enabled it to "understand the situation."

These declarations from the Bench came under my notice at the time, as reported in newspapers.

Perhaps it may be well at this point to quote briefly from Sir Arthur Gordon's Despatches concerning the devastation of Parihaka.

On the 8th November, he asked the ministry to explain an insinuation in one of their memoranda, to the effect that Te Whiti expected the Imperial Government to "interfere in his favour."

After more than five weeks of procrastination, Mr. Rolleston, in whom the task of explanation devolved, was compelled to admit that his assumptions were based on "assurances for the most part verbal," but he alleged, as a kind of proof, that Tohu had once been reported

---

* When asked in Court, in England, in 1886, "Were any of the proceedings which Mr. Bryce was instructed to take at Parihaka, authorized by the Governor?" The most explicit answer that could be obtained from Sir John Hall, (who was the head of the Ministry during the raid upon Parihaka) was –"I say I decline to answer it, yes or no." He could not of course answer effectively, unless he could have said that there had been such an "official act of the Governor." as Judge Gillies had declared essential. By declining to answer, he at least invited the conclusion that the requisite authority never existed.

† When sending to the Secretary of State these extracts from the Judge's observations, the Governor wrote that "his Honour informs me" that the report of his remarks "is substantially correct." (Blue Book. 1882. C. 3382, p. 282.)

to have said, "A stranger shall take care of us." (Blue Book, 1882, C. 3382. p. 279).

Such floundering excuses only proved the hopelessness of the ministry in defending their acts.

The Governor in a Despatch of 3rd December, 1881 (Blue Book, 1882, C. 3382, p. 267) which will repay perusal in full, told Lord Kimberley " It admits of no dispute that natives not excluding many who had borne arms against the Crown, have without molestation retained or resumed possession of much of the confiscated lands; * and that such occupation has not only been tacitly sanctioned, but has received formal recognition by the purchase of portions of the land, and the acceptance by the Crown of regular transfers from the Native owners as its proprietors. The Parihaka lands themselves (on which Te Whiti and some others who had taken no part in rebellion, have lived uninterruptedly from a period anterior to 1865) are in a portion of the confiscated territory in which all white settlement was forbidden by Government, while Natives who had left the district on account of their participation in the War, were encouraged to return to it."
. . . "If I assume with Mr. Rolleston that the natives were 'trespassing in an illegal manner' on the land, and that it had become necessary to show that the statute law of the colony must be observed, I should not the less have deprecated a resort to force. If the law has been broken, it is to the law that recourse should be had in the first instance to redress the wrong; and it is only when that has proved itself inefficient to do so that the employment of military aid is permissible." [There was reason to believe that Te Whiti sought to] " compel the institution of a prosecution on the part of the Crown against himself and other native occupants of the land. If he was indeed a trespasser on the land, liable at any moment to expulsion, it certainly appears to me that it would have been desirable that legal proceedings should have been taken against him, and the question at issue decided by the highest and most impartial tribunal before which it could be brought. Against such a proceeding nothing could be said ; but *the employment of military force, the arbitrary arrest of hundreds of persons, the confiscation of private personal property, the destruction of dwellings and cultivation, and other measures for which an Act of Indemnity may not impossibly be required,† appear to me unhappy methods of teaching that the statute law of the colony must take its course.* . . . Had I therefore been in the colony I should have experienced great difficulty in complying with a recommendation to sign a proclamation which appears to me

---

* Roughly the lands might thus be alluded to: but Sir A. Gordon had in his long-suppressed Despatch of 26th February 1881, quoted Sir F. Dillon Bell's clear declaration, that it "was untrue to say " that the land had "been confiscated. It never had been confiscated." Sir D. Bell's speech is quoted, supra, at page 88.

† Such an Act was passed in 1882. The above passage was not printed in italics in the Blue Book, but is worthy of them.

to embody an injudicious policy, to contain disputable statements, and to announce an inequitable intention." *

This Despatch was received by Lord Kimberley, on the 14th January, 1882, but, true to his undertaking to "delay publication if possible," the noble Lord kept it back from Parliament and the public.

"What (wrote Mr. Stout, 5th December, 1881) will the impartial future historian record against us as a race?"

What, the historian may add, may be the measure of hatred inspired in wrong doers by exposure of their deeds?

Soon after the discharge of Titokowaru and Rangi by Judge Gillies, the New Zealand Parliament assembled on the 18th May, 1882.

No despatches were produced with regard to the destruction of Parihaka: but the vice-regal speech proved that the worst suspicions were justified as to the intentions of the Ministry who, it was announced would produce a Bill " to render the trial of Te Whiti and Tohu unnecessary, and at the same time to prevent them from returning for the present to Parihaka."

The speech made no allusion to an Indemnity Bill, but after a few days the Ministry introduced one simultaneously with a Bill enabling them to keep Te Whiti and Tohu in prison, at a Minister's pleasure, without trial. This latter, though really a Bill of Attainder, was called a West Coast Peace Preservation Bill.

Both Bills were passed in the Lower House on June 9th, 1882; and, incredible as it may seem, it is shown by the New Zealand Hansard that even then information had been kept back from the House.

To the very last, the policy of the Ministry, if the commission of acts of violence and their concealment from public scrutiny can be dignified with the name of policy, seems to have been to prevent judicial or constitutional inquiry until it was too late to arrest wrong-doing.

On May 26th the Native Minister moved the second reading of the Attainder Bill.

On May 30th, May 31st, June 2nd, and June 9th, that Bill was discussed in the Lower House, and, together with a sweeping Indemnity Bill, was passed. The English Blue Books show that during the above period the question of producing information on the subject was deliberated upon by the Governor and his advisers. (1883. C. 3689. p.p. 59,60).

On May 31st they advised him to communicate "a portion" of the papers on West Coast Native affairs to both Houses; i.e., Sir A. Gordon's Report of February 26th, 1881, so long suppressed by Lord Kimberley in England, and by the New Zealand Government.

---

* At the risk of being thought iterative I must call attention to the fact that this despatch was received in Downing Street on January 14th, 1882, and was (faithlessly to the public, but) with sinister faithfulness to Mr. Hall and his colleagues, withheld from Parliament, and was only extorted from Lord Kimberley after his predecessor as Colonial Secretary, Sir M. Hicks-Beach, had called for its production. The date of its receipt is printed at the commencement (vide C. 3382, 1882, p. 265).

On June 8th, 1882, (by which time it must have been clear that the Lower House was ready to work the will of the Ministry without obtaining information) the Ministry withdrew their advice that papers should be produced. The Governor declined (8th June) to recall his order already given for the publication of his Report (of February 26th, 1881) to the Colonial Office, but yielded to the advice that other despatches should be kept back—notably his two despatches (both dated December 3rd, 1881), apprising Lord Kimberley of the raid upon Parihaka. (Blue Book, 1882, C. 3382, pp. 223, 265.)

In his memorandum of June 8th, the Governor observed "that there are few legislative bodies which before granting indemnity for past transactions, and adopting measures to restrict the liberty of particular individuals, would not have demanded full explanation;" and " probably few Governments which would not have hastened to anticipate such a demand by placing before Parliament the materials on which to form a judgment as to their conduct." (Blue Book, 1883. C. 3689. p. 60).

It appears from remarks made in the Upper House on June 14th, by Sir G. Whitmore, that the Governor's old despatch of February 26th, 1881, was only laid upon the table on June 13th, 1882; * and from remarks of Mr. Mantell,† on June 14th, that even then no information was vouchsafed, of a later date than July, 1881, as to communications between the Governor and the Secretary of State on the West Coast affairs. Yet, though the Indemnity Bill and the Attainder Bill were before the Council, the Premier (Whitaker, Attorney-General), when Mr. Mantell moved for more papers, opposed the motion on the ground that, "Already there have been laid on the table all the despatches, both from and to the Governor, which the Government consider at the present time can be laid upon the table without inconvenience. . . . Now I declare that it would be inconvenient for the public service that any further despatches should be produced at the present time.‡ . . ."

Thus adjured, the Council rejected Mr. Mantell's motion, and it is difficult to determine when the documents concerning the raid upon Parihaka would have been published, had it not been for the intervention of Sir M. Hicks-Beach, in England, in July, 1882.

The struggles of the New Zealand Ministers to conceal them in New Zealand, even when demanding an Act of Indemnity for what they had done, showed great hardihood, and it has been seen that Lord Kimberley had, by special request, pledged himself to delay publication " *if possible*," in England.

It must not be supposed that no protests were made in the New Zealand Parliament against the deeds done at Parihaka, and against their condonation procured by measures styled—but unworthy of the august name of—law.

Mr. De Lautour, in the debate on the Address, asked, " What was

---

* New Z. Hansard, 1882, Vol. XLI. p. 429,
† ib. p. 428.   ‡ ib. p. 429.

the necessity for open defiance of the law? And then that hypocritical clinging to the law in the very act of illegality—reading Riot Acts, and you yourselves the rioters." Peace had been kept, "not through any wise action on the part of Ministers," but by the natives in the midst of provocation.

Te Wheoro saw "no reason why the Government should have proceeded to Parihaka and broken down the native whares and rooted up their crops. I see that the Government intend to bring down a Bill to indemnify their action in having imprisoned Te Whiti and Tohu. If Te Whiti and Tohu have not been arrested legally, why not release them at once? Why should you bring down a Bill to indemnify the action of the Government for having so arrested them?"

On May 26th, without producing papers, the Native Minister moved the second reading of the Bill for attainder of Te Whiti and Tohu, under the name of a "West Coast Peace Preservation Act, 1882."

As introduced it enabled any justice of the peace to order any assembled "Maoris exceeding *twenty* in number" "to disperse;" on their failing to disperse, they were to be "deemed guilty of an offence;" any justice of the peace might sentence such offenders to "*all or any of the punishments following:*" a fine not exceeding 50*l*.; imprisonment *with or without hard labour* not exceeding twelve months; the finding of sufficient sureties for "good behaviour."

The Bill applied to the whole district between the White Cliffs and the Waitotara river, and therefore to the whole of Te Whiti's ravished lands and the Waimate Plains.

The number *twenty* was afterwards raised to *fifty*, in compliance with suggestions in the House.

On moving the second reading of the Bill, the Native Minister made the usual complaint of the wolf against the lamb, and ventured to assert that the Maoris began the war on the West Coast in 1860.

It has been shown in a previous page (20) that this assertion is at variance with the testimony of an eye-witness, Colonel Carey,* whose word could not be doubted, and who confuted the erroneous statements made in the local papers in 1860, and repeated by ignorant persons.

Without presenting any papers to the House on the subject, the Native Minister after a long statement "to justify the policy of the Government on the West Coast," added, "Te Whiti and Tohu are now arraigned on a charge of sedition. As I am advised that charge could be sustained; but it might not be; I do not know what a jury might do. . . . I have not, I hope, said one word by way of apology; at any rate, I did not mean to say one word." †

Mr. Bracken declared it "a monstrous thing" to hold the chiefs in custody at will, without trial. "Are we living in a free British colony, or under some petty local despot? Will the people of New Zealand allow any man, even though he hold the rank of Native Minister, to ride roughshod over the constitution? Will they allow

---

* Colonel Carey's book on the war was published in London, 1863, Bentley.
† This and subsequent quotations from the debate on the Bill, are taken from the New Zealand Hansard. 1882. Vol. XLI.

any man, even though he be a Minister of the Crown, to suspend trial by jury if it so pleases him?" [The Treaty of Waitangi imparted to the Maoris] "the rights and privileges of British subjects. Well, sir, if they are entitled to the rights and privileges of British subjects, they are entitled to the right of trial by jury. . . . I stand here to protest, although I may be the only one in the House who does so, against this un-English proceeding on the part of the Ministry."

Mr. Hutchison was "not at all astonished at any statement made by the Native Minister," but in his long statement there was nothing "to prove that any single overt act took place which was likely to lead to serious riot. . . . It would require a very imaginative mind to make sedition out of the words he read to us. But suppose the words were used, who heard them used? The only evidence we have is the evidence of certain native interpreters, and I take it that the reports of these native interpreters, for the last few years, have been made to order. . . . I enter my protest against this wrong being perpetrated against these Maoris, because it reverses every rule of generosity by which the strong should be guided in dealing with the weak. With the gloomy reflection that must come across the minds of many members of this House in dealing with a question of this kind, there is one ray of comfort, and that is the illustration which this native question gives us of the power of mind over matter. Here is Te Whiti, a man without a particle of literary culture or historical knowledge, and yet by the sheer force of his intellect and tenacity of purpose, by his honesty and purity, he is able not only to defy, but to a large extent to defeat' the Native Minister and the brute force which was brought to bear against him. I say defeat the Native Minister, because this Bill, bristling as it does with injustice from the preamble to the close, is an insult to every sentiment of freedom in which English men have been cradled. The very fact of its being brought in is a confession of weakness. . . . The Native Minister has no particular liking for the Maoris; but the midnight proclamation, and the hurrying to and fro in hot haste to get up certain arrangements before His Excellency the Governor could reach these shores—all these things were very curious. . . . Standing here as a representative, and speaking under a sense of responsibility, I express it as my conviction that the driving of the natives from Parihaka, the demolition of their whares, and the wanton destruction of their crops—minimized as this last has been by the Native Minister—amount to a gross outrage, to a cruel and arbitrary outrage upon justice. It is now confessed that it has been done against law. . . . There was no legal sanction for the eviction of those people, and it is now found necessary to introduce an Indemnity Bill. It was a cruel and arbitrary outrage upon justice and humanity; and not only so, but the officer who planned the whole procedure presided at it, and evidently liked his work. . . If I remember aright, he made a very great speech at Wanganui, when he was *feted* after his victory at Parihaka, and he said—I am only quoting from memory—that if a single shot had been fired, the time for for-

K

bearance would have been past. Well, what does that mean? This pah was crowded with women and children. . . . Now I venture to say—of course I shall be contradicted again—there was not very much bravery or skill required to go in among a large number of un-armed men, women, and children, when it was perfectly well known there would not be a shadow of disturbance. It was perfectly well known that there would be no risk. . . . From Manaia all the way to Parihaka every native house, friendly and unfriendly alike, was searched: . . . the first individual whose boxes were broken open was the friendly chief who gives the name to that township (Manaia). His boxes were broken open, the contents were scattered about, his money was thrown on the floor, and then they left. The whole thing was a raid of a most illegal and improper character. . . The whole business of this Parihaka raid, got up with all this parade and bravado, has been a sham from beginning to end."

Mr. De Lautour, after demonstrating that "a fraud" had been prac-tised against the Home Government as to alleged confiscation, and that Prendergast's proclamation of October 19th, 1881, presumed to annul all promises made to the West Coast natives "for the past fifteen years," said: "It is no wonder, indeed, that Te Whiti is not brought to trial, for the Government are afraid to leave the issue to our Courts. I say it is true, and the Commissioners (Sir W. Fox and Sir F. Dillon Bell) say the same, that Te Whiti was actuated by the hope of inducing some Government, he did not care which, to face the posi-tion, and share the blanket, as he called it, with him and his people. . . . Then came our Act authorizing arrest and detention without trial; and so sure as day follows night, so soon as we began that policy of wrong, retribution followed. Step by step in this quagmire of wrong-doing we are getting deeper and deeper, and now think by incarcerating two people in a gaol at Christchurch, that we can appease these people without cost, and wait till they die out, and so, in our greed for land, can obtain these lands ourselves. . . . I say, sir, that as the Legislature of this country we shall suffer shame, and stain our history, if we do any such thing without the fullest inquiry. . . . The details are legion. . . . We have gone on in a long course of wrong-doing; on every page of these Reports (Fox and Bell's) that is apparent."

Mr. Bathgate declared that the Bill was "altogether an unwarrant-able interference with the liberty of the subject. . . . I protest against the general principle of special Acts being passed to meet individual cases."

Tawhai demanded to know why "the Bill should be passed in order that Te Whiti may not be tried. . . . If he is not to be tried now, why was he taken prisoner and confined in gaol? I think this Bill is not framed that Te Whiti may not be tried, but is brought forward to cover the fault of the Government. . . . I think the Government of New Zealand have acted illegally. They should have acted according to law; but in this case they have acted apart from the law, and have now come to make their actions legal. If Te Whiti had been of the

English race you would soon have found out a means to get the Government into trouble, but as he is a native you act in quite a different manner."

Mr. Moss said "Nothing could be more unfair than the way in which the bench was filled [at Taranaki, at the committal of Te Whiti and Tohu]. I suppose it would be unparliamentary to say packed, yet that would be most decidedly the proper word. There it was distinctly proved, in spite of all the efforts to the contrary—I should like the House to bear this in mind—that up to that moment when Te Whiti stood in the Resident Magistrate's Court at Taranaki, the reserves intended to be made had never been pointed out. . . . I think for their own honour the Government should seek inquiry by a trial."

Mr. Montgomery considered "Te Whiti a man of great intellect, immense brain power, of a highly poetic temperament, a born orator, as pure and honest as any man in this colony, and without a flaw in his moral character,—a man who has used all his gifts and powers to do what he could to benefit his race. . . . I think Te Whiti ought to be tried. . . . What I find fault with is, that the Native Minister ran that road through native cultivations, where there was wheat growing, and other crops, and any number of cattle roaming about outside the fences. . . . "Think of the precedent we are establishing; and I ask where will be the liberty of the subject if we pass a law like this?"

Major Te Wheoro—he who had adhered to the Queen through evil report and good report, a chief of high lineage, a soldier repeatedly thanked by English generals—declared that Te Whiti ought to be tried by law.

For trifling offences men were entitled to trial. But this is a "far more serious matter. The Government have also brought forward an Indemnity Bill, freeing them from any wrongs they have done at Parihaka, which means that the House should say that those actions taken at Parihaka were not wrong. It is therefore clear that the steps taken there were excessive, and that this Bill is brought forward to justify them.

. . . "These thousands of troops were sent up there under arms, amidst the weak and unoffending women and children. . . . The troops then burnt their houses and rooted up their crops. When Te Whiti and Tohu were being arrested, they told the natives they were leaving behind to remain in peace during their absence, and not make any disturbance. The natives have obeyed. . . . I think Te Whiti is the best friend of the Government, although he is called a fanatic. He has told his people not to take up arms, but to leave wrath in the hands of God. If Te Whiti had told them they were to slay they would have slain. . . . The Government should be careful to act rightly, for the Treaty of Waitangi stated that they should protect the natives, and act fairly towards them. But the Government have not done so. . . . I know that they are strong enough to carry this measure, but I will vote against it."

One of the friends of the ministry, Captain Mackenzie, bluntly described the position thus:—" I think we must all admit that if the foundation of a building is laid in injustice, that building will have to stand for all time upon a basis of injustice. I think the acquisition of land by the European population in this country has been in a great measure based on injustice; but, notwithstanding that, I say it is now impossible for us to hark back. The talk of justice and law now is, in my opinion, simple bunkum. I do not see what advantage is to be gained by such talk. It simply takes up our time to no purpose."

If such were the arguments by which the Ministry was aided, can it be denied that in the page of history a balance of a different kind should be struck?

Mr. Holmes demanded that before the passing of the Bill the proclamation of October 19th, 1881 (Prendergast's), should be withdrawn. "That proclamation . . . remains in force a standing disgrace and shame to the Government; . . . we must have an assurance that that proclamation is withdrawn, not a mere promise but a Bill . . . before we pass the measure under discussion. Until that is done no honourable member will do well by his conscience, or act according to law, to truth, or to justice, if he supports a Bill which seeks to punish those whom the Government call wrong-doers, but to whom I say justice has not been, but should be, done—namely, Te Whiti and his Maoris. . . . I say that if you honourable members of this House pass this Bill before the proclamation is withdrawn, then you put into the hands of the Government a means of plundering Te Whiti and his people."

[Such a consummation as Mr. Holmes reprobated being what some persons desired, one of them immediately cried out, "Hear, hear," and the sincerity of his applause of plundering was confirmed by a subsequent speech in favour of the Bill.]

Mr. Holmes proceeded to argue against the New Zealand Settlements Act of 1863, under which the alleged confiscation of the West Coast district had been made in 1865, and of which he said, "So gross an injustice, so iniquitous a measure would never be passed by any Legislature unaffected by utter fear." (N. Z. Hansard, Vol. XLI. p. 184).

Mr. Steward, in supporting the Bill, was "sorry to say, and I say it with shame as a colonist of New Zealand and a member of this House, that in years past we have accumulated great store of broken promises, and we are now suffering the punishment which necessarily follows from the breaking of faith . . . . during a long series of years we have committed faults, and have done worse than committed faults—we have blundered in the grossest manner possible. We have blundered, and perhaps in times past we have plundered also. . . . I think it has been clearly shown to the House that Te Whiti is a remarkable man, a man almost *sui generis*. It has been shown that he is a man who wields a very extraordinary influence over the Maori mind. It has been shown that he is a man against whose personal character there is nothing to allege. It has also being shown that for years he has kept peace among his people."

On June 1st, Mr. Macandrew presented a petition from an eminent chief, Wi Parata, " on behalf of Te Whiti ; " but on June 2nd the House, at the instigation of the Native Minister refused to allow Mr. Macandrew to found a motion upon the petition.

The Native Minister declared that Mr. Macandrew's proposed motion was "really and actually an amendment " (on his Attainder Bill), and the Government would "not accept any amendment whatever on the second reading of the Bill, whether it is technical or virtual."

Thus, declining to allow information to be put before the House (as has been shown from the English Blue Book, 1883, O. 3689, p. 60), the Ministry prevented a debate which might have afforded information from other sources. (N. Z. Hansard, 1882, Vol. XLI. p. 254.)

On June 2nd, Tomoana resumed the debate on the Bill, and asked that " Te Whiti be brought to the bar of the House, and let us hear what he has to say about himself."

Mr. Turnbull spoke of the surveys conducted by the Government. "Indeed every desire appears to have been manifested to irritate the natives in every possible way. No reserves of their fisheries were made, no reserves of their places of cultivation, *no reserves of their burial grounds.* Everything that could insult and annoy the natives was done, and allowed to be done. . . . Acts of grosser cruelty were never before committed than those which were done to the Maoris with respect to their places of burial. Those places, so much endeared to them, were not secured, and nothing could be calculated to give the Maoris greater offence. In fact, the Government goaded them to rebellion. What do we find ? That these reserves were never pointed out to them, that they were never made acquainted with them ; and that is the reason of all the troubles that have since taken place. . , . The Bill asks this House, if I may judge from the language of the Native Minister in introducing it, to constitute ourselves a Court in the first place. Well, I say that is most unjust, and I object to it. We are not to have an opportunity of hearing evidence, but we are to try Te Whiti. . . . I object myself to be one of a Court to try these men unless we have before us the fullest evidence on the matter. . . . Even in the proclamation which was issued to those natives it was said, The Queen's law must run here as well elsewhere.' I want it to run elsewhere—I want it to run here. I want to see these men brought before a fair tribunal ; and if they are found guilty then it will be for mercy to step in with all its graciousness. But if they are not found guilty, then let us deal justly and fairly with them, and send them back to their homes.* It is said, 'Oh, but that will be very injurious.' But I say not. These men will have seen that there is a reverence for the law—that we have not only preached obedience to the law, but that we are obedient to it ourselves; and in minds

---

* But " homes" at Parihaka had already been demolished.

constituted as theirs are, who are lovers of justice, the most beneficial influence will be exercised."

Mr. Bracken asked the House to accede to Wi Parata's request, "That the person who is charged with such heinous crimes may be brought here, and be allowed to speak for himself. We do not want to hear only a one-sided statement. There was a time in the history of New Zealand when the Maoris, if they had chosen, could with one swoop have swept the European race from this island.* That time was the time of the Treaty of Waitangi. What did they do then? You call them savages, barbarians; but they treated us in a way that should make us blush for our conduct to them, which makes me blush, and should bring a blush to the cheeks of men who are bent upon perpetrating this wrong to a conquered race. I feel very strongly on this matter, and I appeal once more to the sense of justice of the honourable gentlemen on those benches to accede to this little request, and not allow *the finger of scorn to point for all time* at this honourable House, and this adopted country of our race."

Colonel Trimble, though he supported the Bill, said that he knew Te Whiti, and agreed "with everything that has been said in regard to the moral and intellectual qualities of Te Whiti;" whatever might be the purity of a member who had spoken, "I have not the slightest doubt that Te Whiti is just as good as he is, or as any man in this House, and in intellectual qualifications I believe that he exceeds a very large proportion of the gentlemen in this House."

But Colonel Trimble would vote for the Bill to outlaw Te Whiti. "I have heard a great deal" (he continued) "about Magna Charta and and the Bill of Rights, and all that. That may be very good; but Magna Charta and the Bill of Rights imply something more than mere privilege—they imply duty also. I say the same about this *Treaty of Waitangi, which I hope will in future be relegated to the waste-paper basket, which is about the only place it ought to be seen in,*"

Tawhai aptly demanded: "Was the capture of Te Whiti treating him like a subject of Her Majesty? I do not think that the Government have acted up to this particular provision of the treaty—that the same privileges will be conferred upon the natives as those conferred upon British subjects. Is it fair that the wrong should be committed first and legalized afterwards?"

Te Wheoro vainly implored that Te Whiti and Tohu might be "allowed to appear at the Bar of the House;" and by a large majority the House refused to delay the Bill.

The Government rejected a suggestion that the deceptive words in the preamble—*i.e.*, "that the said Te Whiti and Tohu held language calculated to promote disaffection, and which on several occasions led to breaches of the law"—should be struck out.

---

* *Vide supra*, p. 91, where Sir William Fitzherbert declared that (not only in 1840, when the Treaty of Waitangi was made, but afterwards) in 1860, during the unjust Waitara war, the same "unparalleled forbearance" was shown by the Maoris.

The Native Minister also defended the contemplated reduction of the reserve at Parihaka. The Commissioners (Sir W. Fox and Sir F. D. Bell) had recommended a reserve of 25,000 acres there. Te Whiti had elicited before the justices at New Plymouth the fact that when Mr. Hall's government surrounded the peaceful villagers at Parihaka with an armed force, no information of the intended reserve had been made to the Maoris; and the Native Minister urged in the House that "to have told the Parihaka natives that the proclamation [Prendergast's] was an idle threat, would have had a very bad effect indeed."

"It is not," he said, "the intention of the Government to allow a Bill to be passed in this House which shall give to these Maoris those reserves whether they behave themselves or not."

Te Wheoro made one more effort to offer a hearing to Te Whiti, but was defeated by forty-three votes against twenty-two, and Mr. Turnbull indignantly told the House : " I never felt in a more humiliating position than at the present moment—to think that among a body of Englishmen such a thing could possibly occur as actually to deny these men the assistance they require. . . . A greater disgrace was never perpetrated upon the people of New Zealand than at this moment, bringing all your brute force to bear upon them, and denying them that justice which is their right. I regret to say that never before in my life did I feel so much ashamed of an Act of the Legislature as now."

If such was the language of a legislator in New Zealand, could any just historian treat it with indifference?

The Government had no difficulty in passing their Indemnity Bill.

Mr. Montgomery and Te Wheoro suggested that it ought to contain provisions for compensating the natives whose property had been destroyed at Parihaka, but the Native Minister said "it would be impossible to insert such a provision in a Bill of this nature," and he "*thought the Government had not done wrong*."

There were, of course, many differences of opinion, and there was very general ignorance in men's minds even in New Zealand, as to the conduct of the Government.

The Native Minister appears to have seen nothing wrong in it.

Some persons admitted it was wrong, and yet supported it. Many neither knew nor enquired what was done.*

I say nothing here about any one who conscientiously believed that what was done at Parihaka was right.

---

* In a work published in 1883, I was careful to acquit the colonists of active complicity. I wrote (p. 107;) " The cumbering Maoris were to be destroyed. *The bulk of the colonists had no such desires*, but their humanity did not assume the form of controlling the inhumanity of others," Ib. p. 460 ; " It may be that a wider revelation of the wrongs done in the name, but not by command of the Queen, may tend to lighten the oppression which has so long been inflicted upon a race which reposed its trust in her," Not only in New Zealand but throughout Australasia, it may safely be declared that in proportion to its amount, the population has no superiors elsewhere. But in all countries, things are done which it cannot be said that the public conscience approves of: and exposure is the only process which can be resorted to, to prevent their recurrence.

But amongst the supporters of the Government, if not among its own members, there were some who admitted the wrong doing, and nevertheless abetted it. To any of them I would quote words used by Mr. Justice Lopes in an English Court in 1885 :—" I cannot forget that you are an educated man and should have known that the law cannot be broken to promote any good or supposed good, and that the sanctity of private life cannot be invaded for the furtherance of views of an individual, who, I am inclined to believe, thinks that the end sanctifies the means." *

The Indemnity Bill, like the Attainder Bill began with a glaring mis-statement.

"Whereas large numbers of aboriginal natives frequently assembled at Parihaka, in the provincial district of Taranaki, and thereby produced undue excitement, breaches of the law, and disturbance of the public peace ; and whereas with the object of preventing such meetings and preserving the peace, certain measures were adopted by the Government of New Zealand, and carried out under their authority, some of which measures may have been in excess of legal powers, and it is expedient that the persons acting therein should be indemnified. Be it therefore enacted. . . . . Every person whosoever who shall at any time before the passing of this Act have acted under the authority of the Government of New Zealand given *either before or after any act*, matter, or thing done . . . or committing to prison of any person doing or being concerned in, or *suspected of doing or being concerned in* any of the acts, matters, or things following . . . (1) . . . (2) committing any of the offences specified in the West Coast Settlement (North Island) Act, 1880. (3) *Assembling or holding meetings at Parihaka, in the provincial district of Taranaki* . . . (4) *attending any such meeting, and refusing or neglecting to disperse. &c.* (5) . . . and *any person who shall have damaged or destroyed any real or personal property*, or searched for, seized, or taken possession of . . . shall be and is hereby *freed*, acquitted, released, *indemnified* . . . against *all actions*, suits, . . . prosecutions, liabilities, and *proceedings, whatsoever*." To prevent doubt, the Governor was enabled by a special clause " to declare any act, matter, or thing done, to come within the provisions of this Act," and all courts were to take judicial cognizance of such declaration.

In the Upper House the Attorney-General did not scruple to say that " *the Government* felt that if Te Whiti and Tohu were tried and convicted reasonably the sentence would be a short one, and that if they were acquitted they would return to Parihaka. . . . In removing the trial from New Plymouth to Christchurch, one of the objects of *the Government* was to put off the trial until after the meeting of the General Assembly."

Thus the delay of justice, and its final denial, were attributed, not to any legal obstacles, but to *the policy of the Government*.

"The trial " (Whitaker said) "would not have answered our

purpose; if they were convicted the sentence would probably be short, and if they were acquitted our object would be defeated entirely. Therefore it was that their trial was put off legally; it was done according to the law—until the General Assembly had considered the matter." (N. Z. Hansard, 1882. Vol. XLI. p.p. 553-554).

Mr. Whitaker's statements are not dwelt upon in these pages in order to emphasize his responsibility for deeds done at Parihaka. His share of them appears in history. His words are only quoted here because they prove that what was done at Parihaka was acknowledged to be the *policy of the Government*, of which the Native Minister was the head and front with regard to native affairs. The Blue Books and the debates on the Bill for denying a trial to Te Whiti and Tohu, and for keeping them in prison without trial, even though the Government had suppressed all official information, established these facts : viz.. that armed men were marched into a peaceful district : that everything was done to goad the Maoris to violence ; that their lands were seized in defiance of the Governor's proclamations and Donald Mc'Leans guarantee that they might retain them in peace : that roads were taken through their cultivations ; that the Maoris were imprisoned for cultivating ; that they were never told what reserves were intended to be allotted to them, out of their hereditary lands thus ravished from them ; that their peaceful chiefs were arrested while sitting quietly and preaching patience in their village ; that women and children were deported, and families were separated with violence ; that their dwellings were pillaged ; that many of their houses were destroyed ; that their crops were rooted up ; that the Government dared not allow Te Whiti and Tohu to be tried in any court ; that under pretence of changing the venue of trial the Government moved them to a distant place, in order that time might elapse and a special Act might be passed to defraud them of any trial at all ; and that, by an arrangement with Lord Kimberley, official information was suppressed in England simultaneously with its suppression in New Zealand until the New Zealand Government had passed a special Act to enable the Government to hold arbitrarily in prison the chiefs to whom they denied a trial.

The student of history may see a remarkable difference between the fate of this Indemnity Bill, and that of a similar Bill in 1866.

In 1865 a bill " for indemnifying persons acting in the native insurrection," was sent to England, and Mr. (now Sir) E. Stafford, the Premier, sent with it a minute, stating that proceedings, commenced and threatened against persons, military and civil, necessitated the passing of the Act.

The Ministry in England did not at once advise the allowance or disallowance of the measure. There were two years within which such power might be exercised by the Crown. The Stafford Ministry passed a second Indemnity Bill in 1866.

The Secretary of State announced, in May, 1867, that the Bill of 1865 would be allowed, but that of 1866 would be disallowed :—
" First, that it was so worded as to indemnify not only civil and military

authorities and persons acting under them, or under the authority of the Government, but *all and every other person and persons whomsoever* who shall have done, or ordered, or directed any matter or thing to be done, &c. Secondly, that owing to the disjunctive form in which the 2nd and 3rd sections are drawn, the destruction of the property of a person *suspected to be concerned* in the insurrection would be covered by the Indemnity given by the Act, even though such destruction may have been wanton and reckless, and not inflicted or ordered in or about the suppressing or quelling of the insurrection. Thus if a private individual acting *under no authority* has wantonly or recklessly destroyed or ordered the destruction of the property of those *whom he may have chosen to suspect . . .* he would be protected under the terms of this Act, though such destruction in no way directly or indirectly tended to quell the insurrection, and though the person whose property was destroyed should have proved that he was in no way directly or indirectly concerned in it." *

Thus did a Secretary of State write, when the late Lord Derby was Prime Minister in England:—he who had in 1843, informed the New Zealand Company that "as long as he has the honour of serving the Crown, he will not admit that any person, or any government acting in the name of Her Majesty can contract a legal, moral, or honorary obligation to despoil others of their lawful and equitable rights."

The Bill of 1866, had morever been preceded by war—unjust no doubt, but still war—, which was erroneously styled an insurrection.

In 1881, there was neither war, nor insurrection. Te Whiti asked for nothing more than to be let alone on his native lands, the possession of which had been guaranteed to him by Proclamations, and by solemn pledges of the government through a long series of years. All that the Maori members of Parliament asked for was that the Supreme Court should be appealed to, as to titles on the West Coast.

The attack upon Te Whiti was wanton; and a Judge of the Supreme Court had, almost in terms, declared it unlawful, inasmuch as it was not preceded by the "official act of the Governor" which could alone justify any subordinate in doing the things which were done at Parihaka.

But in 1883, Mr. Gladstone was Prime Minister in England. It was true that he had said in Parliament (9th Feb. 1848) "as far as England was concerned there was not a more strictly and rigorously binding treaty in existence than that of Waitangi." But there is hardly anything which Mr. Gladstone has said at one time, which he has not contradicted at another. His colleague, Lord Kimberley, had undertaken in 1881, to "delay publication if possible," of papers already promised to Parliament, about Te Whiti, and Parliament with or without consciousness of wrong, had submitted.

---

* Whether governments usually consult their law officers with regard to Indemnity Bills, I cannot say. The Attorney General in Lord Derby's ministry in 1867, was Sir John Rolt. The Attorney General in Mr. Gladstone's ministry in 1882, was Sir Henry James.

The Indemnity Bill of 1882 was allowed to become law, without objection.

Yet it sinned against all those reasons for which the Bill of 1866 was disallowed; and all the unjust acts which it condoned were wantonly done in the invasion and desolation of a peaceful village.

In the Upper House, the Indemnity Bill was passed without difficulty, but more than one member objected to the allegations in the preamble to the Bill for denying a trial to Te Whiti and Tohu, and Mr. Mantell complained that " we have no information whatever laid on the table by the Government of what action was taken from October 19th, 1881, to April 17th, 1882, under the West Coast Settlements Act of last session. Now, it has been customary in former times to lay on the table telegrams, despatches, and reports from officers of any exciting events that occur; but during this recess nothing appears to have reached the Government which they thought worth laying on the table." (N. Z. Hansard ,1882. Vol. XLI p. 563.)

Mr. Buckley, a lawyer, asked the members "not to disgrace the Legislature by allowing themselves to pass, without a solemn protest, an Act for punishing people who cannot be punished by the present law."

Dr. Pollen, though he would vote for the Bill, said he did " not believe that to kidnap political opponents and shut them up was the best way to bring them to their right mind."

The Bill was passed by a large majority, although Sir G. Whitmore, among others, rebuked the glaring statements of the preamble.

Mr. Mantell recorded a formal protest against the Bill, " because it appears to me inconvenient, if constitutional, to pass a measure so seriously affecting the liberties of any of Her Majesty's subjects without full and complete evidence of its necessity and justice; and because *from the refusal or omission of the Government to place before this Council any official reports of those recent occurrences on the West Coast*, which are alleged to require such legislation, it can only be inferred that those occurrences have not been of a nature to justify such severe provisions as are contained in this Bill."

Captain Fraser also recorded his protest against the Bill—

" 1. As *ultra vires* of the General Assemby of New Zealand, inasmuch as it is repugnant to the English statute law, and deprives British subjects of the privileges granted them by the Habeas Corpus Acts.

" 2. It declares men guilty of sedition without trial, and *without any evidence of their guilt produced before the Parliament*.

" 3. It declares men guilty who have not been allowed to be heard in their defence before Parliament.

" 4. It will tend to create disaffection amongst the Maoris, and foment bitterness and strife amongst the colonists.

" 5. It is punishing Maoris, who, if guilty, would be punished by the judicial tribunals of the colony.

" 6. There is no reason for suspecting that if any evidence could be produced against Te Whiti and Tohu before the Supreme Court a jury would not convict them."*

Prendergast was again administrator of the Government when these protests were transmitted to England on June 28th, 1882, and he slightingly told Lord Kimberley—" Ministers to whom I have communicated these protests before forwarding them to your lordship, desire to make no observations upon them."

He enclosed a copy of the Act in his despatch of June 28th, and it was received by Lord Kimberley in August, 1882; but in the spirit of his promise to the New Zealand Ministry to delay publication of a former despatch about Te Whiti, "if possible," Lord Kimberley did not permit the publication of the Act or of the above protests in 1882, although there was in that year an autumn session. They appeared in a Blue Book in July, 1883, when Lord Derby had become Secretary of State for the Colonies. (C. 3689. 1883).

The " West Coast Peace Preservation Act, 1882," 46 Victoria, No. 5, *alias* the "Act of Attainder of Te Whiti," &c. enabled the Governor in Council to deny a trial, to hold Te Whiti and Tohu in prison, to release them, and to *re-arrest and imprison them at pleasure*, in defiance of Magna Charta, Habeas Corpus Act, or any other safe guard of the liberties of the subjects of the Queen.

Te Whiti and Tohu were accordingly with more or less restraint, kept as prisoners in the Middle Island. They were so calm in their manner that it would have been difficult to find excuse for harshness in dealing with them, and the man to whose care or custody they were confided, declared in a published journal that he only once used force to prevent them from walking whither they would, though he afterwards kept two armed men to support him.

Te Whiti and Tohu were released in March, 1883; but were still subject to arbitrary arrest under the Act 46, Victoria, No. 5, and in September, 1883, a brief " Continuance Act" renewed its provisions.

Mr. Hall, the head of the ministry under which the raid upon Parihaka was conducted in 1881, retired on 21st April 1882; and Mr. Whitaker (Attorney General in the Hall ministry) became premier, the other members of the Hall ministry retaining office.

Whitaker resigned in September 1883, and Major Atkinson who had been Treasurer in the Hall and Whitaker ministries, became premier, his other colleagues remaining with him.

In August 1884, the Atkinson Ministry was expelled from office, and after some oscillations Mr. (now Sir) Robert Stout formed (in September 1884,) a ministry which did not renew the Act relating to Te Whiti; but furnished an instructive commentary on the " Raid upon Parihaka" of 1881.

In July, 1886, Te Whiti and others were committed for trial for promoting disturbance at Hawera, on the West Coast.

In October, 1886 they were fined and imprisoned. Thus Sir R

* These protests are printed in the Blue Book, 1883. C. 3689. p.p. 8. 9.

Stout vindicated the soundness of his opinion that the ordinary law only should be availed of. If it be said that the necessity to prosecute Te Whiti in 1886 shows that he was of an unruly nature, let it also be remembered that between 1881 and 1886, he had been unlawfully seized and imprisoned: that his house and his church had been destroyed, his fields had been laid waste, and given to strangers. "Surely oppression maketh a wise man mad." So long ago as 1880, when armed men were sent into the district by the Native Minister, Te Whiti said "I want not war; but they do. The flashes of their guns have singed our eyelashes, and yet they say they do not want war. . . What say they of me? That I am a fanatic, a fool, and a madman. " But I am none of these things. The land is yours; but that which I have lately seen—the armed swarm which has been poured upon it—is enough to distract my brain."*

On one subject members of the New Zealand Parliament groaned on behalf of their Maori friends.

Throughout the New Zealand wars, which ended in 1865, the English troops were aided by friendly chiefs, who clung to the belief that the pledges of the Queen would be fulfilled, and that it was proper to aid in asserting the supremacy of the Crown, trusting to the honour of its Governors and servants.

Sir George Grey had in early years adopted the principle of contributing to the importance of chiefs who possessed no money but had hereditary claims on large tribal lands; and, when the wars were at an end, many Maori allies received pensions to which the faith of the Colony was pledged.

The subsequent up-risings of The Kooti and Titokowaru were in no sense Maori wars. The savage natures of both of them were provoked by misconduct of the Government or of its officers, and both of them were eventually crushed by the Maori chiefs, Rangihiwinui, Topia Turoa, Ropata Wahawaha and others, rather than by European forces.

Swords of honour were sent to the Chiefs as presents from the Queen, and pensions were awarded in some instances.

After Donald McLean became Native Minister there was no danger of war, or even of serious tumult or violence in New Zealand.

Te Kooti had taken refuge in the territory of Tawhiao, the so called Maori King, but McLean had established friendly relations with Tawhiao, and the runaway was harmless.

---

* The wild and mystic language of Te Whiti excited various feelings. His prophetic pretensions were accepted almost universally among his people- How he maintained his reputation was shown by Mr. Sheehan in 1882.—A Maori complained in open meeting that a promise to raise the dead had not been performed by Te Whiti, who retorted, "Do you not remember that I promised to do so if for twelve months you were all sober, temperate, pure and chaste in your lives?" "Yes." "Have you been so?" "No." "Then, do you think I would disgrace your ancestors by bringing them back to a people like this?" [N. Z. Hansard, Vol. XLI. p. 143.]

The colonists who remembered Te Kooti's ferocious raids on the East Coast in 1868-9, and the reward, of £1000 for his body dead or alive, offered by Mr. Stafford and his friends, were not well-pleased at Te Kooti's impunity, but while he was out of sight he was not much spoken of. Early in 1883 his name was on many tongues.

An Amnesty Bill, often asked for in former years was passed in 1882. Mr. Scotland in the Upper House, while supporting the Bill, thought it undesirable that "Te Kooti and Purukutu should be allowed to come amongst us, and perhaps be met by Government officials, and have their hands shaken by those officials."*

The honourable member was prophetic.

An English Blue Book (1883, C. 3689, p. 67) contains an account of a meeting (12th February, 1883) between Te Kooti and the Native Minister. The latter furnished the account for the Governor's information. "Te Kooti shaking hands with Mr. Bryce said, "Mercy and truth have met together; righteousness and peace have kissed each other," &c.

Which virtue was embodied in Te Kooti and which in the Minister the enigmatic Maori did not say. There was food, and then conversation, at the end of which "Mr. Bryce (ib. p. 68) walked over and shook hands with Te Kooti. After a lapse of a few minutes, Te Kooti rose and sang a waiata (song) and said, as everything is now settled, I will come and shake hands with you. He then advanced and shook hands with the party. . ."

Writing on the 13th February to the Governor, the Native Minister said "I think the result must be considered satisfactory." (ib. p.

It was not considered satisfactory by some Colonists.

When the Parliament met afterwards, Mr. Montgomery said—"We can extend a free pardon to Te Kooti, the man of blood, the man guilty of the vilest atrocities. We can shake hands with him. Here is a man of peace—Te Whiti—and we are asked to extend the law by which this man can be arrested at a moment's notice, not for any new offence, but simply at the will of the Minister of the day. I say it is an outrage upon humanity.†"

The relations between the Minister and Te Kooti were not in themselves perhaps deserving of remark, and I shall not comment upon them; but they assist to explain the debate which took place with regard to the stoppage by the former of pensions of the chiefs who had aided the colonists in the field.

---

* N. Z. Hansard, 1882. Vol. 43. p. 914. "As I have no personal knowledge of Mr. Scotland it is grateful to me to notice that in 1883, he said in Parliament, "From what I have heard of Mr. Rusden I believe him to be a good Christian and a gentleman, and I do not think he would put anything on paper respecting this Colony that he did not think was true. He may have been led into errors, and a great many historians have been. It would have been easy for him to write a popular book by praising up the country, right or wrong, but he was too honest." N. Z. Hansard, 1883, Vol. 46, p. 481.

† N. Z. Hansard, 1883, Vol. 46, p. 158.

The extent of these stoppages was described in the Legislative Council * by one of his own colleagues.

His statement was made when Sir G. Whitmore brought before the Upper House the treatment of Ropata Wahawaha by the Government. Sir G. Whitmore† said that in the war of 1865 " no officer of European troops, and no native chief was more distinguished than Ropata Wahawaha; who from that time until 1873 had been the unflinching ally of the Europeans, and a hard-working officer of the native corps on the (East) coast.

" There had been a great many instances in which that chief had shown personal devotion and courage of the highest order; and at the time of the massacre at Poverty Bay (by Te Kooti) the whole of the inhabitants of the district might be said to have looked upon Ropata Wahawaha as their protector and their shield. . . It was upon his (Sir G. Whitmore's) recommendation that Ropata was made a major of the Militia, and obtained the honour of the New Zealand Cross. . . Ropata was employed in driving the rebels out of the Uriwera Mountains under the most terrible extremes of cold and privation, passing through hardships and difficulties which he (Sir G. Whitmore) did not believe Europeans could have surmounted; until at last he stamped out the embers of rebellion, and drove Te Kooti from the Uriwera Mountains to the asylum (Tawhiao's territory) in which he had since remained, . . It was thought right by that Native Minister, who most relied on and employed his services —the late Sir Donald McLean—to show the people that the country considered these services entitled him to a sufficient pension to enable him to keep up a high position. It was therefore decided to give him £300 per annum. (The Government had interfered with the allowance thus made.) All classes of Europeans and natives had held meetings, and a very strong feeling was displayed on this subject The chief had spoken to him (Sir G. Whitmore). He said, " Ah ! I am now useless, and I suppose I am not worth any further thought; and so I have my pension taken away; while the enemy of public order (Te Kooti), whom I was employed specially to keep down, has had a property purchased for him, and perhaps the money taken from me is devoted to that purpose.' "

Sir G. Whitmore, endeavouring " to see that faith was kept with the Maori people," moved for " all papers in connection with: (1) the reduction of the pension or salary of the Chief Major Ropata Wahawaha, N. Z. C., from £300 to £100 per annum; (2) all papers connected with the purchase of a farm or block of land for the recently pardoned outlaw Te Kooti."

A member of the Government (Mr. Oliver) in a lame defence of the treatment of Ropata, said, " Since my colleague the Hon. Minister for Native Affairs has been in office, he has stopped absolutely no less than seventy-four of these so-called pensions, and has reduced no less than fifty others."

---

* N. Z. Hansard, 1883. Vol. 47. p. 10. † ib. p. 8.

The Hon. Wi Tako Ngatata supported Sir G. Whitmore's motion. "He thought it was not fair to reduce the reward after the time had passed when the assistance was given for which the reward was given. And why, also, had they honoured Te Kooti, who murdered the children of both Europeans and Maoris?"

The Hon. Mr. Waterhouse declared that when he read that these allowances were to be withdrawn, "he was free to confess that it had sent through his system a thrill of indignation and grief. . . he had not heard this subject referred to by any one, whether a friend or foe to the Government, who had not spoken of it in terms of indignation and grief."

The Hon. Captain Fraser said that "if Sir E. Stafford had been now Premier, he (Captain Fraser) could imagine with what scorn he would have heard any proposal to commit an act of injustice to a man who, in the hour of utmost need, came forward to save women and children from the ruthless murderer, Te Kooti. (Sir Donald McLean had introduced to him, Captain Fraser) "Ropata as one of the greatest soldiers in the colony. He was a man whom the Queen had delighted to honour; he had been given a sword of honour and the Cross, which in any other country would have carried a pension with it, as was the case with the Legion of Honour. He was afraid that the granting of a reward to the ruthless murderer Te Kooti, and acting as they were now doing to the man who had driven him into his lairs in the Uriwera country, would add another dark chapter to . . . (the) History of New Zealand."

The Hon. Colonel Brett declared "that the Government had broken faith with an old, distinguished, and gallant officer. If this occurred in India, we should lose the country. . . Major Ropata wore the the distinguished honour of the New Zealand Cross; and were they to sit quietly and calmly, and listen when the honourable gentlemen on the Government benches said they had robbed him of a certain sum of money, and had robbed seventy others similarly? Were they quietly to submit to this injustice."

Sir George Whitmore's motion was carried.*

In the House of Representatives Sir G. Grey alluded to Ropata thus :—

"What has become of the allowance made to a chief on the East Coast? Is it fair that without any accusation being made against the chief, without there being some tribunal to hear what cause there is for taking his pension from him, one individual should have the power by his mere writing to strip a man at once of a pension of that kind? Who is more worthy of respect, the man who does that, or the chief who says, 'You may take away my pension; you may ruin

---

* The Ministry which thus dealt with pensions encountered an adverse vote on June 12th, 1884, and a general election took place. Under an administration of which Mr. Stout became the head, and in which Mr. Ballance was Native Minister, Ropata's pension was restored, with arrears. Mr. Ballance read a statement to that effect to the House. The statement showed also that the sum appropriated by the Atkinson Ministry for purchase of "land for Te Kooti" was £600.

me ; but there is one thing you cannot do, you cannot make me disloyal ' ? Which is the greater man of the two ? I say the native who can make an answer of that kind, and can act in that manner, is infinitely the greater person, and the one that we should most admire." (N.Z. Hansard, 1884. Vol. XLVII., p. 121).

The various deprivations of emolument to which Maori pensioners were subjected by the "policy" of the Ministry were noticed from time to time in the newspapers.

No thoughtful traveller acquainted with the traditions of the Maoris, their ancestral cult, their veneration for the bones of the dead, and the seclusion in which Maori manners demanded that those hallowed relics should be preserved, can have stood near one of the ancient burial-grounds and seen without compunction those relics scattered in fragments on the earth.

To a Maori of old time such a sight would have stirred the feelings by which an Englishman or a Roman might be moved if Westminster Abbey or St. Peters were rent and rifled, and the ashes of the dead were sprinkled like dust over the spot where they once rested in the odour of sanctity.

In many cases, so numerous were the burial places of the tribes, it would have been impossible for the march of what is called civilization to take place without inflicting pain upon the inheritors of the soil.

Many excellent public men in the colony always strove to respect the feelings of the remnants of the tribes : and by Bishop Selwyn, Chief Justice Martin, and others, efforts were made to lighten inevitable blows, and to avert sufferings which were not unavoidable.

When land was acquired by the Crown, it was usual in early days to guard against the desecration of burial grounds.

Independently of sentimental considerations, there were difficulties in clearing up questions of title, interlaced as they were between families and sometimes with tribes

Bill after Bill was passed upon the subject after its treatment devolved upon the New Zealand legislature, and doubtless in most cases their framers were actuated by a sense of justice.

It was when a coveted possession assumed so concrete a form as the Maori Reserve at Prince's Street, Dunedin, that the moral natures of some persons could not bear the burden which justice to the Maoris would have imposed.

Prominent among those who never veiled their eyes from the light of justice was the good Chief Justice, Sir William Martin. Whether frowned on by Lord Grey in 1847, or reviled by Governor Browne's advisers in 1860,—in office or out of office,—his advice was always ready when sought for, though it had been rejected with such contumely on the occasion of the Waitara war.

L

As lately as in 1871, Donald McLean consulted Sir William (who had retired from office) as to the terms of a Bill to amend the existing Land law.

Sir W. Martin received "the best thanks of the Government for the arduous labour" undertaken, but the reward which would have been most grateful—the adoption of his proposals,—was not accorded.

To describe fully the various Native Land Acts would require a treatise. A few facts may be stated. One of the Acts (1862) waived (so far as it could) the pre-emptive right which under the Treaty of Waitangi was reserved for the Crown, and there was much conflict of opinion as to the wisdom of this step. Its validity was questioned by those who deemed that the Treaty could not in such a manner be tampered with. All the Acts contemplated proof of Maori ownership, when blocks of land were submitted to the Court to ascertain the titles.

The joint tribal title, and intricate interests derived from descent and marriage, unfortunately induced the legislature to strive to cut the Gordian knot by a proviso (1865) that "no certificate of title should be ordered to more than ten persons:" but there was no care taken that those ten persons should be trustees in a proper sense for the many scores, perhaps hundreds of persons who had interest in the land. The consequences might easily be foreseen.

An objectionable provision in one act enabled a single native to call upon the Court to deal with a claim to land, although the vast majority of the tribe were opposed to its being brought before the Court. It would be tedious to dwell on the various Acts, in 1867, 1873, 1880, 1882, 1883, and other years.

Two instances of hardships suffered will be given in these pages; but some prefatory quotations may be made from speeches in the New Zealand Parliament on the Acts, and on the manner in which they were administered.

A high official, Colonel Haultain, furnished a Report to the effect that, from the date of surrender by the Crown of exclusive power as to the sale of land, certificates or Crown Grants, up to the end of 1870, had been issued for 2,400,000 acres in the North Island. He added, "The Maoris have always been loth to part with their fertile land, and it is *chiefly by confiscation* that we have obtained any large tracts of really good land."

Moreover, the Acts were not translated for the information of the Maoris, and a Native Assessor (in the Land Court) testified that the "natives would gladly read the Acts if they could get them, and there are intelligent men amongst them, well able to explain the Acts to others." He, like other unsophisticated Maoris, objected to the enormous law-charges, and would banish lawyers from the Court, as "it was to be expected that they would prolong cases in order to get more fees."

Donald McLean confessed in Parliament in 1871 that, in a matter affecting tribal rights, the natives ought to have been made acquainted with the law in their own language, and that they had been left unacquainted.

On one point Sir William Martin, Mr. Fenton the Chief Judge in the Court, and Mr. Sewell the Minister of Justice concurred in 1871, viz., that in order to prevent the sanctioned mischief created by facilities given to an individual to plunge his tribe into litigation without their consent, it was essential to provide that there should be a thorough investigation before any title could be brought under the operation of the Court.

Dr. Pollen,* said in the Upper House in 1863, "I was present when the Treaty of Waitangi was proposed, and an attentive and anxious listener to all that passed. I heard Her Majesty's representative arguing, explaining, promising to the natives, pledging the faith of the Queen and of the British people to the due observance of it ; giving upon the honour of an English gentleman the broadest interpretation of the words in which the Treaty was couched. . . . The ink was scarcely dry on the Treaty before the suspicions which had been temporarily allayed by the promises of the Governor were awakened with redoubled force, and I need scarcely remind the Council that from that time (1840) to this, *every action of ours affecting the natives* had presented itself to their eyes, and had been capable of that interpretation, as showing that *our object and business* in this Colony was to obtain possession of the lands of the natives, *recte si possimus, si non quocunque modo.* Before we talked of the duties of the natives to us in this Colony, we ought to be able to show that some of the duties which the Crown undertook to discharge to the native people have been so discharged. I ask any one to point out on the statutes of this Colony, *or on the records of Native administration,* any of those measures which might fairly be said to have fulfilled *those obligations* which devolved upon the Crown at that time." . . . (N.Z. Hansard, 1863, p. 872).

In 1873 Dr. Pollen was the Ministerial leader in the Legislative Council; and Mr. Mantell, who had carried a resolution in 1872 that all Bills affecting the Maoris should be translated for their information moved for a Return of the Bills so translated. Dr. Pollen confessed that the Return would be *nil*, and his confession was confirmed by the Return.

Nor was this all. Wi Tako Ngatata told the Council in 1873, "It is thirty years since the European came here, and there is this difference between him and the Maori, that it was the European who had the desire to rob the native:" and Dr. Pollen said "I have, myself, seen natives hovering about the streets of Auckland, who owned an estate of 30,000 acres, against which there was a surveyors charge of some £150 or £200, and I have known that estate sold for one shilling an acre *to pay the surveyors.* The unfortunate proprietors left the town without a sixpence in their pockets feeling that their estate had been *unjustly and ruthlessly sacrificed.*" (N.Z. Hansard, 1873. Vol. XV., p. 1378).

---

* Dr. Pollen has held high office in New Zealand. Long a member of the Upper House, he has frequently been a member of ministries,—and was Prime Minister in 1875.

To prove how Maoris had been made "victims of licensed interpreters, land-sharks and lawyers," Dr. Pollen cited a case of a large block of land batween Napier and Taupo. "That land (he said) was let, or purpoited to be let, by the native owners—for what, did the Council think ?—£18 a year ! 48000 acres for £18 a year ! In the document which purported to be the lease, there was a covenant inserted to the effect that at the termination of the lease the natives should pay to the lessee compensation for every kind of improvement he might have effected upon it during the term of the lease. What did that mean but absolute confiscation of the land? But there was more to be said about this particular transaction. The clause which he had just referred to in the deed was ruled over with a black pigment of some kind as if it were meant to be an erasure. There was not the usual memorandum in the margin, showing that the erasure had been effected at the time the deed was signed; there was nothing to show when or how it was done. The whole affair seemed very remarkable. It struck him that the colour of the ink was unusual, and he took the document into a survey office, and having asked one of the draftsmen what was the character of the ink, he took a sponge and showed that it was quite possible to wipe out the erasure by simply washing it over. That *came within his knowledge in his capacity* as Commissioner. It was an extreme case, but it illustrated the system of fraud *under the authority of the law the natives had been subjected to for years.*" (ib. p. 1379).

Maoris petitioned in the same year (1873) against a proposed Land Bill— "We have suffered from mortgages, from sales of land, and spirituous liquors ; . . . we trust you will permit our land to abide with us, for such was the Queen's promise at the Treaty of Waitangi in 1840. The same promise was renewed by Governor Browne. Friend, Mr. Speaker . . . the Queen has certainly no desire to see her Maori people, her New Zealand subjects, live without estate. Should you nevertheless sanction these laws, then our very existence will be crucified. . ."

Henare Matua and his friends on the East Coast were no doubt right in saying that the Queen had no desire that they should be robbed.

That they *were* robbed Dr. Pollen conclusively proved; and no denials, whether on oath or in the large license of public speaking, can shake the testimony of such a witness.

It may be urged that Dr. Pollen spoke in 1873 ; and that, though the acts he exposed were possible then, matters afterwards improved.

Mr. Swanson, however, spoke thus in 1881 in the House of Representatives, "I appeal to every member of the Public Petitions Committee if we had not a case before us this week in which a man was given a bribe to rob and swindle the Maoris, and we actually recommended that it should be paid. . . I am ashamed at the grasping desire shown to get possession of the land which still belongs to the natives. Talk about equal rights ! The Maoris are taxed enough, fleeced enough, and robbed enough."* Did anyone impugn Mr. Swanson's authority? By no means. On the contrary, the Premier, Mr. (now Sir) John Hall, replied that there was "no man better qualified to speak upon the Maori representation question than his honourable friend" Mr. Swanson.

Wrong doings which cause groans among Maoris may therefore be vehemently, and with impunity, denounced in New Zealand; but if a public writer denounces them in England, Hall and his congeners are indignant.

In 1877, three thousand Maoris petitioned against a Land Bill of which Mr. Whitaker, the Attorney-General, said "the object should be, not only to have the surplus land dealt with, but to put the whole under a Crown title, whether retained by the natives or not, because it is of the greatest importance that the native title should be extinguished as speedily as possible."

Mr. Whitaker groaned—not for the Maoris but—over the difficulties which obstructed European speculators: "By the time the purchaser gets perhaps the signatures of twenty, some of the other owners may die. The consequence is that the purchaser has to go to the Native Land Court and get successors appointed. By the time these successors are appointed, other natives will be dead. All this renders the land in point of fact inalienable."

Living or dying the Maori was a stumbling-block to some persons, and sensitive minds must deeply commiserate the woe of so important a functionary,† if when the echoes of Maori groans become faint and few, the page of history should record that they were once loud and multitudinous.

Transactions on the East Coast, which it was difficult to hush up, caused the appointment of a Commission in 1873.

---

* N. Z. Hansard, 1881. Vol. XL. pp. 359, 361.

† Mr. Whitaker had a special trouble about a land-claim, and complained that he was "badly treated" in the matter of a Piako Land Exchange Bill. A Select Committee investigated the case which arose with regard to claims for many thousand acres dating from an alleged purchase of land in 1839 (not by Mr. Whitaker, but by an antecessor) before the Colony was founded. The alleged purchase was not recognized, and was, in fact, done away with by Sir G. Gipps, who limited to 2,560 acres the claims which the Government would consent to sanction, founded as all such claims were upon unauthorized and unlawful transactions. The case is not deserving of lengthy comment: but one item of Mr. Whitaker's claims put before a Select Committee in 1877, is grotesque:—

Date, Nov. 15th, 1854: Purchaser (original) Abercrombie. Acres, 5000. Price, £2000· Date to June, 1876—21 years, 199 days.
Simple interest at 10 per cent £6,309 0s. 10d.
Compound interest at 10 per cent £15,609 7s. 10d.

I presume that if the Maori inheritors of the land ever saw this claim they uttered groans, but I have no information on the subject. They justified their reluctance to quit their birth-place, by alleging that "their ancestors and chiefs of the tribe were buried there, and they did not wish to give it up." It may be added that the wide claims which were extinguished or reduced by Sir G. Gipps, included more acres than there were in the island.

Mr. C. W. Richmond, a judge of the Supreme Court; Mr. F. Maning, a judge of the Native Land Court; and two Maori Assessors, officiated. Maori Assessors had no voice in deciding, but they could ask questions. Their crippled position was the subject of constant complaint and of petitions from their countrymen.

It was urged that their presence might be held to imply approval of decisions from which, nevertheless they dissented to the uttermost. Some went so far as to say that they ought to have a potential voice in matters which they understood better than their colleagues.

The proceedings of the Commission occupied 256 pages in a New Zealand Parliamentary Paper.

Fraud and illegality of various kinds, secret gifts to procure signatures, deceptive doings by interpreters, appropriation of part of the alleged "purchase-money to pay off old scores for spirits," were blots brought forward by the Maori counsel.

As it was a distinct breach of the law to apply the money to pay debts for spirits, Judge Richmond's ruling on the point may be mentioned at once as a notable cause for grief amongst all temperate Maoris, who neither indulged in intoxicating liquors, nor desired to see the heritage of their countrymen squandered by traffickers in vice, of whichsoever race.

Judge Richmond said :—"Whatever the law may say on the matter, it appeared to us (not including the Maori assessor who protested) that it would be unconscientious on the part of a native who had received *value in this shape* to attempt to rip up the transaction. At all events, that the law allows repudiation, cannot make repudiation honourable or right. On this ground we determined that the native vendor was *in foro conscientiæ* debarred from this objection. . . . That a breach of law should be remunerated by allowing one of the offenders to break a contract is an anomaly with which it is to be hoped that the native people will not be allowed to make practical acquaintance, as it would tend doubly to weaken their still feeble sense of legal and moral obligation.

It would make the matter worse that to the Maori should belong *all the pleasure and the profit* while on the Pakeha would fall the whole penalty of wrong-doing. No worse lesson could be given to a people who have yet to learn that they must themselves bear the burden of their own follies and misdeeds."

If the object of counsel for the Maoris had been to enable a Maori drunkard to recover land obtained from him in his own right, because the transaction was absolutely unlawful, Judge Richmond's contention even if irregular, would be intelligible.

But this was a case in which ten Maori owners had been registered by the Land Court. They were not personally owners, but were trustees for the tribe; for the old and for the young, for the sick and the needy.

The corrupt debaucher knew better than the drunken debauchee that the payment in spirits was unlawful.

The innocent owners had no share in the breach of law : they had none of what the Judge called "the pleasure and the profit : " but by vilipending the law (and creating a forum which ought to be set up in Maori conscience) he gave the profit to the briber. Resolute against a decision which might weaken the moral sense of a drunken Maori trustee, he gave legal effect to his unlawful acts, and in so doing rewarded the unlawful and immoral act of the debauching and corrupt Pakeha. To him the Judge awarded the profit of the debauch. From the widow and the orphan that award may have torn the means of living.

The Maori assessor, Hikairo, protested that the ten grantees were only " chosen as trustees," and that they were not to sell. He complained that the alleged purchase bore fraud upon its face. The evidence showed that undue pressure had been brought to bear on the trustees, " sometimes on the roads, sometimes in public-houses, sometimes in bed-rooms, sometimes upon the sick. I do not think this was a proper way of making a sale of land."

Hikairo protested in vain.

On another point,—the receipt of special sums from the buyers (irrespective of their authorized fees) by the interpreters.—the Judge seemed to agree that Hikairo's objections were reasonable ; but in the Heretaunga case the objection was not allowed, although the Judge said that the double functions assumed by the interpreters would have " strongly affected his mind " if he had doubted whether the sellers knew what they were doing. What would have been the result of his "mind being affected," did not appear.

The evidence taken by the Commission was voluminous. One trustee was persuaded, without consulting his co-trustees, to assign his interest to a butcher who was to assign it to a lessee. Originally there had been an invalid lease of the land for twenty-one years, but this was afterwards converted into a valid one and devices were then resorted to in order to induce the trustees to sell the freehold.

One witness (a well known public man, and a member of Parliament at various periods) was asked whether an after-payment given to one Maori was understood to be a secret matter. He replied, "No. My understanding was that we had to pay a bribe to secure his co-operation, and the simple question in my mind, was whether it was worth doing so or not."

Another witness (afterwards a member of the New Zealand Parliament) was asked if he paid away a sum shortly after an arrangement about Pahoro's and Paramena's claims. He answered—"£250 for a steam-threshing machine. I suspect it had been bought previously with Paramena's money." Then (said counsel) he had the satisfaction of paying for it twice over.

" *I believe so* " responded the witness. *

Why did you retain Pahoro's money instead of paying it over ?

---

* The proceedings were published in a bulky pamphlet—"Hawke's Bay Native Lands Alienation Commission, Napier 1873.

" He has never asked for it. . . There is a small balance of £40 or £50 still."

Is he aware of this ? "I believe he is—as much a man can be aware who is almost constantly drunk."

One of the trustees deposed that to escape the importunity of a lessee and an interpreter, he hid himself in a willow-tree one day, and in a loft on another day, so as to avoid giving his signature ; but that finding others were signing he also submitted and signed, and was afterwards told that the promised £1,000 to which he became entitled was swallowed up in paying his previous debts.

One wonders who might be described as having *the pleasure and the profit* in this case. The man's debts were incurred without regard to the Heretaunga land. He purported to convey the interest of others, women and children, in that land.

It is to be hoped that the " sense of legal and moral obligation " in the minds of those who obtained his signature was not weakened by the decision of the Commission.

Mr. Sheehan was counsel for members of the tribe who disputed the validity of the transaction which deprived them of the Heretaunga block.

He said, in Parliament, in 1877, that a Maori girl, eight years old, was induced to "sign a deed of mortage to secure payment of certain sums of money " and that an interpreter endorsed the deed with a " solemn declaration that he had explained the deed, and that the child fully understood it. " This, he added, " is one of scores, absolute scores" of the Hawkes Bay Transactions.

When light was poured upon some of them, the alarmed purchasers strove to effect private compositions ; and it was alleged that in one case where the original purchase had been secretly arranged for £2000, a further sum of £17,500 was paid to "quiet" the title.

The Hawkes Bay transaction may serve as a sample of the manner in which families, *hapus* (or sub-tribes,) and even tribes, saw their birth-places wrested from them and their burial places desecrated, in spite of the solemn guarantee of the Treaty of Waitangi which was so often appealed to in vain.

It must not be supposed that the bulk of the colonists approved or even knew of the arts of which the Maoris were victims. The plotters would not have worked secretly if they had not in some degree dreaded exposure.

In a debate in the New Zealand Parliament (on 6th July, 1886) Sir Robert Stout, Attorney-General and Prime Minister of the Colony, alluded thus to the Hawkes' Bay transactions, which included the Heretaunga affair.

" We are to have in this country all the jobbery and disgrace which has disgraced New Zealand in the purchase of native land in the past. Let honourable members read the report of the Commission which sat at Hawkes' Bay, if they want to know what has been done in the past. It will be a disgrace to some settlers for some years to come, the way in which the Maoris have been treated in respect of their lands. (An hon. Member, No.) Does the honourable Member want me to say how the Maoris have been made drunk and made to sign deeds, *how infants' names have been forged* to deeds, and how men have been lodged in gaol because of the forgeries ? If the honourable Member wishes me to go into that, I will give the whole facts. I know them; I know what has been proved in the Courts; I know what has been proved before Commissions. I say these cases will be a lasting digrace in the history of the Colony for years to come."

Nor is this weighty statement unsupported by admissions of those politically opposed to Sir Robert Stout.

Mr. Bryce, when Native Minister in 1880, spoke thus on the second reading of a Native Land Sales Bill * for which he was responsible.

Its provisions proved the grasp of the Government over the Native Land Court.

The Act of 1865 had accorded to the Judges a tenure during good behaviour. The Act of 1873 had substituted a tenure during pleasure; or, practically, at the will of the Native Minister. The subjection of the judicial office to the precarious behests of the Executive Government it was proposed to continue; and when the singular function exercised by Mr. Hall at Christchurch in 1868, with regard to the Ngaitahu Deed is remembered, it must be admitted that a Member of the Cabinet might largely control the operations of the Court.

Mr. Bryce declared that the policy of the Colony had "been a very crooked one;" that in 1871 "there commenced a course of conduct on the part of agents both of the Crown and private individuals, which I think has done more to demoralize and degrade the Maori race than all our efforts at colonization can ever redeem;" that he "despaired of being able to make the House understand *the terrible iniquity of the system* which had been in vogue during the last few years;" that "however great the iniquity in which we, as Colonists, have been guilty, we have not succeeded in attaining the † desired end, we have not gained the reward of our iniquity;" that "the natives, *as a rule, do not get the goods that are charged against them;*" that (a Public Auditor had reported "that in *innumerable instances* monies charged as paid to natives were paid in fact to storekeepers for goods supplied" to Europeans, and "in some cases *large sums were charged to natives who never had goods at all;*") and that he hoped his Bill would "relieve the Government from the *miserable necessity* of becoming hucksters, *and being always ready, as it were, to take advantage of the necessities of the Maoris.*"‡

Mr. Bryce is one of those who has voted against the maintenance of the New Zealand Hansard; but for historical purposes it is well that a record of such speeches is preserved.

---

* N.Z. Hansard, 1880. Vol. XXXV., pp. 267-271.

† If Mr. Bryce was correct, the Government had not been so fortunate as the practitioners who broke the law at Heretaunga, and were nevertheless enabled by the Heretaunga Commission to reap the coveted crop of their labours.

‡ N.Z. Hansard, 1880. Vol. XXXV., pp. 267. *et seq.*

Before the debate was resumed, the Maori Prisoners Bill of 1880, already described in these pages, was passed.

When the Land Bill was again discussed, Te Wheoro complained that it guarded against none of the evils of the past, but seemed " to tie the hands and feet of the Maoris so that the Pakehas might take their lands from them." The nominal purchase-money would be dissipated. " Part will be taken to pay the surveyors; fees of Court, and costs ordered by the Court, will have to be paid; also expenses of advertising and duties payable to Her Majesty; also an amount to the receiver of land-revenue, and five acres in every hundred; also the sum to be paid for the Crown grant, and an amount for roads; also fees of lawyers and interpreters.

" l believe that these amounts, when added together, would amount to more than the £100 from which they have to be deducted. What would fifty owners of a patch of land, sold for £100, get in return for their land?

" This reminds me of an ancient Maori proverb, ' He with the dishevelled hair shall have nothing, while he with the fine head-dress will take all;' which I interpret thus, the host who is at home gets nothing, he fasts while the guest has all the food.

"Observe that the land taken for road purposes is not taken to make roads through native lands, but through lands which have been sold and which have gone to Europeans. These deductions are made to form roads on lands in the hands of Europeans. Now, do you believe that Europeans would submit to a law of this sort? I think not. I believe that if you were to pass a Bill affecting thus the lands of Europeans, that would be the day when a host would come into the House as Oliver Cromwell did into the Parliament of England."

Other Maori Members spoke, and Sir William Fox said: "I must congratulate the House upon the able manner in which the Native Members have upon this occasion addressed us. It is very gratifying to hear so much intelligence exhibited, and so much study and reading displayed." (N.Z. Hansard, 1880. Vol. XXXVI. p. 380).

Mr. Reader Wood moved a resolution to give to the Maoris some power in dealing with their lands. " I ask (he said) whether a native of New Zealand is not, in every attribute that becomes a man, equal to the European who has come into these islands, with the single exception, of course, of acquired knowledge, and of that wretched varnish which has been called civilization? Taking man for man, I ask whether the native is not equal to the European?"

Mr. Hall, the Premier, vehemently supported the Bill, but it did not emerge from Committee.

The Session, however, was by no means barren of results oppressive to Maoris, as the Ministry obtained on the 23rd July, 1880, the Act (No. 4) to " provide for further detention " of Maoris in prison without trial; on the 6th August, 1880, the Act (No. 6) authorizing similar " detention;" and 1st September, 1880, the Act (No. 39) called the " West Coast Settlement " Act, creating new offences, and setting all British safeguards of liberty at nought. These preliminaries to the Raid upon Parihaka have already been described.

Friendly expressions of sympathy uttered by Mr. Scotland, a Member of the Upper House, may be quoted here. He knew well the district of Taranaki. He asserted that there were grievances there. "A neighbour of mine, an excellent native, who never was in rebellion, who has never even visited Parihaka, a cousin of the honourable Mr. Ngatata, who can corroborate what I say, *has been despoiled* of everything he had, has lost 4,000 acres of land—*lost the property of his father and the property of his mother.* He ought to be able to live in as much comfort as I live in, and perhaps more, and it pains me to see the good-natured fellow going along the road, driving his cart of firewood into town for sale."*

Thus could Mr. Scotland groan for his fellow-men. In the same Session, however, the Native Minister said there were " probably no grievances to speak of" in the district. His point of view differed much from that of Captain Fraser, who, in the Upper House, said of the West Coast Settlement Bill of 1880 that its "second part (creating offences) breathed the harsh and hostile spirit of a Minister towards the native race."†

In the twelfth paragraph of a memorandum furnished on 12th December, 1882, to Sir J. Prendergast, Administrator of the Government, by Whitaker, the Premier, there is a sentence worthy of notice. It was written for the purpose of being sent to Lord Kimberley, and may be found at page 39 of the Blue Book, C. 3689, 1883.

" When laws have been made applicable to the people of the Colony the object has, in many instances, been to except the Maoris from their stringency ; and there is no instance in which they have been placed in a less favourable position than the European population."

The cynical inaccuracy of this statement is ineffable. Though a very high functionary has recently styled me a "master of language," I confess that I want words to express the extent to which Mr. Whitaker's words might, although unintentionally, mislead persons unacquainted with the history of New Zealand.

He was one of the Ministry which in July, 1881, entreated Lord Kimberley to keep back from the British public the Governor's Report on affairs at Parihaka, although that Report had been promised, and Lord Kimberley admitted the promise while making a fresh promise irreconcileable with his first.‡

Mr. Whitaker and his colleagues passed the various Acts for imprisoning and denying trial to Maoris, and he was jointly responsible

---

* N.Z. Hansard, 1879. Vol. XXXIV., p. 868.
† ib. 1880. Vol. XXXVII., p. 652.
‡ Vide in New Zealand Parliamentary Papers, 1882, A. 8. p. 16, Lord Kimberley's telegraphic message that he would "delay publication if possible, but that, as the papers had been promised, they must be published if pressed for." He kept them back for more than a year.

for the raid upon Parihaka. When he penned the above inaccuracy, Te Whiti was held under an Attainder Act, which denied him a trial; women and children had been haled away in hundreds from their homes; Te Whiti's village was desolate; and the Native Minister had stated in the House that he did not know whether, under his orders, Te Whiti's house had been pulled down, but "if so, it was a very good thing, &c."*

Mr. Whitaker and his colleagues had approved the pulling down of Te Whiti's sacred medicine house, or church, as described by the Native Minister himself;† and yet Whitaker prepared a formal document to assure the Secretary of State that there was "*no instance*" in which Maoris had been "placed in a less favourable position than the European population."

Was it self-deception, or some bolder quality that prompted such a statement?

I must leave the qualification to the reader.

That the statement was an erring one, no one who reads the Blue Books of 1882 and 1883 can for one moment doubt.

That Mr. Whitaker knew it to be untrue, I do not assert.

His sensibility must, however, have been probed in 1881 by Mr Mantell, who obtained some Returns in the Legislative Council concerning the Himatangi block of land. Pending examination of ownership money had been paid as rent by occupiers, and the Government which impounded the rents had, amongst other failures to do right, failed to pay over the rents to the rightful owners.

When it was found that the owners had been thus treated, Mr. Mantell asked the House to declare that payment "to the recognized owners should no longer be delayed." Some money, it was supposed, had been paid to wrong persons.

Mr. Whitaker (then Attorney-General and in the Cabinet) was indignant. He admitted that "Mr. Mantell had stated the facts pretty well as they occurred," but insisted that it was only "a tribal business." Some Maoris had received something, and a portion of the impounded rents still remained in the hands of the Government. "Whether the people who were subsequently found by the Native Land Court to be owners of the Himatangi block had received their share (Whitaker) did not know. . . . If such matters were to be rooted out and brought up again under circumstances such as these, they could have no finality to transactions between Government and natives."

Mr. Mantell retorted: "Well, I intend that there shall be none. I am determined, while I have a seat in this Council, that there shall be no finality so long as this dishonest action on the part of the Government continues. . . . If a lawyer had acted with his client's money as the Government had acted with the money they

---

* N.Z. Hansard, 1882. Vol. XLI., p. 438.

† Blue Book, 1882. C. 3382, p. 262.

collected on behalf of these natives, the chances are that he would cease to be a lawyer." (N.Z. Hansard, 1881. Vol. XL., p. 642).

For the latest instance brought to my knowledge of the hardships inflicted on Maoris I am indebted to members of both Houses in New Zealand who forwarded to me copies of a very remarkable Bill introduced "to provide for a re-investigation into the Native Title to Lands known as Owhaoko and Kaimanawa—Oruamatua." The Bill was brought in (1886) by Mr. Ballance, Native Minister in a ministry of which Sir Robert Stout was Prime Minister and Attorney General.

The preamble declared that the Governor on the 4th Feb., 1880, ordered a re-hearing in the Native Lands Court of the claim of Renata Kawepo and others to the Owhaoko land. The re-hearing was ordered to take place within three years from 31st. October 1877.

The Order recited that " at a sitting of the Native Land Court . . . held at Porangahau on 2nd Dec., 1876. the claim of Renata Kawepo and others to Owhaoko was heard and decided and that a certain order was on 31st Oct., 1877, thereupon made by the Court;" that thereupon, 31st Jan., 1878, application was made " on behalf of certain aboriginal natives" for a rehearing of the claim, and the Governor under powers of sec. 58 of the Native Land Act, 1873 (Donald McLean's Act) *ordered a re-hearing*. The preamble continued thus, "And whereas the said period of three years from the 31st Oct., 1877, was allowed to elapse *without the rehearing so ordered being had*, though in *pretended compliance* with such Order the Native Land Court afterwards *unlawfully assumed, after its authority* under the said order in Council *had expired*, to deal with the said decision :

And whereas it would be just and right that the benefit of the re-hearing ordered should not be denied to the natives interested, by reason of the omission or delay aforesaid : And whereas by decision of the Native Land Court acting under the Native Land Act 1873 land known as Kaimanawa Oruamatua was on evidence before it, apart from any voluntary arrangement, declared to be owned by certain natives whose names were entered on a memorial of ownership as the owners of such land ; and whereas in the evidence upon which such decision was arrived at it was *stated and not disputed* that Natives besides those so declared to be owners had a claim on the land and there is good reason to suppose such evidence was true ;—and whereas application for a re-hearing in respect of the said decision was made, but by reason of an insufficient knowledge of the premises not granted :

And whereas it would be just and right on the premises that there should be a re-investigation into the title to the said lands :— Be it therefore enacted," &c.

The second clause declared the lands named to be within the jurisdiction of the Native Land Court and provided against giving the benefit of the Act to any Natives already recognized as owners.

The Bill itself consisted of two pages only, but attached to it was a memorandum by Sir Robert Stout, narrating the facts which led to the introduction of the Bill. The memorandum extended to twenty-six pages, and must be astounding to any one inclined to adopt the opinion that the Maoris have been treated with exceptional kindness.

Bad as the Owhaoko case is, it cannot be put forward as unusually harsh or unjust. Extracts already made from speeches of Dr. Pollen, Mr. Sheehan, Mr. Bryce, and others, show that, whether from malice or proclivity to blundering, injustice to the Maoris was common; and Dr. Pollen went so far as to assert in 1873 that they had been "subjected for years" to a "system of fraud under the authority of the law."

The specialty in the Owhaoko case is that it was carefully analyzed by a lawyer, the Prime Minister of New Zealand.

It must be borne in mind that usually when natives applied to have their lands brought under the operation of the Court there was an intended lessee or purchaser in the background, and that he had much to do with promoting the case.

Sir R. Stout's memorandum declared that in September, 1875, a Native Land Court was held at Napier, under circumstances which made it impossible for some of the natives (interested) to be present; that evidence given in Court showed that there were such interested natives; that in December, 1875, some of them petitioned for a hearing; that, owing to the absence of maps, or other causes, no order was made at the particular time at which it was afterwards pretended that an order had been made; that contradictory entries were made in the Minutes which purported to record the proceedings of the Court; that again in January, 1878, Maoris applied for a hearing as to their title; that on the 26th March, 1879, a re-hearing was sanctioned by Sheehan, the Native Minister, but that on 2nd April, 1879, he arrested it; that Sheehan being out of office in 1880, and Bryce being Native Minister, the re-hearing applied for in January, 1878, was directed on Mr. Bryce's recommendation, by the Governor on 4th of February, 1880; that it was fixed for 30th June, 1880; that on the 10th June it was postponed by a notice giving no reasons, and fixing no other date; that various communications passed subsequently between officials of the Land Court Office and the solicitor employed by the lessee, who opposed the re-hearing; that some of those who had in January, 1880, applied for a re-hearing were persuaded to sign a paper of withdrawal (of their application), which was sent to the Court in October, 1880, by the solicitor who opposed the re-hearing, and thus seemed to act for both sides; that some Maoris whose names appeared in the withdrawal wrote in November, 1880, that they had been "cajoled" to sign their names to it; that another wrote that his name had been appended "secretly without his concurrence;" that, though the Governor's order in Council directed the re-hearing within three years from 31st October, 1877, it was not so held, but that on the 1st November, 1880, the counsel for the lessee who opposed the re-hearing, informed the Court that he "held a retainer from the natives" who had "applied for the re-hearing," and that he was "instructed to withdraw their application;" and that on the 3rd November, 1880, the Judge dismissed the case.

Then came appeals to the Native Minister which (p. 17 of Mem.), appear not to have been replied to.

But the case was not clear. The Judge who had on 31st October, 1877, signed the Order of the Native Land Court about Owhaoko had referred to an order in the case made at a sitting of the Court on the 2nd December, 1876, and no such order had been made. On the contrary, there was an entry about that time (p. 417 of the Minutes and page 5 of Stout's memorandum), " Owhaoko : *No order*, Map to be altered and put into Court."

But, though ownership of natives may be brushed aside, as in the case of Heremaia Mautai at Christchurch in 1868, or that of the Dunedin Maori Reserve, the titles of colonists must be more carefully considered, and a case was stated for the Supreme Court in order to ascertain under that august sanction whether the Judge of the Native Land Court could make an order in the case.

If any one imagined that the Maori petitioners for a re-hearing would profit by the scrutiny of the Supreme Court, he was wofully disappointed.*

The judgment of the Supreme Court was a dry decision that " where an order has been made for a re-hearing, and the applicants subsequently abandon their application, the Native Land Court has power to affirm the original decision." (Stout's Mem : p. 19).

This seems, as an abstract statement, irrefragable ; but, as far as can be gathered from it, the particulars of the Owhaoko case were not even put before the Court. The singular circumstance that to the " document cancelling the application for a re-hearing " names were affixed without the knowledge of the supposed signers, and that the document was transmitted to the Native Land Court Judge by the the lawyer employed on the other side, cannot be deemed to have been sanctioned by the terms of the judgment of the Supreme Court.

Rawiri Kahia's letter of 10th November, 1880, affirming that his name "had been appended without his knowledge," may not have been seen by the Court.

According to Sir Robert Stout's summary of the case, no order had been made at all by the Native Land Court, and the applicants had not abandoned their application for a re-hearing.

The concluding words of Sir Robert Stout's Memorandum were :—

"1 In my opinion, no valid orders regarding the Owhaoko blocks have ever been made by the Native Land Court.

"2. That, as regards the Kaimanawa-Oruamatua block, the order was improperly made; for the Court was informed that other persons had interests in the land.

---

* We must remember how Taiaroa and Parata strove to cause the Waimate and Parihaka Land Question to go before the Supreme Court; how the West Coast Commissioners "refused to hear counsel " as to the validity of the confiscation; how, when an appeal to the Privy Council seemed imminent in the Dunedin Maori Reserve case, a sum of money was paid by the Government to quash the proceedings.

" 3. That the Native Land Court—first, in adjourning the Court *sine die ;* second, in not meeting until after the three years mentioned in the order in Council had expired—namely, on the 1st November, 1880 ; and third, in dealing with the question of withdrawal of the re-hearing in the absence of the natives concerned, acted both improperly and illegally.

" In order to do justice to the Natives concerned, the Government ought to introduce a special Bill ordering a re-hearing of the whole of the blocks.

" I do not care to comment upon the conduct of the various persons whose action I have had to allude to in this Memorandum.

" The facts are sufficient without comment. Let me only add that if this case is a sample of what has been done under our Native Land Court administration, I am not surprised that many natives decline to bring their land before the Courts. A more gross travesty of justice it has never been my fortune to consider.

" ROBERT STOUT.

" Premier's Office, Wellington, 18th May, 1886."

The Bill was carried with modifications. The confessions of wrong-doing in the preamble were excised. Nevertheless, under Sir R. Stout's leading, a great step towards the idea of justice had been made since the days when, in 1868, Mr. John Hall framed his Order of Reference about the Ngaitahu Deed at Christchurch; and, from 1855 to 1877, those remarkable proceedings occurred with regard to the Maori Reserve at Prince's Street, Dunedin, which have been chronicled in these pages.

If anything I have formerly written has conduced to make public men more studious than of old to extend justice to the Maoris, I have something to be grateful for.

Often when injustice was done it was unknown to the majority of the Colonists ; and, though it is dangerous for a writer to arouse the wrath of wrong-doers, yet, if he can mitigate oppression, he is not without his reward. I am persuaded that whatever ill-deeds have been done towards the Maoris by persons dressed in a little brief authority, the community had no immoral complicity with them. There is, perhaps, no more estimable community under the British Crown than that in New Zealand, and many recorded ill-deeds would not have been done if only the moral watchfulness and sense of justice of the public had been rought to bear upon wrong-doers at the time.

Would the public in England have consented to the vain and broken promises, the tortures of delay, the studied betrayal, which brought about the death of General Gordon ?

Was not the public conscience shocked when that martyr to duty, standing alone on the ramparts of Khartoum, fell a victim, not to local difficulties (which he could easily have surmounted, if not re-strained by Lord Granville and the Prime Minister) but to instruc-tions, and died " doing his best for the honour of his country " ?

It will not be the people of England upon whom posterity will heap the shame of Gordon's death, and it is not to the people of New Zealand that I impute those wrongs which have caused the groans of the Maoris.*

Failing to make impression upon certain minds in New Zealand, some Maori chiefs, Parore and others visited England in 1882, with a petition, hoping to lay their grievances before the Queen, whose kind words had often been made known to them, and whose paramount power they revered.

They were members of the Ngapuhi tribe always staunch to the Queen.

After some delay they were permitted to see Lord Kimberley at Downing Street, on the 18th July, 1882, (five days after the Despatches about Parihaka *so long withheld by that nobleman* had been promised to Parliament in reply to the request of Sir Michael Hicks-Beach).

Parore was admitted to be of high lineage, even by those who vilipended the deputation.

The petition glanced at the desire of the Maoris to secure the protection of the Crown under the Treaty of Waitangi; "at the evil brought upon them by the Governor himself, who, without any grounds, drove Wiremu Kingi Te Rangitake from his own lands at Waitara." . . . On this occasion, O mother, the Queen! the grievous lamentation of this island was raised."

(The war of 1863 in Waikato was attributed to the desire for land.) "When the Waikatos were overpowered" "armies went forth to the East and to the West against the Maoris. "The motive impelling the projectors of these deeds to execute this work was a desire to confiscate the Maori lands, and to trample under the soles of their feet the Treaty of Waitangi. While these proceedings were being carried out, the sorrowing people wept, the lamenting people groaned, the tortured people were in agony, the sad people were in darkness of heart, but still they held the Treaty of Waitangi as a foundation on which the voice of the Maoris could be made known to you, O Queen!

But the Europeans of New Zealand declared that the fighting, and the confiscation† of land, which brought calamity, and made your Maori children orphans, were sanctioned by you, O Queen. We did not believe these utterances as to the wrongs we suffered, that they were brought upon us by your Queenly authority; but our opinion

---

* Reference to General Gordon is not out of place in pages devoted to an effort to temper the severities of "civilization."

Writing to me from Palestine in October, 1883, he said "Men like —— do things and never think of the true hearing of them, and are horrified when their actions are depicted. . . . I do not in the least imagine civilization has made man more compassionate in himself : he fears the criticism, but when that is wanting he is as ruthless as ever."

† The term used by the Maoris to render the word confiscation, is well-known to readers of Maori history as Muru, plunder or robbery :—but it is a word for which no one English word is an equivalent.

M

was that such acts were not sanctioned by you, O Queen, whose benevolence towards the Maori people is well known.

The disorderly work we refer to has been done so that a path might be opened up to the Europeans to seize Maori lands."

The memorialists described the raid upon Parihaka as a "new plan" devised "to enkindle strife." "Armies were sent to Parihaka to capture innocent men; to seize their property and money; to destroy their growing crops, to break down their houses, and commit other unjust acts." So the petitioners had wandered across the ocean to pray that the Queen would appoint a Royal English Commission to abrogate existing evils; to put a bridle in the mouth of Ministers for Native Affairs, who might act as Ministers had done at Parihaka; so that all might be brought back to obey the Queen's laws.

The labours of such a Commission would (the petitioners hoped) restore lands unlawfully confiscated in violation of the Treaty of Waitangi, and would "draw forth from beneath the many unauthorized acts of the New Zealand Parliament, the concealed Treaty, that it may now assert its own dignity."

The Maoris themselves reared a stone memorial at the Bay of Islands, and caused the Treaty to be engraved on it. They requested the Governor to unveil the Stone Treaty. He declined. "Perhaps," the petitioners said, "his disinclination arose from the fact that the Europeans had disregarded the principles embodied in the Treaty, because in you, O Queen, is vested the sole authority affecting the Waitangi Treaty. . . It is believed by us, O Queen, that you have no knowledge as to the deeds of wrong that gave us so much pain, and which create lamentation among the tribes. O mother, the Queen, there are no expressions of disaffection towards you by the Maori tribes, including the tribes of the King; but they revere, only revere your Majesty; and the search after you, O Queen, has induced us to send this petition to England by the hands of the persons appointed by our committee who will see* your very countenance, and hear your words."

The petition summarized the many causes of Maori groans.

1. The avarice of the New Zealand Company which brought on the affray in which Captain Wakefield, Mr. Thompson, and others fell at Wairau in 1843, while wantonly assailing Rauparaha and his people.

2. Alleged unlawful executions of Rangihaeata's followers.

3. Occurrences at the Bay of Islands with regard to Heke and Kawiti, in 1844.

4. Occurrences in which Te Hapuku was concerned in 1848.

---

* It may have been a sanguine but it was not an unnatural expectation that a Ministry of which Mr. Gladstone was the head, would strive to gratify the deputation by aiding them in their desire to see the Queen. Once under Sir R. Peel, he had advocated justice to the Maoris. But in 1882, he transferred his sympathy to Africa. Besides accommodating the Boers in a startling manner, he and Lord Kimberley aided Cetewayo in visiting Her Majesty in 1882.

5. The unlawful seizure of Te Rangitake's land, at Waitara in 1860.

6. The invasion of Waikato in 1863.

7. Other troubles in 1879.

8. "The capture of 200 innocent men of Te Whiti in 1879-81.

9. The incarceration of Te Whiti and his people (in 1881-2) who were guiltless of any crime." . .

O mother, the Queen, these things, and many of the laws which are being carried into effect, are, according to Maori ideas, very unjust, creating disorder amongst us, giving us heart-pangs, and sadness of spirit to your Maori children who are ever looking towards you, most Gracious Queen; and it is averred by men of wisdom that these matters which weigh so heavily upon us are in opposition to the great and excellent principles of the Treaty of Waitangi.

May you be in health, O mother, the Queen! May the Almighty bring down upon you, upon your family, and upon the whole of your people, the exalted goodness of Heaven, even up to the termination of your sojourn in this world, and in your inheritance in the home of sacred rest."

When the Maori chiefs presented the petition to Lord Kimberley they were accompanied by Sir T. Fowell Buxton, Sir Robert Fowler, and other Members of Parliament as well as by Mr. F. W. Chesson, and others.

I have described the reception elsewhere It is sufficient to say here that Lord Kimberley's manner was disingenuous and evasive. When reminded that successive Secretaries of State had commanded successive Governors through a long series of years to inform the Maoris, and that they had accordingly been informed, that the Queen would cause the Treaty to be scrupulously and loyally respected, the Earl* merely mumbled something about "a matter of construction."

After a time the noble lord received from Sir J. Prendergast (the Administrator pro. tem. of the Government in New Zealand) a Despatch enclosing a supercilious memorandum from Mr. Whitaker, the Premier. (Blue Book, 1883, C. 3689. p. 39).

That functionary prudently abstained from dwelling on the Treaty of Waitangi. To that ghost of past honour some men are prone to say—Avaunt, and quit my sight.

Mr. Whitaker thought it not beneath the dignity of his position as a lawyer to assure Lord Kimberley that the land legislation in the Colony was "not restrictive but enabling;" "that the general legislation of the Colony as to the Maoris has been more than just, it has been exceptionably favourable to them;" and that "*there is no instance in which they have been placed in a less favourable position than the European population.*"

While he wrote these words, Te Whiti was held a prisoner under

* He sent a brief Report of the Deputation to the Governor of New Zealand (vide Blue Book, 1882, C. 3382, pp. 287-291), but he said nothing about the pledges of his predecessors.

the Act of Attainder described in these pages. Te Whiti's fields had been ravaged, and his house and place of worship had been ruthlessly destroyed.*

Whitaker's memorandum appears (by its date) to have occupied him several weeks in preparation. Governor Sir W. Jervois forwarded it without comment to Downing Street, where Lord Derby had succeeded Lord Kimberley. The new Secretary of State was not so repellent as his predecessor. He did not grant the prayer of the petitioners, but he told them that it had been "laid before the Queen who was pleased to receive it very graciously" though Lord Derby had been "unable to advise Her Majesty to give any directions for a compliance with the prayer of the memorialists."†

As the groans of Parore and his companions were unavailing, the Maoris, pierced to the heart by consciousness of the wrongs done to them, sent another deputation to England.

The so-called King, Tawhiao, was accompanied by chiefs who traced their descent from the noblest families which led the Maoris in the fleet which first bore the dusky Vikings of the Pacific to the shores of New Zealand.

Tawhiao and Wiremu Te Wheoro were of the best blood of Waikato. Pataru Te Tuhi was Tawhiao's cousin.

Topia Turoa claimed to represent the tribes from Taupo to Wanganui. Hori Ropihana represented the Ngatikahungunu tribe between Wellington and Hawke's Bay. Te Wheoro had always fought for the Queen. Topia Turoa had been active in suppressing Te Kooti. Hori Ropihana declared "My tribe has ever been loyal and obedient, and yet we find that together with the other tribes we are suffering from the wrongs done by the New Zealand Government."

Mr. (now Sir John) Gorst introduced the deputation on the 22nd July, 1884 to Lord Derby, whom he reminded of the late Lord Derby's noble declaration with regard to the Maoris, that while he had the honour of serving Her Majesty, he would "never admit that any person or any government acting in the name of Her Majesty" could contract any obligation "to despoil others of their lawful and equitable rights."

He reminded him also that Mr. Gladstone had fervently declared in the House of Commons that "as far as England was concerned there was not a more strictly and rigorously binding Treaty in existence than the Treaty of Waitangi."

He reminded him also that in the existing Constitution Act of New Zealand (15 & 16 Vict. cap. 72) the Crown had distinctly retained the power to make provision to protect the Maoris from ill-treatment.

---

* Moreover Mr. Whitaker was a minister in 1863, when the Suppression Bill, and the New Zealand Settlements Bill were passed in 1863. For their "exceptionally" humane character *vide supra*, pp. 25, 26 *et seq.*

† Blue Book, 1883, C. 3689, p. 40.

Tawhiao in supporting his petition avowed his loyalty to the Queen. Te Wheoro alluded to his own loyal services as an unpaid magistrate in 1857; as a paid magistrate in 1860, "as a captain of militia in 1863," as Assessor of the Land Court in 1866, "but when I saw the corruption of that Court I left it (he said) in 1872;" as a major in 1873, as a Maori Commissioner in 1875, "and then I saw more clearly the unfair dealing of the Government towards the natives and I gave up the post in 1879; and in the same year I was made a Member of Parliament, thinking that there perhaps the rights of the Maoris would be respected, but when I saw that the Maori Members were ignored, and that the whole Maori race was under oppression, I came to England with Tawhiao to lay our wrongs before Her Gracious Majesty, for we are weary of laying our complaints before the New Zealand Government who refuse to consider our case, and who continue to trample upon us, and we look to you for redress. May God preserve you."

The petition itself is in an English Blue Book, C. 4413 of 1885. It referred to the Queen's faith plighted in the Treaty of Waitangi, in "tender regard" for the Maori race. The Treaty secured all rights of chieftainship, and all Maori lands, villages, forests and fisheries, and it solemnly guaranteed protection of the Maoris under British law.

"But these contracts have been trampled upon by the Government without exception." In 1855 they were violated. Afterwards the Waitara land was seized under pretence of purchase, Wiremu Kingi Te Rangitake, "the paramount chief of that tribe, forbidding the sale" . . "and the Government waged war (1860) throughout Taranaki and confiscated the land."

Though Te Wheoro and his people aided the Government (1863) in the Waikato war "their lands, amounting to about 200,000 acres, and property were confiscated, and a very little portion of the land was returned."

Donald McLean, when Native Minister made arrangements about the West Coast Lands, and promised to purchase what the Government required from the Maoris.

But—afterwards "the Government began to seize the land without any pretext, arrested Te Whiti and people in their homes, destroyed their houses, rooted up their crops, and removed their goods, surveyed the land, put it into the market, and it was bought by the English, and very small portions were returned to the natives."[*]

---

* Sir W, Fox and Sir F. D. Bell, Commissioners on the West Coast in 1880, had recommended reserves for the Maoris, at the Waimate Plains 25,000 acres, at Parihaka 25,000 acres. In a final report (as sole Commissioner in 1882) Sir W. Fox declared that the Government (Mr. Bryce being Native Minister) "determined to reduce the continuous reserve on the Waimate Plains by 5,000 acres," and that a similar reduction by 5,000 acres, of the Parihaka reserve "has been effected by your Excellency's Government." Blue Book, 1883, C. 3689, pp. 10, 11. And yet some people do not shrink from saying that no "reasonable exception can be taken" to the treatment inflicted on the Maoris.

For months Te Whiti was imprisoned and was never tried.

The refusal to redeem the pledges to reserve lands in the Middle Island was complained of. (These unfulfilled promises are described *supra* pp. 61 to 63.)

The grievance of issuing certificates of title to ten selected persons of a tribe, was complained of as coercing the majority of the tribal owners "to rest satisfied with no land to live on, and the lands were ultimately alienated by purchase. Another rule was set up by the Court, that if the claimants failed to present themselves to the Court *the land should be handed over to others*, and thus the lands were sold, including the lands, the homesteads, and the plantations, and the real owners of the land were left destitute. When the Maori race asked that they *might be allowed to deal with their own lands by means of their own Committees*, the Government declined·*

In cases where Europeans purchased land from Maoris who received money *for lands not theirs*, the purchase thus made was established to the purchasers. Assessors were indeed appointed for the Courts, but they had no power to say anything with regard to the lands dealt with by the Court. . . "The rights of the chiefs over their own lands were disallowed by the Government." . . .

Therefore we pray for our Maori race that the Queen may cherish us, and accede to our prayer."

They craved that Maoris "living on their own lands, on those of their ancestors, and within the limits of Maori territory," might be unmolested, and that a "Maori Commissioner" might be appointed by the Queen to mediate "in matters touching the leasing and selling of the lands of the Queen's Maori subjects."

They wished that "the greater portion of the taxes levied" on the Maoris might be returned to them.

They wished Maori authorities to supersede the European Judges in the Native Land Court, but so that all the Maori determinations might be submitted through the Queen's Commissioner to the Governor "for confirmation," that at any rate some Commissioner from England should investigate the "wrongs done, and if he finds them in accordance with what we have now presented before you, that then he should decide whether the lands of your wronged subjects should be returned, or a compensation be made for part of it. We, your Maori race, confidently rely on the Treaty of Waitangi, on its provisions and force . . . and we pray in the presence of the Queen, that she will confirm her words given in that Treaty, that it may not be trampled upon by the Government of New Zealand in anything they may do to annul that Treaty. Let the Queen live. May God preserve you."

* After the expulsion, in 1884, of the Ministry containing members responsible for the raid upon Parihaka, a Ministry of which Sir R. Stout was the head, brought forward a Bill on the terms of which the Maoris were consulted, and containing provision for exercise of some power by Maori Committees, with regard to lands, to be acquired from the tribes. How far that provision will be operative remains to be seen.

When the Maoris framed their supplication (which was duly translated by the Rev. F. H. Spencer son of an early Missionary to the Maoris) they would appear to have expected that they might be permitted to "pray in the presence of the Queen."

Cetewayo had aspired to that honour and under Mr. Gladstone's auspices had obtained it. But no such grace was accorded to the high-born Maoris whose genealogies could be traced as far back at least as the days of the Plantagenets.

Lord Derby treated the chiefs courteously and declared that it was the "desire of Her Majesty's government to treat with equal justice natives and Europeans, and not to allow native rights to be over-ridden where it is in our power to help it." "I concur (he said) in the sentiments expressed by my father forty years ago, that a treaty is a serious and binding thing whether contracted with natives or with Europeans." "I do not forget what has been said as to the Treaty of Waitangi." He added that after hearing what answer might be sent from New Zealand to the complaints made— "we will so far as our power goes, endeavour to do justice."

Referring to Sir John Gorst's citation of the Constitution Act of New Zealand and the reservation of power by the Crown he hinted that there were "many things in a country and a Government like ours which though they may be strictly legal, are yet so contrary to constitutional practice, and to that which has been for so many years understood to be the law, that it would be very difficult to act upon them, whatever the state of the law may be."

With a fine forgetfulness of that active section of politicians spoken of by Governor Gore Browne as coveting Maori lands and resolved to obtain them recte si possint, si non quocunque modo— the noble lord said he had "no doubt" that the colonial legislature would be "quite willing" to "remedy any injustice which they may have involuntarily committed."*

A singular scene occurred as the deputation left the Colonial office. They were in various groups in the quadrangle, and discussing their reception, when Mr. Gladstone, the Prime Minister, passed, and entered into conversation with one of the English members of the deputation. Mr. Gladstone was not only aware that Tawhiao and his friends were before him : he knew that they had been imploring his colleague to regard loyally that Treaty concerning which Mr. Gladstone himself had averred in Parliament that "as far as England was concerned there was not a more strictly and rigorously binding Treaty n existence than that of Waitangi."†

As I watched his countenance those words flashed through my mind, and I was curious to observe how that lip service of former years would be wrought into action in 1884.

I saw a furtive glance : I saw an expression more of aversion than of pity ; of indignation at being shown to walk crookedly rather than

* A report of the discussion was published in "The Aborigines Friend," December, 1884.

† Hansard, 1848, vol. 96, p. 342.

of a desire to walk straightforwardly—and finally I saw the leader of the House of Commons stride away as if he had been injured by having an opportunity of using his great gift of words in alleviating the sorrows for which he had made himself in some degree responsible when he "indulged a hope" that Governor Gore Browne would be able to set aside the decision of Governor Fitzroy at Taranaki, and take those steps which led so disastrously to the unjust war of 1860.

I made no remark, but I heard epithets, not loud but deep, as the Premier flitted from the scene.

The fate of the Petition of the chiefs may be inferred, but must be told briefly.

Lord Derby transmitted it to the Governor of New Zealand.

On 28th March, 1885, the Governor forwarded a Memorandum from his Ministry, which Mr. Stout had recently formed. That Memorandum insinuated that if there had been any infraction of the Treaty of Waitangi before 1865 the Imperial Government was culpable : it insinuated that the powers reserved for the Crown under " Sec. 71 of the Constitution Act 15 and 16 Vict. cap. 72 " must be held to have been not intended to endure : and it referred to former Memoranda and former Despatches as rendering it unnecessary to discuss the "allegations of the petition."

The Governor enclosed copies of Acts respecting Native Lands, the virtue of which,—read by the light of Sir Robert Stout's careful statement with regard to the Owhaoko lands—was often of questionable character when put to the proof.

The same Blue Book (1885, C. 4413) which contains the above Despatch of 1885 contains a singular Despatch of 1st March, 1884, enclosing a Memorandum from the Native Minister in the previous Cabinet (Mr. Atkinson's) on the subject of a letter from Te Wheoro, Tomoana, Tawhai, and Taiaroa (all Members of the New Zealand Parliament) to the Secretary of the Aborigines Protection Society in London.

The writer conceived that the chiefs' letter did not "contain the sentiments" of its signers. One sentence in the Memorandum deserves to be preserved   When the reader remembers the performances at Parihaka of the Native Minister in 1881-2, he will appreciate the spirit in which that functionary wrote in January 1884, " for the past four years every effort has been directed to reducing to a minimum matters within the control of the Native Minister."

The Governor's Despatch concerning Tawhiao's petition was answered on 23rd June, 1885, by Lord Derby, who requested the Governor to transmit the Ministerial Memorandum to Tawhiao. While there was much sympathy with the Maoris in the English Parliament, there appeared to be a feeling that the Imperial Government could only "use its good offices with the Colonial Government with the view of obtaining for the Natives all the consideration which can be given to them." . . Although therefore Her Majesty's Government cannot undertake to give you specific instructions as to the applicability at the present time of any particular stipulations of a Treaty which it no longer rests with them to carry into effect, they are confident, as I request that you will intimate to your Ministers that the Government of New Zealand will not fail to protect and promote the welfare of the Natives by just administration of the law, and by a generous consideration of all their reasonable expectations."* . .

The Aborigines Friend (Journal of the Aborigines Society)† somewhat sadly contrasted the performance of the Despatch with the Earl's words to Tawhiao that the Government would "as far as our power goes, endeavour to do justice"—but there was a large improvement upon the demeanour of Lord Kimberley towards a previous Maori deputation.

Sympathy and sneering " are of two houses."

The matter was mentioned in the House of Commons in July, 1885, in a discussion upon the Estimates.

Sir John Gorst reminded Mr. Gladstone of his testimony to the sacredness of the Treaty, and besought the Government to mediate in order to secure for the remnant of the Maori race the rights and the justice to which they were entitled.

Lord Randolph Churchill intervened, and complained of the keeping of information from the House.

On this Mr. Gladstone, in a speech which was nothing to the purpose, unless deception be laudable, had the effrontery to declare that the Government *had really provided information sometimes earlier than was altogether justified."*‡

It is useless to complain, however, of anything said by Mr. Gladstone, who spends half his time in explaining that he never said what every one believes that he has said, and which he cares not to repudiate until the need to appear in a new character before the footlights has commended itself to his Protean mutability.

He was still a power in the House, and the curtain fell, with his words, upon the last appeal from the Maoris to the Imperial Government.

I once wrote that if in the dreary records of injury done to the Maoris there could have been found one word of rebuke, or even of remonstrance, on the part of Lord Kimberley against wrong, he might escape censure for complicity in the raid upon Parihaka.

Mr. Gladstone deserves more than hypothetical censure. Lord Kimberley may have been incapable of seeing that the maintenance of good faith in the name of the Queen was an Imperial duty, and, therefore, may have been stolid enough to suppose that he treated the matter properly when he told the deputation which accompanied Parore to the Colonial Office (in 1882) that "the Queen was advised by the Ministers of the Colony with regard to these matters, and not by himself."

---

* Blue Book, 1885, C. 4492, p. 43. † May, 1886.
‡ *Times* Report. Contrast this with Lord Kimberley's telegram in July, 1881, that the Governor's Despatch of 26th February, 1881, should be delayed "if possible, but that, as the papers had been promised they must be published if pressed for,"— and the result that they were not published until late in the year, 1882.

That such a washing of his hands could fail to relieve him of responsibility if wrong were done in the name of the Queen during his tenure of office may not have occurred to the noble Lord. But Mr. Gladstone was in no such fool's paradise. He had solemnly declared in the House of Commons that "as far as England was concerned there was not a more strictly and rigorously binding Treaty in existence than the Treaty of Waitangi."

He had never (so far as I know, though some people may wonder if there is anything which he has not said)—he had never committed himself to the doctrine that the Crown or the Imperial Government could be called upon to tolerate or to sanction a breach of faith.

He has very recently expounded his opinion on the subject. In a speech made at a private house, but reported in the *Times* and other newspapers (on 4th July, 1887) he declared that the doctrine which seemed sufficient to Lord Kimberley was disgraceful, and even revolutionary.

Lord Hartington had said, or was reported to have said, that practically the Crown did not interfere with colonial legislation, and that practical separation of Ireland from England would be entailed if a separate legislative body such as that of a Colony were set up in Ireland. Mr. Gladstone retorted thus :—

"Then Lord Hartington goes on to something more than a slip of the memory, in a passage which I feel it my duty to grapple with rather broadly, where I find him the propounder of what I call rather a strong revolutionary doctrine .   He says if we refuse the presence of the Irish members we shall lose   the only title by which Parliament has the right to concern itself with Irish affairs. Did he for a moment consider to what a doctrine he was giving utterance when he used those words ?

Have we any representatives in the House of Commons from the Colony of New South Wales? Have we renounced the right under that circumstance of interfering in the affairs of New South Wales? I say on the contrary, we have conceded to New South Wales the right of local self-government. That right of local self-government has been given upon the assumption that it would be well used, reasonably used; and it has been reasonably used, but Parliament has never abandoned its right to interfere if it saw cause upon Imperial grounds in the proceedings of any of the Colonies of this country,(Hear, Hear). And it is in my opinion a doctrine which we might have heard from the most transcendental Radical, from the most ultra-revolutionist, that we were to lose our only title of interfering in Ireland if Irish members should not sit in the House of Commons : .   but gentlemen, I will simply say this to you—that never at any time, under any circumstances by any terms, or by any implication—have we abated in the smallest degree the Imperial powers and prerogatives of the Imperial Parliament over the whole of the Empire of Her Majesty, and Lord Hartington if he does not know that has not learned one of the elementary principles and parts of the question he proposes to discuss. . . .

We believe and are convinced that nowhere will there be an abuse of the powers so conceded: but if I am to take into view the odious supposition that such an abuse may happen in which I do not for a moment believe, I may remind Lord Hartington of what I happen to recollect, that Sir W. Harcourt, in making a very able speech on the second reading of the Irish Government Bill last year, pointed out to the House of Commons that in case of such a misuse of power, the power of Parliament remained intact and the right and duty of Parliament would revive. Well, so much for slips of memory, and so much for what I must say is in my opinion a revolutionary doctrine; and of those who say it is not a revolutionary doctrine I would like to ask what are the present rights of Parliament with regard to the Colonies of New South Wales, Queensland, and Victoria, and half a score of others?"

From which it follows, that not having renounced the power to do right, Mr. Gladstone formally sanctioned the doing of wrong. The consciousness of what he was doing or leaving undone may have caused the scowl with which he eyed Tawhiao and his followers in the Downing Street Courtyard.

The failure of Tawhiao's appeal to the Colonial Office has made it necessary to resort to the tribunal of public opinion.

Exposure of past wrongs may be a warning to those who may be tempted to sin hereafter. In his own day a historian may have tribulation, but he is cheered by the knowledge that the tribunal which will really value his work is the serene judgment of the future.

If these pages purported to be a history of New Zealand, they ought to contain due censure of deeds condemned by the judgment of the historian.

Who can estimate so accurately the evil or the good done as the writer who has assiduously followed the current of events in all their windings, although many of those windings may seem to him too trivial to be dwelt upon in his pages?

They aid him in forming his judgment of men and manners just as numberless developments of temper and capacity aid individuals in forming judgment with regard to friends and acquaintances in private life.

A history which awards no censure must be either a dull catalogue, or a ghastly simulacrum.

Who would recognize or prize the pages of the monarch of Latin historians, if robbed of the burning words with which he branded the vicious careers of the despots or the traitors marshalled before him as he probed the records of the past?

But these pages do not pretend to be a history Their object is only to gather together a few facts which caused lamentation amongst the Maoris.

Moreover, as to the responsibility of actors in such scenes as are here depicted, there may be differences of opinion. Long arguments have been used, ere now, as to the extent of complicity in wrong doing, even where complicity is admitted. The existence of any complicity may be denied by one person, in a case where to another it seems clear.

I shall not attempt to define the extent, if any, of the complicity of Mr. Gladstone or Lord Kimberley in violating the Treaty of Waitangi.

I am content to show that the former solemnly declared it to be rigor ously binding on England, and that a few months ago he as solemnly declared that the right and duty of the Imperial powers and preroga tives remained in full force to repress wrongs or abuse, if anything so odious should require restraint.

But though I abstain from laying down the law myself, I may put before the Maoris and their friends an opinion given about complicity by no less an authority than a Queen's Counsel, who has more than once held high legal office.

At a Liberal Unionist assemblage on 7th December, 1886, in the presence of Lord Selborne, and other illustrious persons, Sir Henry James thus spoke* of the terrible scenes enacted in Ireland by conspirers against law:—"I look upon what has taken place in Ireland as representing almost the individual responsibility of the leaders of the liberal party as it was. There are some of my friends around me who will understand legal phrases. They will recognize what are accessories before the fact, and what are accessories after the fact. We have to-day to deal with accessories during the fact. (Loud cheers.)

There are men who it is said represent the national power in Ireland, and can control that power, and the attacks which are made upon society, and upon law and order, and who yet wilfully remain silent. It is to these men that we are asked to hand over the loyal subjects of the Queen who represent the minority. (Hear, Hear)."

Commenting on this and other words spoken at the same place, the *Times*, in a leading article, said, "Mr. Gladstone is at least tacitly abetting a system of downright robbery, no longer veiled under the pretence of agrarian injustice:" nothing that Mr. Gladstone can now say can obliterate the fact that he has tacitly if not explicitly approved the use in this cause of weapons which every honest man must reprobate."

The raid upon Parihaka was committed while Mr. Gladstone was Prime Minister and Lord Kimberley was at the Colonial Office. The facts were reported without delay by the Governor, and if the ministry incurred responsibility, individual such as Sir Henry James described, or collective as Ministers, it was not diminished by the fact that Sir Henry James was their Attorney General, whom they may not have consulted.

The chief prayer of the Maori deputation in 1884 was that the Treaty of Waitangi might be respected. No man had more strongly insisted than Mr. Gladstone upon its binding nature, but he sent them empty away.

He did not even give them words. Of words, at least, his store was always unlimited before.

It may be said that there is now no room left for doing justice to the Maoris

---

* *Times*, 8th December 1886

But the Treaty has never been abrogated, ana there is a remnant o their ancestral lands still under their own control.

When the Waikato tribes were smitten by the English troops, and shrunk back in sullen isolation to what was called the King country, (or Tawhiao's territory), they were left undisputed masters of it; and after a time Donald McLean obtained much credit for renewing friendly intercourse with them.

But their mastery of the territory was not disputed by him, nor by his successors in office.

Occasional paragraphs, and casual sayings, complained that the existence of an isolated district in which the Government possessed no land was an intolerable check to civilization; but the pledges of successive Governments had been so frequent and so unguarded that it seemed shameful, while any respect for treaties or promises remained, to suggest that all past guarantees should be boldly broken or disavowed.

The burden of the complaint of the self-styled votaries of civilization was always—"the country must be opened up."

In May 1879, Sir George Grey being then Premier visited the district, and a great conference of tribes was held at Kopua.

The proposals made by Sir George Grey did not, in spite of his eloquence, and the support of many chiefs, commend themselves to those councillors who held sway over Tawhiao's conduct.

In January 1882, Tawhiao with his leading advisers visited Auckland. Mr. John Hall was then Premier, Major Atkinson Treasurer, and Mr. Bryce Native Minister.

The opinions of those who desired to "open up the country" were thus expressed in a journal which had supported the ministry during the raid upon Parihaka:—

"Our progress it is sad to say means the decadence of the Maori race, or at all events it has meant that . . . The country held by the Waikatos and the Ngatimaniapotos beyond the Aukati (boundary) line has been left undisturbed till now, but cannot long so remain. Millions of fertile acres are lying waste, while a most profitable and necessary line of railway is blocked. We cannot sit down contentedly while there is no communication through the interior. The Maoris cannot keep up a separate territory and separate kingdom for ever. They must find a means of living in amity with us."

The visit of Tawhiao caused much speaking, but it was looked upon as preparatory to a conference about to be held in his own district in March.

On the 31st January 1882, Mr. Hall, the Premier, was reported by the New Zealand Herald (1st February) to have affirmed previous pledges to the Maoris by saying to Tawhiao himself—

"This Government did not in any way interfere with him and his people, so long as they wished to remain living by themselves."

More meetings took place. In November 1882 (Whitaker being then Premier) the Native Minister, Mr. Bryce, made propositions, at

Whativ hatihoe, to Tawhiao which, after discussion, were declined under the potent advice of Wahanui a leading Ngatimaniapoto chief.*

In 1881 a Bill, called a Crown and Native Land Rating Bill was brought forward by the Hall Government. It enabled the Governor to proclaim districts within which Native lands were to be rated, and enabled the Treasurer of the Colony to pay such rates out of money appropriated for the purpose : and whenever such native land might thereafter be "sold or exchanged for the first time" (or leased) then the amount paid by the Treasurer was to be repaid to him, and payable as a "duty on such sale exchange or lease."

Te Wheoro thought "the principles of the Bill monstrous as far as the Natives are concerned. (It) merely means a system of mortgage which is to be exercised over Native lands. . . . I know the object it will attain will be the confiscation of the Maori lands. The Maoris will not be able to sell their land with all these rates upon it which will go on increasing until ultimately the land will be taken to pay for the rates which the Government have placed upon it. Who knows that the Government may not bring in another Bill to take all the Maoris prisoners*—to arrest them on their own properties for for unpaid rates? Why do you not call this Bill at once the Mortgage and Confiscation of Native Lands Bill? The Bill is altogether opposed to the provisions of the Treaty of Waitangi."

The Bill encountered opposition. One European member who did not object to it altogether—pointed out that it was unjust in proposing "practically to confiscate the Native Lands."

In 1882 a Bill with the same title was passed, but Major Atkinson, the premier of a Ministry formed in 1887, announced the intention of the Government to repeal it and to deal with the whole subject of "the Maoris paying rates upon their lands in settled districts as their fellow settlers of the European race are doing." (N.Z. Hansard, 1887. Vol. lviii. p. 98.)

It is obvious that the subject may be dealt with in a Treaty-respecting or in a Treaty-violating manner. It is equally obvious that if there be a desire to proclaim districts in which a law may operate so as to confiscate Maori lands which the Maoris hold under the terms of the Treaty of Waitangi, and of which their separate occupation has been always respected since the war of 1863-4, that desire is ungenerous and unjust.

There have been many ways already in which Maori lands have been taken from them.

Soldiers were sent to seize Te Rangitake's lands at the Waitara in 1860.

---

* The New Zealand Herald thus described him " by his intelligence, by force of will and character, and by his high chieftainship, really the foremost man, . . very tall, . . is a splendid orator. He has a fine command of language, with all those graces of poetic allusion and quotation, of references to ancient tradition, and the deeds of famous ancestors, essential to the Maori orator."

* N.Z. Hansard 1881. Vol. xxxviii. p. 576. The spirit of prophecy was upon Te Wheoro. He spoke thus on the 20th July 1881, and in November the raid upon Parihaka was made and more than 2000 Maoris were dealt with as already told in these pages.

Waikato was invaded by an English general with ten thousand troops in 1863 ; and a proclamation of confiscation in Waikato followed the war.

Dr. Pollen (supra p. 147-8) described in Parliament some of the more hidden ways in which some Maoris lost their heritage. The Heretaunga Commission revealed other successful arts.

A power to proclaim districts within which new laws shall operate might cover almost any ground.

That the Maoris have cause to shrink from the clutch of new laws none can deny who have studied the past.

When Wahanui gave evidence before a Select Committee of the House in 1884 as to the best route for a North Island Trunk Railway (which would traverse the so-called King-country) he declared that he would willingly co-operate with the Government with regard to the railway, but that he and his people " wished that all the final arrangements connected with our lands should be settled first." (Report of Committee, p 16).

Before the same Committee Major Atkinson (p. 62) in comparing two lines, used the remarkable words—" it seems to me we should get at the *troublesome natives* practically as well by one line as by the other."

Major Atkinson was a member of the ministry which uprooted Te Whiti's settlement in 1881, and he is now the premier of the colony.

Who the troublesome natives were, who were thus glanced at, it might be difficult to define. The trouble of the natives is well-known. They yearn to be left unpersecuted ; to live, and at the appointed time to die, on the lands solemnly guaranteed to them by Treaty.

If their term of existence as a human family be brief, at least they might be allowed to gather their robes around them and depart in peace.

They did not trample on Europeans when they were powerful, and it would be tyrannous to mete to them a measure which they were too magnanimous to apply to others.

Proposals have been made from time to time to temper the hardships which a ruthless advance would inflict upon the Maoris in that isolated domain which for more than a quarter of a century has been respected as peculiarly their own. In 1882, when the chief Parore was treated by Lord Kimberley with civilized contempt, a scheme was propounded for forming an Association to purchase the Maori lands and distribute perpetual annuities amongst the Maoris.

The scheme is set forth in a Blue Book of 1883 (C. 3689, p. 1) and honoured names are amongst its propounders.

The Secretary of State forwarded it to Sir Arthur Gordon, then Governor of New Zealand, and the Governor's prudent comments upon it are on the 35th page of the same document.

Other schemes, of more or less kindred character, have been proposed.

There is but one solution of the problem which can be honourable to England or the colony, and just to the Maoris.

It is not a scheme; it is a duty.

The prayer of the Maoris, when Mr. Gladstone passed by on the other side at Downing Street in 1884, was that England would respect the Treaty on whose terms the Maoris relied.

To respect that Treaty ought to be the pride, and is the duty of all honourable Englishmen—of all subjects of the Crown.

These brief pages are my own contribution towards a consummation, devoutly to be wished for, which the public men of New Zealand have still the power to bring about, if they will be just and fear not.

Manifesto to the Maori tribes interested in the lands confiscated by the Government in consequence of the wars between the Maori and the European peoples.

WE, THE COMMITTEE appointed to inquire into and to take proceedings for testing the validity of the laws under which the said lands have been confiscated, and are now claimed by the Government, and to enquire into and test the validity of the acts done by the Government under the provisions of those laws, SEND GREETING:

KNOW YE, that we have consulted lawyers at Port Nicholson touching these matters, and we are informed as follows :—

THAT, in the month of December, 1863, the General Assembly of New Zealand passed a law authorizing the Governor, whenever he was satisfied that any Maori tribe or hapu had been engaged in war against the Government since the first day of January, 1863, to declare and fix the boundaries of Districts within which the lands of such tribe or hapu were situated, and then to set apart any of such lands as sites for settlement; and, by the said law, every site so set apart, was to become the property of the Government, freed from the title of the Native owners of the same.

BUT it was by that law provided, that compensation should be made for the taking of such lands to any of the Native owners, who had not been engaged or concerned in the war for which the same had been confiscated.

NOW we find that the Government purporting to act under the provisions of that law, and of other laws passed by the General Assembly in connection therewith, have created Districts in various parts of the North Island of New Zealand, and claim to hold the lands of the Maori people within those Districts, on the alleged ground that the said lands have been lawfully confiscated by reason that the owners thereof had been engaged in wars against the Government since the First day of January, 1863.

WE know that the right of the Government to confiscate those lands, and to retain the same, has long been disputed by the Maori owners thereof, but that no proceedings have ever been taken in any Court of Law to test the validity of the Acts of the General Assembly under which they have been taken, or of the proceedings of the Government under those Acts, or the right of the Government to retain any portions of the lands, so taken which have not been set apart as sites of settlement.

WE, therefore, having been appointed to enquire into these things, have been advised that the proper course for the Maori people who object to them is, to commence proceedings in the Supreme Court of New Zealand, in order that the following questions may be heard and determined by law :—

1. WHETHER the Acts of the General Assembly, authorizing the confiscation of the Maori lands, are valid Acts or not ?

2. WHETHER those Acts, if valid, authorized the Government to confiscate any of the Maori lands by reason of wars which happened after the Third day of December, 1863 ?

3. WHETHER those Acts, if valid, authorized the Government to retain any of the lands within the proclaimed districts, which had not been specifically set apart as sites for settlement before the Third day of December, 1867 ?

4. WHETHER the proceedings of the Government, under those Acts, have been regular and proper, so as to bind the Native owners of the lands taken ?

5. WHETHER, if those Acts be valid, proper compensation has been made to those who had not been engaged or concerned in the wars ?

THESE are the principal questions which we have been advised by our lawyers to bring before the Supreme Court but there are many others in connection therewith, which will also have to be decided, and all such questions will be duly raised in the interests of the Maori people.

WE have also been advised, that if we are not satisfied with the decision of the Supreme Court upon any of these questions we shall be entitled to appeal to the great Court of the Queen of England, by which the case, will then be fully heard and decided.

Now, in order that these things may be properly done, we, the Committee, call upon you to assure the Government that you will not commit any deed of violence or attempt to assert your claims to those lands by force, and that you will leave your rights to be settled by the law and not by the sword. And we will urge upon the Government, on the other hand, not to proceed with the surveys or to deal with the disputed lands until the law has decided the questions we raise in respect of the same.

AND we further make known to you, that acting in the belief that it is your wish that these things should be peaceably done, we intend at once to take steps for bringing all questions touching your claims to the confiscated lands before the Supreme Court.

From the Committee,

HORI KEREI TAIAROA M.L.C.,
President.

WI PARATA TE KAKAKURA,
Secretary.

WI TAKO NGATATA, M.L.C.
MOKENA KOHERE, M.L.C.
HENARE TOMOANA, M.H.R.
HORI KARAKA TAWITI, M.H.R.
IHAIA TAINUI. M.H.R.
MAIHI PARAONE KAWITI.
KEEPA TE RANGIHIWINUI,
Major, N.Z. Militia.

PEETI TE AWEAWE.

Sir W. Fitzherbert's general testimony as to several of the chiefs who signed the above manifesto has been given at page 91.

When Wi Tako Ngatata died in 1887, and the Legislative Council adjourned in consequence, Dr. Grace, a member who had served in the English army in New Zealand, said: (LEGISLATIVE COUNCIL. *Thursday,* 10*th. November* 1887.)

"I wish to say that I find it impossible to avoid taking advantage of this opportunity of saying a few words with reference to the distinguished chief who has passed away. Sir, it is impossible for me to consider the disappearance of a man like Wi Tako Ngatata from our midst without giving expression to the boundless feeling of admiration I entertain for men of his type. I say, Sir, that if we have not sufficient greatness of soul to set the proper value on the services rendered to this colony by men like Wi Tako Ngatata we have not been worthy of the services which they have been rendered,—we are not worthy of the security which we enjoy, and owe so largely to their services. There was a time when Wi Tako held the balance of power between the Maori King Potatau and the English Queen; a time during the war when he had two thousand armed men under his control. and had he thrown his tomahawk to the right or left, and lent his influence to the Maori King I do not know what would have become of this settlement. I say we have lost in him one of the greatest Natives this country, rich in great men, has ever borne. What sacri fices did the honourable gentleman make for the benefit of the Europeans ! He imperilled by his loyalty to us the whole of his influence with the Native race. Every one must know how the spirit of nationality with a volcanic throb moved the Maori people at that time. Who is there that can fail to see the greatness of soul which actuated Wiremu Tamihana when he conceived the idea of a Maori nationality, and who, realising this, can fail to admit the nicety of the balance of power between the races that existed at that time ? It was then Wi Tako, failing to be carried away by the passing impulse of the moment, holding the scales between the two races, gave us the full advantage of his sympathy and, ultimately of his support. I have heard the late Dr Featherston say of him, "Wi Tako is the cleverest man, black or white, in the country." That was his estimate of the man's skill, and his appreciation of Wi Tako's power of controlling the wild races he held in the leash. I know that forty years ago, at a time when Native troubles were balanced with the greatest nicety in the Hutt, Wi Tako was always found protecting the right of the European. His word was as trusty as ever his tomahawk had been, and, as was well said of him, he had no two tongues—what he promised he performed. I have seen many aspects of the late war: I have seen the Arawa, the Waikato, the Ngatiawa, the Ngatimaniapoto, the Ngatiporou, the Ngatipukeko, the Ngatiruanui, and all the warlike tribes engaged either on one side or the other; and I remember to-day with glowing admiration the chivalry, valour, and magnanimity of this great race of people, who are dying out from our midst, leaving but the memory of their achievements behind them."